War

KNIGHTS AND PEASANTS

THE HUNDRED YEARS WAR IN THE FRENCH COUNTRYSIDE

Warfare in History

General Editor: Matthew Bennett
ISSN 1358–779X

KNIGHTS AND PEASANTS

THE HUNDRED YEARS WAR IN THE FRENCH COUNTRYSIDE

Nicholas Wright

THE BOYDELL PRESS

First published 1998
The Boydell Press, Woodbridge

Transferred to digital printing

ISBN 978-0-85115-806-8

The Boydell Press is an imprint of Boydell & Brewer Ltd
PO Box 9, Woodbridge, Suffolk IP12 3DF, UK
and of Boydell & Brewer Inc.
668 Mt Hope Avenue, Rochester, NY 14620, USA
website: www.boydellandbrewer.com

A CiP catalogue record for this book is available
from the British Library

This publication is printed on acid-free paper

CONTENTS

ILLUSTRATIONS

GENERAL EDITOR'S PREFACE

> But if on both sides war is decided upon and begun by the Councils of the
> two kings [of England and France], the soldiery may take spoil from the
> kingdom at will, and make war freely; and if sometimes the humble and
> innocent suffer harm and lose their goods, it cannot be otherwise; . . .
> Valiant men and wise, however, who follow arms should take pains, so far
> as they can, not to bear hard on the simple and innocent folk but only on
> those who make and continue war and flee peace.
>
> (Honore Bouvet, *The Tree of Battles*, Part Four, ch. 58)[1]

This was the reality of warfare as it seemed to a serious commentator at the end
of the fourteenth century; it was certain that, even in a war fought legitimately
between two sovereign princes, the 'humble and innocent suffer'. Much of what
Nicholas Wright describes in this book bears out this premise. His exploration of
how war bore down upon the peasantry of France, necessarily chronicles misery
and oppression by a military caste striving to maintain its own status in troubled
times.

Yet the picture is far from one-sided, as Dr Wright shows. The ability of peasant
communities to defend themselves, to organise physical resistance, to fortify
buildings and churches, to pursue malefactors through legal process, is also
apparent. While the balance of power, whether in the fields or in the courts, usually
lay with the lords and their military servants, it was possible for the social
underdogs to take their revenge, in many circumstances. Nor does one have to
believe in the legendary resilience of 'Jaques Bonhomme', as romantically interpreted by nineteenth-century French historians, as Dr Wright shows convincingly.
The true picture is more nuanced, for resistance and co-operation, opposition and
alliance were interwoven in the relationship between those seemingly irreconcilable archetypes: Knight and Peasant.

In fact, as the author makes clear, the social conflicts operated at many levels
within French communities he has studied. While many peasants sat and suffered,
others 'went for a soldier' – willingly or unwillingly – sometimes to return to their
original village as potential marauder, often also as protector, or co-ordinator of
defence against oppressors in the locality or the kingdom's enemies. Generally,
war produced nothing but sorrow, turning good husbandmen into brigands and
undermining or destroying the agricultural economy; but to understand the com-
plexities of the relationship between the warriors and the producers an historian

---

[1] *The Tree of Battles of Honore Bonet*, trans. G. Coopland (Liverpool, 1949). See also p. 32
below.

must examine it at local level. This is what Dr Wright has achieved in his analysis of what he calls the 'more familiar rhythms of medieval society' (p. 126).

He shows that the success of peasant resistance was very variable. Fortified churches could act more as larders for marauding soldiery than reliable defences. The creation of extensive subterranean refuges shows to what extremes a terrified population was driven. Yet, the author makes the point that in Joan of Arc, the assertive peasant class had its justification, with her as its representative it did save France from the English where generations of noblemen had failed. Her virgin femininity and divine inspiration stood in direct contrast to the vicious and voracious image of that 'Great She-Devil War' which beset her country and its ordinary, farming population.

Matthew Bennett
Royal Military Academy Sandhurst
November 1997

ACKNOWLEDGEMENTS

Although a short book, this one has been a long one in preparation. Many debts have been incurred over that period. The first is to the History department at Edinburgh University where I was introduced to this topic as I worked towards my 1972 doctoral thesis on Honoré Bouvet and late medieval war literature. Bouvet's fascination with the subject of conflict, out of which he created the metaphor of a tree of battles and his absorption in the high ideals of late medieval chivalry and religion, and in the contrasting practical day-to-day affairs of the soldiers themselves, undoubtedly infects this present work. It was Kenneth Fowler who inspired this interest and who guided me through the long research, and I have always been grateful to him. I am equally grateful to Christopher Allmand for his helpful criticism of this (in its early stages), and of other related works. His encouragement has always been appreciated; his advice equally so.

The writing of this book has been completed in Woodbridge, in the deceptively appealing status of "independent scholar", but much of the research for it was done while I was teaching medieval history at the University of Adelaide. I am grateful to that university and to the Australian Research Grants Council for funding several research expeditions to France. These latter were enjoyed by all my family, Jackie, Duncan and Ben, as we travelled from archive to archive and from one historical site to another. There were other times when my family had to be patient with the inevitable unsociability and selfishness of scholarly activity. My wife, Jackie, was always patient and supportive, and I am at last able to be properly and ungrudgingly grateful. This book would not have been completed without her help and tolerance. Ben has also been helpful with some of the painful editorial tasks.

Although drafts of this work have been read by Richard Barber, Matthew Bennett, Christopher Allmand and Maurice de Soissons, all of whom made very necessary suggestions for their improvement, the final version is entirely my own responsibility. I have a strong feeling that each of them could have written a different and better book, but, although not slow to take their advice, I have persisted with my own.

Some of the material in this book first appeared in my contributions to a number of historical journals and collections of essays and I am grateful to their editors for granting permission to reprint it in a revised form here. The relevant publications are: "The 'Tree of Battles' of Honoré Bouvet and the Laws of War" in *War, Literature and Politics in the late Middle Ages*, ed. C.T. Allmand, Liverpool University Press, 1976, pp. 12–31; "French Peasants in the Hundred Years War" in *History Today*, vol. 33, June 1983, pp. 38–42; " 'Pillagers' and 'brigands' in the Hundred Years War" reprinted from the *Journal of Medieval History*, vol. 9, pp. 15–24 with kind permission from Elsevier Science; "Feudalism and the Hundred Years War" in *Feudalism: Comparative Studies*, Sydney Studies in Society and Culture, vol. 2, eds. E. Leach, S.N. Mukherjee and J. Ward, Sydney, 1983, pp. 105–23; "Ransoms of Non-combatants during the Hundred Years War", reprinted from the *Journal of Medieval History*, vol. 17, 1991, pp. 323–32 with kind permission from Elsevier Science; "The Fortified Church at Chitry" in *Fort*, vol. 9, 1991, pp. 105–23.

I am also grateful to Michael Jones for permission to reproduce the maps on pp. x–xii and to the Bibliothèque Royale Albert Ier, Brussels, for permission to reproduce the tree of battles from, BR Ms 9079, fol. 10v on p. 10. David Poole's assistance with the plans of the fortified churches on pp. 109–10 is also much appreciated.

NARW
Woodbridge, August 1997

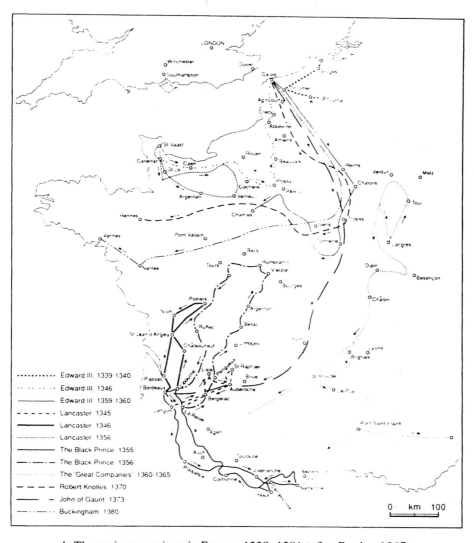

1. The main campaigns in France, 1339–1381 (after Fowler, 1967)

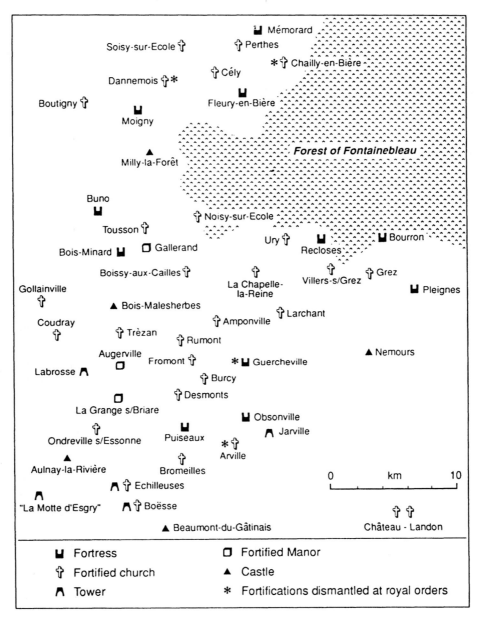

Mémorard

Soisy-sur-Ecole

Perthes

Chailly-en-Bière

Cély

Dannemois

Fleury-en-Bière

Boutigny

Moigny

Milly-la-Forêt

Forest of Fontainebleau

Buno

Tousson

Noisy-sur-Ecole

Bois-Minard Gallerand

Ury Recloses Bourron

Boissy-aux-Cailles

La Chapelle-la-Reine

Villers-s/Grez Grez

Gollainville

Pleignes

Bois-Malesherbes

Coudray

Amponville Larchant

Trèzan

Rumont

Augerville Fromont

Guercheville

Nemours

Labrosse

Burcy

La Grange s/Briare

Desmonts

Obsonville

Ondreville s/Essonne

Puiseaux

Jarville

Arville

Aulnay-la-Rivière

Bromeilles

| 0 | km | 10 |

"La Motte d'Esgry" Echilleuses

Boësse

Château - Landon

Beaumont-du-Gâtinais

Fortress	Fortified Manor
Fortified church	Castle
Tower	* Fortifications dismantled at royal orders

2. Fortifications in the area south of Fontainebleau Forest in 1367
(after Contamine, 1972)

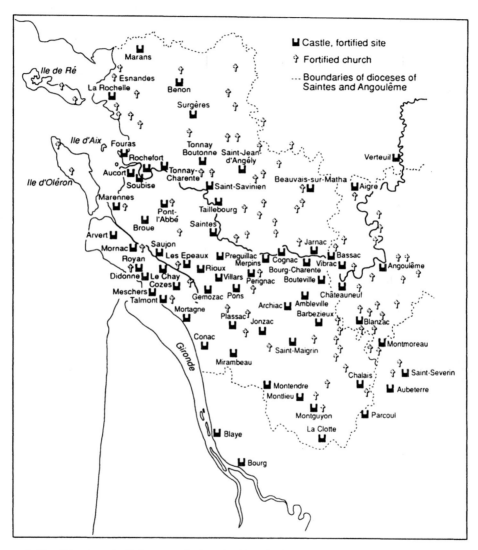

3. Fortifications in Saintonge during the Hundred Years War (after Favreau, 1986)

INTRODUCTION

The Hundred Years War

AS A HISTORIOGRAPHICAL concept, the Hundred Years War is impregnable. Few of its historians, however, have failed to acknowledge its roots in much more ancient disputes over land and sovereignty between the kings of France and of England, which vastly pre-date the opening of "the" war, in 1337. Nor have they ignored the fact that the English Crown persisted in its claims to France long after the conventional close of the war in 1453, and that no English monarch, in the century which followed, neglected to undertake some military adventure in France. The defiance of Edward III, as duke of Gascony, towards his sovereign, the king of France, was no novelty of 1337; the conquest of English Gascony by forces loyal to the French Crown, in 1453, was not considered by anyone at the time to be the end of the story.

In political and military terms, the Hundred Years War has often been described. Edward III, having defied the French king "Philip of Valois, who calls himself king of France", started the war by landing in Flanders and by defeating the French navy at Sluys in June 1340. The English assault on the French kingdom from its periphery continued with their intervention in the war of succession in Brittany, between the Montfort and Blois families, during 1342. In 1346 Edward III, on a march through northern France, met and defeated the French army at Crécy and proceeded to besiege, eventually to capture, the town of Calais which was to remain in English hands long after the end of the war. In 1356 Edward's son, known to history as the Black Prince, on a campaign which started in Gascony, a possession of the English Crown since the twelfth century, won another victory, at Poitiers, in the course of which the king of France, John II, was captured. A period of unprecedented political collapse followed in France, as the kingdom was torn by urban and rural revolt, and by fighting between the supporters of the Regent Charles and those of the king of Navarre. An attempt to conclude a final peace between England and France at Brétigny in 1360 secured nine years of uneasy truce which spared the French people from English campaign armies but exposed them to armies of freebooting discharged soldiers, known as the Great Companies. When the French king, Charles V, assisted by his able brother, Louis of Anjou, and his constable, Bertrand du Guesclin, renewed the war in 1369, there began a decade of reverses for the English Crown which eroded its French possessions to little more than the territories immediately surrounding Bordeaux and Calais. The *coup de grace*, however, was not delivered by the French at that time and a new generation of political leaders on both sides of the Channel negotiated a peace between the young kings, Charles VI and Richard II, in 1393.

Peace endured uneasily until Henry V ascended the English throne in 1413.

Determined to take advantage of the civil war in France between the supporters
of Charles, duke of Orleans and John, duke of Burgundy, Henry renewed the war
in alliance with the latter. In 1415 he established a foothold in Normandy, at
Harfleur, and went on to defeat the French at Agincourt. In 1417 he and his
Burgundian allies began the systematic conquest of northern France which forced
Charles VI, in 1420, to come to terms at the Treaty of Troyes and to recognize
Henry as heir to the French throne, thus officially disinheriting Charles' own son,
the dauphin. The dauphin, the future Charles VII, however, became a rallying-
point (initially of a rather feeble kind), from his capital at Bourges, for those who
refused to accept the arrangement. The opponents of the 1420 settlement could do
little at first to check the Anglo-Burgundian advance which was continued, after
the death of Henry V in 1422, by his brother, the duke of Bedford. After the battle
of Verneuil in 1424, the conquering English armies moved into Anjou and Maine.
By 1426, however, a stalemate had been reached, and, following the failed siege
of Orleans, in 1429, in which Joan of Arc played a spectacular rôle, the English
found themselves for the first time on the defensive. The defection of the duke of
Burgundy from the English side, at the Treaty of Arras in 1435, and the death of
the duke of Bedford in the same year, compounded their difficulties. By 1448, the
English had been cleared from Maine. In 1449 began the rapid reconquest of
Normandy by the armies of Charles VII, and, two years later, the process was
repeated in Gascony. Bordeaux, the capital of English Gascony, fell in 1453 as a
result of the defeat of the English expeditionary force at Castillon. The English
Crown, for the first time since 1066, was left with virtually no territory in France.[1]

Even such a brief outline of the Hundred Years War suggests that this was no
straightforward struggle between the emerging nation-states of France and England, and that it was enmeshed, from start to finish, in what we might now call
civil wars within the French kingdom and in the more generalized disorder of
freebooting. The "great game" (if we may call it such) was the struggle for power
between the French Valois kings and their most powerful neighbours and most
recalcitrant vassals, the English Plantaganet and Lancastrian kings. It was fought
largely on French soil over irreconcilable territorial claims and it forced people,
willy-nilly, to take sides. It was a game which was characterized during much of
the fourteenth century by the destructive raid in force, known as *chevauchée*,
which might find its climax in a battle or a major siege, but often did not. The
fifteenth-century phase is more recognizable in terms of an English conquest
followed by a French reconquest. This "great game" is the background to the
Hundred Years War which is described in this book. Never was the game entirely
buried beneath the host of lesser conflicts. Occasionally its campaigns, its battles,

---

[1] The classic account of the Hundred Years War is that of E. Perroy, *The Hundred Years War*
(London, 1965), which appeared originally, in French, in 1945. Its enduring appeal (having
been written in exceptionally difficult circumstances) is a tribute to its author. The first
volume of a fundamentally new account is J. Sumption, *The Hundred Years War*, 1, *Trial by
Battle* (London, 1990).

its sieges, its treaties and its truces intruded into the foreground: most obviously when armies attempted to lay waste, or conquer, the territory of their enemy.

It has often been pointed out, most recently by Michael Jones,[2] that, if warfare on French soil during the Hundred Years War period had been confined to these chronologically and geographically isolated campaigns, then most Frenchmen would have had no experience of it. Unfortunately for them, there was a great deal more military activity than that which was directed personally by the kings and their immediate subordinates at the head of armies of several thousand men-at-arms, bowmen and infantry, assembled for the purpose. The weakness of the French monarchy during much of this period encouraged private wars between lords who might dignify and legitimate their actions by associating them with the wider Anglo-French (or other) conflict but who had more local scores to settle. The weakness of both the French and English Crowns also encouraged the activity of military adventurers whose freebooting enterprises could similarly be disguised as loyal service to one or other of these warring sovereigns. Thus, as our focus shifts to encompass more of the detail of military activity during this period, we may observe a France studded with tens of thousands of castles, fortified churches, fortified farm houses, walled towns and villages, whose often tiny and impoverished garrisons fought for local power with each other and with the local people. For long periods, this conflict might be pursued with little, or no, reference to what was happening elsewhere.

This form of warfare could vary considerably in status. On the one extreme, it might clearly be seen as a continuation of the "public" war by armies which had dispersed into garrisons along well-recognised frontiers. On the other, it might have been an undisguised, atavistic exploitation by armed men of the profits of local power for their own private ends and with only the most cynical reference to the war-aims of their nominal sovereigns. Most of the soldiers who fought in France with any degree of continuity during this period, whether noble or non-noble, whether English or French, moved, according to political and personal circumstance, between these two extremes.

This is an aspect of the Hundred Years War with which, as historians, we are much less familiar, but whose features are instantly recognizable by those with experience of wars in the so-called "Third World" of today. At its centre were ill-paid and ill-disciplined soldiers, scattered over the land of France in a large number of fortified bases, engaged in a very bitter struggle for survival, not only between themselves, but also with a more numerous and impoverished peasantry. Their own "Englishness" and "Frenchness" was the justification rather than the reason for the murder and mayhem in which they were all engaged, and, although their existence as soldiers may have been a product of the "great game", they did not always play by its rules. Their motivation, by and large, was much more

---

[2] M. Jones, "War and Fourteenth-century France", *Arms, Armies and Fortifications in the Hundred Years War*, ed. A. Curry and M. Hughes (Woodbridge, 1994), pp. 105–6.

personal and immediate: hunger, greed, self-preservation, revenge, group loyalty, family pride. This is the war which is described in this book.

Christine de Pisan, writing at the French court in the early years of the fifteenth century, observed that in the time of Charles V it was necessary to maintain soldiers on a continuous basis on "five or six" frontiers of his kingdom[3] and Philippe Contamine has estimated that the principal French garrisons north and south of the Garonne, on the Gascony frontier, in September 1340, contained no less than four thousand men-at-arms and footsoldiers.[4] Soon after the capture of Calais by the English, in 1347, there were fourteen French and seven English fortresses within a forty kilometre radius of Calais.[5] Siméon Luce catalogued 855 fortified places which were occupied either by French or by Anglo-Navarrese soldiers in northern and central France during the eight years after the battle of Poitiers in 1356, accounting for well over ten thousand soldiers.[6] At much the same time, but in Brittany, there were no less than forty-four major Anglo-Breton garrisons confronted by a dozen or so French ones.[7] Although the French monarchy was experimenting with permanent armies during this period, notably under Charles V in the 1360s and 1370s, when up to six thousand soldiers were for a while in permanent paid service, and under Charles VII in the late 1440s when similar numbers were recruited into the *compagnies d'ordonnance*, it was, for the most part, quite incapable of absorbing professional soldiers into its service on this scale. Charles VI, in 1390, had to make do with less than half these numbers, and even these may not have been paid regularly.[8] The English Crown, throughout the fourteenth century, and during the latter stages of the war, was even less able to pay the soldiers it required to defend its interests in France. Most soldiers, if they were employed at all by a "public" authority, were engaged on short-term contracts, known to the English as indentures and to the French as *lettres de retenue*. When their services were no longer required in a field army or in a strategically important garrison, they were simply dismissed at the end of their contracts. They then, very often, became part of that mass of ill-paid or unpaid

---

3   *The "Livre de la Paix" of Christine de Pisan*, ed. C. Willard (The Hague, 1958), p. 110. She explains that Charles V had to contend, not only with the king of England, but also with the king of Navarre and the duke of Brittany: "pour lesquelz guerres convenoit tenir continuellement gens d'armes en v. ou en vi. lieux, es frontieres et par le royaume ou mesmement sur mer".

4   P. Contamine, *War in the Middle Ages*, trans. M. Jones (Oxford, 1984), p. 221. Map 3 shows the principal French garrisons in this area, of which eight contained at least 200 soldiers each, 14 with at least 100, 38 with less than 100.

5   K. Fowler, *The Age of Plantagenet and Valois: the Struggle for Supremacy 1328–1498* (London, 1967), p. 72.

6   S. Luce, *Histoire de Bertrand du Guesclin et de son Epoque: la Jeunesse de Bertrand, 1320–1364* (Paris, 1876), pp. 459–509. My figures are based on the assumption that, allowing for consecutive occupations, the average garrison strength was about a dozen soldiers: a conservative estimate.

7   Fowler, *Plantagenet and Valois*, p. 70.

8   P. Contamine, *Guerre, Etat et Société à la Fin du Moyen Age* (Paris, 1972), p. 210. Fowler, *Plantagenet and Valois*, pp. 134 and 137.

troops which sought-out, or created, frontiers of war in the hope of a share of those profits which came from the occupation of land and which awaited the next time that indentures were signed and wages began to flow again.

Clearly, in these frontier areas where English and French soldiers were concentrated in a large number of fortresses, the "great game" established some sort of continuity in the relatively small-scale confrontations of border warfare. Nevertheless, because it was a rare circumstance for a garrison soldier, on either side of these frontiers, to be paid a regular and sufficient wage, the notion of a frontier between "friendly" and "enemy" territory was in constant danger of collapse into meaninglessness as the fundamental imperatives of survival took precedence over the rules of the great game. For unpaid soldiers, the difference between friends and foes, especially amongst the non-combatants, was likely to be of little immediate relevance to their constant search for profits and sustenance. Similarly, a peasant who saw his livestock being driven away by unidentifiable armed men towards a fortified place had neither the capacity nor, one would guess, much incentive to determine whether the plunder was for the benefit of an English or of a French garrison. In these circumstances, the hundred or so years of war which was the day-to-day experience of people who lived in France during the later Middle Ages cannot always, or even usually, be related to the great game which was played by the kings and whose rules were made by their lawyers. A large amount of military activity took place (to use a popular contemporary expression) "under cover" of these wars. Lift the covers and we find a very serious lack of centralized control of military activity and a bewildering diversity of small-scale conflict. The Hundred Years War was as much a state of affairs, a condition of chronic instability, as the story of an Anglo-French power-struggle.

The diversity of conflict is reflected in the chronicles of the period. Making the best of his enforced idleness as a prisoner in Edinburgh castle during the middle years of the fourteenth century, Sir Thomas Gray endeavoured to place on record the deeds of arms done by his contemporaries in France. Like Jean Froissart after him, however, who travelled incessantly in search of stories lest he miss any important ones, he was overwhelmed by the sheer quantity of his material. "In the same season, truce having been struck as aforesaid, numbers of Englishmen who lived by the war invaded Normandy, plundered castles, seized manors, and carried on such warlike operations in the country . . . They were scattered in so many places over different parts of the country that nobody could recount the combats and deeds of arms which befel them during this time; but they so acted that all Christian people were filled with astonishment."[9] His intention had been to present an heroic account of the deeds of the English in France and elsewhere, but his *Scalacronica* quickly degenerates into a catalogue of disconnected skirmishes only elevated to the heroic plane by a tendency to exaggerate numbers and

[9]   *Scalacronica: the Reigns of Edward I, Edward II and Edward III as Recorded by Sir Thomas Gray*, ed. Sir H. Maxwell (Glasgow, 1907), pp. 130–1. *Chroniques de Jean Froissart, publiées pour la Société de l'Histoire de France par Siméon Luce (et al.)*, ii (Paris, 1869), p. 236.

by a mildly partisan spirit. The Carmelite friar, Jean de Venette, viewing the same phenomena from behind the walls of Paris, but with considerably less sympathy for what was going on, had the same thing to say: "For enemies multiplied throughout the land, and robbers increased to such a degree that they despoiled the inhabitants of country villages in their own houses . . . Highways and roads were almost everywhere uncertain and dangerous on account of freebooters and robbers."[10] Jean Juvenal des Ursins, in the following century, suggested that to describe the sufferings of the French people since the English invasion of 1415 would need a book as long as the Bible, "too long to recite".[11] Whether one wanted to praise the noble deeds of noblemen, as was the purpose of Froissart and Gray, or to damn the military class for its iniquities, as Venette and Ursins intended, one was confronted with the overwhelming problem of diversity.

The same sort of desperation is detectable in more recent accounts of the war by historians who have attempted to survey the whole field of war while doing justice to its complexity. Henri Denifle, the great Dominican historian, as he contemplated from the vantage-point of the nineteenth-century Vatican archives the destruction of churches and monasteries in France during the Hundred Years War, described the war as "an endless and grimly monotonous succession of massacres, fires, pillaging, ransoms, destructions, losses of harvests and cattle, rapes and – to make an end of it – of every sort of calamity".[12] Half a century later, Robert Boutruche, professor at the University of Strasbourg, attempted to comprehend the devastation of war with these words:

> Although the destruction was vast, its degree varied from region to region and, within each region, from one locality to the next . . . The variables are countless and in the current state of knowledge of regional history they cannot be assessed in their entirety.[13]

In describing the war in Gascony, he commented that this was far from being war on a continuous front, but was rather characterised by a multiplicity of ambushes and skirmishes, which were only occasionally drawn into the wider conflict.[14] Indeed, how could it have been otherwise in a province which, even before the war had begun, contained approximately one thousand castles and *maison-fortes*?[15]

We are dealing here with chroniclers and historians who did not shirk the task

10 *The Chronicle of Jean de Venette*, trans J. Birdsall, ed. R. Newhall (New York, 1953), p. 66.
11 Jean Juvenal des Ursins, *Les Ecrits Politiques de J.J. des U*, ed. P. Lewis, 3 vols. (Paris, 1978–92), iii, p. 109.
12 H. Denifle, *La Désolation des Eglises, Monastères et Hopitaux en France Pendant la Guerre de Cent Ans*, 2 vols. (Macon, 1897), i, p. 1.
13 R. Boutruche, "The Devastation of Rural Areas during the Hundred Years War and the Agricultural Recovery of France", *The Recovery of France in the Fifteenth Century*, ed. P. Lewis, trans. G. Martin (London, 1971), p. 29.
14 R. Boutruche, *La Crise d'une Société: Seigneurs et Paysans du Bordelais Pendant la Guerre de Cent Ans* (Paris, 1947), p. 165.
15 M. Vale, "Seigneurial Fortifications and Private War in later Medieval Gascony", *Gentry and Lesser Nobility in Late-Medieval Europe*, ed. M. Jones (Gloucester, 1986), p. 134.

of describing what they knew of the Hundred Years War in some of its diversity. They were merely facing up to the common problem of the serious investigator whose knowledge makes him only the more acutely aware of his own ignorance. As the focus shifts from the relative certainties of the "official" war of the great military campaigns led by the rival kings and their commanders, and from the battlefields where, on very rare occasions, they confronted each other, the multitude of smaller incidents which concerned smaller people comes fitfully and partially into view. These were the deeds of people who were fighting hardly at all for their king, still less for their country, but for themselves, their families, their communities, their companions. A study of the Hundred Years War, such as this present one, which seeks to create a better understanding of the impact of a very long war on a society of fifteen million souls within a territory of about 420,000 square kilometres, is bound to seem impressionistic and anecdotal because it relies heavily upon what the nineteenth-century Jules Michelet liked to call "voices" from the past and trust that they are representative.[16] But it is only by listening to the voices of concerned contemporaries and individual participants that we can penetrate into the painful business of day-to-day survival as soldiers and non-combatants confronted and adapted to each other during this period.

In terms which would have made sense to an educated person of the later Middle Ages, the difference between the two sorts of war, the "official" and the "unofficial", might be expressed as that between just and unjust wars.[17] The official war was waged on the authority of competent persons, namely sovereign princes; it was fought for good reasons, either for the defence of the national territory or to maintain the prince's rights; it was fought by soldiers whose principal purpose was to render their lord the service which they owed him and not, primarily, for their own vain-glory or private profit. The major campaigns of the Hundred Years War may not always have satisfied all of these criteria of the just war which had been invented by the theologians of the previous century and which had been incorporated into many a text-book of canon law. They did, however, come close enough, or could be sufficiently disguised, to be identifiable in such terms. There was no sharp distinction in real life between this war of princely campaigns and the kind of war which filled the gaps between them, as soldiers moved out of royal field armies into the static warfare of garrisons or the varied freebooting activities of the *routiers*. Soldiers moved easily between royal field armies, royal and private garrisons, and freebooting companies, as circumstances required. In these latter sorts of war, however, as soldiers approached and perhaps crossed that delicate boundary between loyal service and armed criminality, the self-interest motive inevitably became more prominent at the expense of

---

[16] For the size of fourteenth-century France, see P. Contamine, *La Vie Quotidienne Pendant la Guerre de Cent Ans: France et Angleterre (XIVe siècle)* (Paris, 1976), chapter 1. On Michelet's "voices", see J. Le Goff, *Pour un Autre Moyen Age* (Paris, 1977), p. 20.

[17] On the "Just War" theories of the period, see F. Russell, *The Just War in the Middle Ages* (Cambridge, 1975). Also M. Keen, *The Laws of War in the late Middle Ages* (London, 1965), esp. chapter 5, "The legal theory of Just War".

the war-aims of the sovereign princes. The distinction between the two sorts of war was a moral and a legal one, with penalties of an appropriately eternal and temporal kind promised for transgressors. The just warrior of the legal theorists was, ideally, the man-at-arms who had responded to the summons of his sovereign prince in his hour of need and had returned home when he had completed his service. It was acknowledged that he should be rewarded with pay and a share in the so-called "profits of war": booty and prisoners taken from the enemy. His motivation, however, was expected to be service rather than reward. At the other extreme was the armed robber, the *routier* or *companion*, who fought in unjust wars. This was the soldier who had slipped the traces of princely control and was engaged in a company of freebooters who made war "without reason", either because of his own cruelty and greed, or to support the cruelty and greed of another who was engaged in a private war. There were few soldiers aspiring to be truly professional, permanently occupied in the military calling within the kingdom of France, who did not stray into the area delineated by the lawyers and theologians as criminal.[18]

In terms which make more sense to us today, the "official" war is the Hundred Years War in its politico-strategic aspect. The "unofficial" Hundred Years War is the war in its socio-economic context. The key to an understanding of the latter is to follow the activities of the large numbers of soldiers who, for one reason or another (not all of them dishonourable), were unwilling to lay down their arms and go home as soon as their prince no longer required their services in the field or in a regularly paid garrison. It is a context which historians have often urged upon others and, more and more, are confronting themselves. Guy Bois, for example, has done this for the eastern parts of Normandy and it is a study which treats the war as only one part of a general social upheaval.[19] The French peasantry, instead of assuming the rôle of a restless but ineffectual ghost hinting at something unpleasant beneath the surface glitter of chivalry, as is its part in many histories of the Hundred Years War, is introduced as a key actor. From this point of view, the Hundred Years War loses some of its clarity as a political conflict carried on by military means but is more clearly presented as a struggle for survival between soldiers and non-combatants: between knights and peasants. "The Hundred Years War" in the French countryside, of my title, is mainly about this conflict.

---

[18] C. Rogers, "By Fire and Sword; *Bellum Hostile* and 'civilians' in the Hundred Years War", unpublished paper presented at "Civilians in the Path of War" Conference, Ohio State University, November 1993, pp. 41–42, attempts a distinction between war-like activities which were "elements" of the Hundred Years War and those which were merely "results" of this war. In this analysis, those who fought in the name of the king of France or of England (including the *routiers* of the late 1350s) fall into the former category, while the Free Companies and (presumably) those engaged in other wars on French soil fall into the latter. It is argued in this present work that such a distinction is easier to maintain in the context of law-courts and political commentaries than it is in the circumstances of individual warriors "on the ground". [Rogers' significant contribution to the subject has, unfortunately, come to my notice too late to incorporate its findings into my text.]

[19] G. Bois, *Crise du Féodalisme* (Paris, 1981).

Knights and peasants

If the commonly accepted notion of what is, and is not, "the" Hundred Years War is affronted by an interpretation which relegates political and strategic issues to the side-lines, the "knights" of my title might also be seen as something of a challenge. Of the soldiers who fought during the Hundred Years War, only a very tiny, and declining, proportion were knights.[20] Even amongst the ranks of soldiers who were called men-at-arms – that is to say, those who normally fought on horseback with the accoutrements and according to the rules of chivalric warfare – only about one in every ten had been through some form of initiation into the ranks of knighthood. The rest, the squires, felt no need to acquire the title of "Sir" or "Messire" and had several good financial reasons not to do so. As for the mass of common soldiers, the archers, crossbowmen, pikemen, varlets and pillagers, who normally fought on foot and were protected by lighter armour, the gulf which separated them from the knights was much wider and, without an extraordinary measure of luck and ambition, unbridgeable. Contacts between knights and peasants, whether friendly or hostile, were, as we shall see, extremely rare. The commissariat function of armies in enemy territory, and of garrisons, was largely carried out on a much less exalted level, by the personal servants of the men-at-arms, known as *valets* or *pillars*, whose social origin was much closer to that of their victims than to that of their masters.[21] The Tree of War, or of Battles, was a popular allegory at that time and later for the hierarchy of military affairs in which the princes and knights occupy the upper branches and the common soldiers the lower ones which were closer, in more ways than one, to the earth. Honoré Bouvet's *L'Arbre des Batailles* was a famous and widely dispersed example of the fourteenth century, with the rival popes at the top, the warring kings and princes on the next level, and the commons at the bottom.[22] Grimmelshausen's later vision, as described by his Simplicissimus the Vagabond, is a more developed version of the *genre* and drawn from the author's own extensive experience of the Thirty Years War.[23] The roots of this tree are the peasants who give it strength; its

---

[20] P. Contamine, "The French Nobility and the War", chapter 6 in *The Hundred Years War*, ed. K. Fowler (London, 1971), esp. p. 145.

[21] N. Wright, " 'Pillagers' and 'Brigands' in the Hundred Years War", *Journal of Medieval History*, ix (1983), pp. 15–24.

[22] *L'Arbre des Batailles d'Honoré Bonet*, ed. E. Nys (Brussels, 1883), pp. 2–3, where the author describes the meaning of his "arbre de dueil". This can also be read in *The Tree of Battles of Honoré Bonet*, trans. G. Coopland (Liverpool, 1949), p. 79. On the spelling of the author's surname, Bouvet or Bonet, see G. Ouy, "Honoré Bouvet (appelé à tort Bonet) Prieur de Selonnet", *Romania*, lxxx (1959), pp. 255–9. Also N. Wright, "Honoré Bouvet and the Abbey of Ile-Barbe", *Recherches de Théologie Ancienne et Médiévale*, xxxix (1972), p. 113, n.1. To complete the confusion, several historians now insist, inconveniently, but with some reason, upon the form "Bovet".

[23] Grimmelshausen, J. Christoph, *Simplicissimus the Vagabond*, trans. A. Goodrick (London, 1912), pp. 32–4. The author, Johann Jacob Christoph, otherwise Grimmelshausen, was born c. 1621 and died in 1676. By his sixteenth birthday, he had been captured by Croatians and

lower branches are occupied by the common soldiers known as "henroost-robbers" and "coat-beaters", insolent, swaggering and vile; in the upper branches sit the "higher folk" who could fill their pockets with the fattest slices cut from the roots, but who are separated from the teeming lower branches by a smooth place on the tree trunk "greased with all manner of ointments and curious soap of disfavour, so that no man save of noble birth could scale it".

It may, therefore, seem perverse to persist with the word "knight", in the title, when only the upper branches of the late medieval tree of war were peopled by men of this sort, and when so much of the activity described is that of "henroost robbing" rather than the clash of heavily-armoured horsemen. The term "soldier" might seem to be a wiser choice. This latter has not, however, been used in the title for several reasons. The medieval origins of this simple, catch-all, term have confusing implications. As *soillar* it would have excluded altogether the noble category of men-at-arms who dominated the war from start to finish, for the author of the fourteenth-century *Complaint on the Battle of Poitiers* makes a clear distinction between men-at-arms and "their *soillars*".[24] A soldier, in this sense, could easily have been of peasant background, either taken into the service of a man-at-arms to fetch and carry for him as a *pillar*, *valet* or *page*, or as part of a parish contingent of footsoldiers responding to a general call to arms. He was the occupant of the lower branches only. As *soudier*, payment for service would have been a defining characteristic, which, as has already been seen, could never actually have been taken for granted.[25] It has, moreover, been the cause of much comment on the warfare of the later Middle Ages, both then and now, that the ethos of the knightly warrior known as chivalry was very much at odds with the kind of warfare which most of the military class were actually engaged in for most of the time. The contrast between this great ideal of the sublime life, conducted according to strict rules of honour, which belonged, *par excellence*, to the knights, and the grubbiness of the daily experience of war, was a rich mine for contemporary clerical satire and an important theme of this present book. As everyone knew at the time, the people who controlled the activity of pillage and of forced contributions from non-combatants, and the people who gained the lion's share of the proceeds, were the knights and their fellow men-at-arms, the squires, who were in most respects indistinguishable from them. Although there were some half-hearted attempts, especially by laymen, to blame common soldiers for the crimes which were committed to provision and to enrich men-at-arms at the

Hessians and recruited into imperial service. He had then seen military service during the last dozen years of the 30 Years War. His *Simplicissimus*, written in 1668, has no medieval parallel.

24 "Complainte sur la Bataille de Poitiers". ed. C. de Beaurepaire, *Bibliothèque de l'Ecole des Chartes (BEC)*, ii (1851), p. 261.

25 The word is derived from the name of the Roman coin, the *solidus*, and that of the French *sol*.

4. A Tree of Battles: Bibliothèque Royale, Brussels, ms 9079, fo. 10v.
(Copyright Bibliothèque Royale Albert Ier, Bruxelles)

expense of non-combatants,[26] the main target for criticism was the nobility in arms, the knights themselves. They failed, according to many clerical commentators, not only at the level of effective soldiering (in that they failed to win the war), but also, and more significantly in the context of this present book, at the level of lordship (in that they attacked, rather than defended, their people). Any study of the Hundred Years War in the French countryside which fails to place the subject of territorial lordship at its centre is in danger of missing the mark; and any study of territorial lordship which does not have the knights at its core is equally wide of the mark.

The term "soldier" will, however, be used in the chapters which follow in the modern sense of "one who takes part in military service" because there is no serious alternative when a need to imply a distinction between commoner and gentleman is *not* required. Where such a social distinction *is* indicated, the term "man-at-arms" will be used to denote both knights and squires: those whose weapons and equipment, whose assumptions and aspirations, if not always their birth, set them apart from the common soldier.

The term "peasant" is, alas, not without its own attendant difficulties. This is not because we lack an adequate definition of the term in its medieval context. Indeed, Rodney Hilton has listed five or six "essential elements" of this class in his famous study of the English peasantry of this very period.[27] Nor is there a problem that contemporaries did not recognize and use the notion of a class of agricultural farmers and workers which they called "labourers" and "rustics". This social class or "order" was quite clearly acknowledged by all as the economic foundation of their society. The French of this period even had a name for the quintessential peasant: it was *Jacques Bonhomme*. The problem for historians, however, is in determining whether the "non-nobles", "laboureurs", "povres laboureurs", "gens du plat pays", "laboratores", "populares", "rustici" of their documents and other source materials possess any or all of Hilton's essential characteristics. The ambiguities associated with these terms have, for example, recently brought that great Peasant Revolt of the fourteenth century in France, the *Jacquerie*, into question as a "peasant" revolt because of the presence of people who were clearly not agricultural labourers within the ranks of the *jacques*.[28] It is obviously important to make distinctions when distinctions can be made, but we should not be disheartened if the softness of our evidence refuses to

[26] Sir Thomas Gray, for example, described the Free Companies as "but a gathering of commons, young fellows who hitherto had been of small account", *Scalacronica*, p. 131. Alain Chartier also has his knight, in the *Quadrilogue Invectif*, ed. E. Droz (Paris, 1950), p. 33, attribute many of the outrages of war to people of low estate. Interestingly, Jean Gerson's description of the Seven Deadly Sins, in his famous Vivat Rex sermon of 1405, describes them as accompanied by "les aultres detestables sodoiers et crueulx pillars sans nombre". *Jean Gerson, Oeuvres Complètes*, ed. Mgr. Glorieux, 10 vols. (Paris, 1960–73), vii, p. 1150.

[27] R. Hilton, *The English Peasantry in the later Middle Ages: the Ford Lectures for 1973 and Related Studies* (Oxford, 1975), pp. 12–13.

[28] R. Cazelles, "La Jacquerie: Fut-elle un Mouvement Paysan?", *Academie des Inscriptions et Belles Lettres, Comptes-rendus* (July–Oct. 1978), pp. 654–66.

be accommodated within hard categories. The people denoted by the "peasant" label of the title are the inhabitants of the French *plat pays,* the "flatlands" of the open country which existed outside the walls of the great towns and castles.[29] The exact nature of their livelihood, whether agricultural labour, small farming, rural craftsmanship, petty officialdom, or a combination of each or any of these, is usually impossible to determine. Nevertheless, if the knight was the archetype of the late medieval warrior who set his stamp upon the conduct of military activity during the course of the Hundred Years War; so, also, was the peasant the archetypal non-combatant, the one who supported the military establishment and was at times consumed by it.

Sources

It must be admitted that the sources for a systematic study of the relationship between combatants and non-combatants during this period do not exist. The people who described the horrors of late medieval warfare were, for the most part, clergymen, whose descriptions are not of first-hand personal experience and are often over-blown and formulaic. The men with personal experience of warfare, and provided with the will and capacity to describe that experience in literary form, were so preoccupied with the chivalric ideal of warfare that they tended to ignore its darker and ignoble dimension. Whereas chronicles of the war are often richly illustrated with pictures of armed men in direct conflict with each other, they very rarely show an armed raid on a village. There is nothing from this period which remotely approaches the harsh realism of Jacques Callot's etchings in his seventeenth-century *Misères et Malheurs de la Guerre,* nor the engravings of Romeyn de Hooghe which illustrate Myron Gutmann's study of soldiers and peasants in the early-modern Low Countries.[30] By the standards even of sixteenth-century wars, historians of the "civilian" dimension of late medieval warfare are woefully ill-equipped. There are, however, some exceptions and surprises.

The careers and aspirations of noble warriors are well represented in the chroniclers, like Jean Froissart, who identified with their way of life and determined to record their deeds of arms.[31] His purpose and that of Jean Monstrelet who followed him was to describe, for the inspiration of future generations of men-at-arms, the "great enterprises, fine feats of arms, which took place during

---

[29] This problem of classification is discussed in C. Gauvard, *De Grace Especial: Crime, Etat et Société en France à la Fin du Moyen Age,* 2 vols. (Paris, 1991), 1, pp. 411–15 and 422. The non-nobles involved in the Jacquerie of 1358 were often called "gens du plat pays" and they included masons, coopers, blacksmiths, wheelwrights, quarrymen, country clergy and petty officials.

[30] M. Gutmann, *War and Rural Life in the Early-modern Low Countries* (Assen, 1980)

[31] The best, but still incomplete, edition of Froissart's *Chroniques* is the multi-volume edition for the *Société de l'Histoire de France,* edited by S. Luce and others. A good English language abridgement is *Froissart, Chronicles,* ed. G. Brereton (Harmondsworth, 1968).

the wars waged by France and England".[32] Fortunately for us, their histories of
the war are not limited to such matter, nor were their authors so besotted by the
colourful and glorious aspects of knightly warfare that they refused to recognize
and describe any other aspect. Nevertheless, their admitted purpose was to present
the glorious and honourable activities of noble warriors and, although we should
never discount these records of deeds of arms, they do create a misleading
impression that the Hundred Years War was fought largely by men-at-arms
according to the conventions of knightly warfare. The chivalric hagiographies of
military commanders, like that of the Black Prince by the herald of his friend, Sir
John Chandos, and that of the French marshal, Boucicaut, and of Louis II, duke
of Bourbon, also have the stated purpose of setting on record the honourable deeds
of their real-life heroes for the example and benefit of other knights.[33] Because
the biographers are a great deal more single-minded than the chroniclers, who are
more easily distracted, their works tend to be less revealing both about their noble
subjects and about their society.

Much more important for our purpose within what might be called the "secular" literature of the period are the works of knights who had the chance to reflect
upon their own experience either in a contemplative old age, like Philippe de
Mézières, or because they had achieved such high status as military commanders,
like Geoffrey Charny or Jean de Bueil, that they commanded a natural respect.
Many, as the fifteenth-century squire, Stephen Scrope, charmingly expressed it,
were men who had spent the greater part of their days in "dedys of chevalrie and
actis of armis" but who had, in old age, turned to "gostly chevallrie off dedes of
armes spirituall, as in contemplacion of morall wysdome and exercisying gostly
werkys".[34] Mézières' concern, in several works of which the *Dream of the Old
Pilgrim* is undoubtedly the most important, was with steering a reformed knighthood away from the internecine war between Christians towards the crusade
against the Turk.[35] His military experience as a knight during the early years of
the Hundred Years War and the political wisdom derived from the councils of the
kings of Cyprus and of France gave him a breadth of view and a depth of
understanding very rare in this period. Charny and de Bueil were both military
commanders, the one of the early years of the war until his glorious death at
Poitiers bearing the sacred *Oriflamme* banner of France, the other who ended the

---

[32] Froissart, *Chroniques*, ed. Luce , i, p. 1.
[33] *Life of the Black Prince by the Herald of Sir John Chandos*, ed. M. Pope and E. Lodge
    (Oxford, 1910). *Le Livre du Bon Messire Jean le Maingre dit Boucicaut, Mareschal de
    France et Gouverneur de Genes*, ed. C. Petitot (Paris, 1819). See also D. Lalande, *Jean II
    le Meingre dit Boucicaut 1366–1421: Etude d'une Biographie Héroïque* (Geneva, 1988). J.
    Cabaret d'Orville, *La Chronique du Bon Duc Loys de Bourbon*, ed. A. Chazaud (Paris,
    1876).
[34] *The Epistre of Othea to Hector, or the Boke of Knyghthode, Translated from the French of
    Christine de Pisan with a Dedication to Sir John Fastolf, K.G., by Stephen Scrope, Esquire*,
    ed. G. Warner (London, 1904), p. 1. The quotation is from the dedication.
[35] Philippe de Mézières, *Le Songe du Vieil Pelerin*, ed. G. Coopland, 2 vols. (Cambridge,
    1969). The best biography of this writer is still N. Jorga, *Philippe de Mézières, 1327–1405,
    et la Croisade au XIVe Siècle* (Paris, 1896).

war in his capacity as the French commander at the battle of Castillon in 1453.[36] Each, in his own way, was concerned with the problem of how a young man-at-arms, eager for a military career, might find an honourable path. Their concern in the matter belies the impression which Froissart and others unwittingly project that the knights of the Hundred Years War were all either self-seeking mercenaries or frivolous glory-hunters. They show that honour in warfare, a delicate plant in any age, was no less in need of careful nurturing in this so-called Age of Chivalry.

Mézières is certainly not typical of what might be called "secular" writers, and his semi-enclosure in the Paris Celestine convent during the latter years of his life was not a retirement which every military veteran would contemplate easily. When he died, in 1405, he was buried in the convent chapel, dressed in the Celestine habit, after his body had been dragged, feet-first, into the church and bound to a hurdle. Such, at least, were the demands which he made in his will of 1392.[37] The canvas of the "Dream" of this most untypical of knights is the entire society of western Christendom and, as such, inevitably includes the peasantry and its problems and grievances. For the most part, however, these secular writers were concerned with the matter of chivalry which was the affair of men-at-arms exclusively. The concerns of peasants were not only irrelevant to this matter of chivalry but the very antithesis of it: base, ignoble, unrefined, clod-hopping. It was a fact of life, almost too obvious to be worth mentioning, that the glorious lifestyle of the knightly warrior was founded upon the wealth produced by peasants. This was part of the divine order of things. If peasants, or their advocates, complained about the high level of taxation and the plundering activities of men-at-arms; these latter were not without their own complaints. They were obliged, it was argued, to throw their lives and their fortunes into the defence of the king and his non-combatant subjects while the priests and peasants amassed wealth and refused to pay properly for their own defence.[38] The argument may seem disingenuous to us, but, to men like Geoffrey Charny or Jean de Bueil, it may have seemed no more than a statement of fact based upon their own hard experience. Neither of them could have been ignorant of the terrifying ferocity of a peasantry aroused to rebellion and both were familiar with the hardships and dangers of the military life.

Although of little interest to the chroniclers of chivalry like Jean Froissart, and of still less interest to the biographers of knightly heroes like Jean Cabaret d'Orville, the peasantry and its grievances had a much more sympathetic showing in the rich political and didactic literature which flowered in France during the

---

[36] The most useful recent survey of Charny's military career may be found in M. Keen, *Chivalry* (New Haven, 1984), pp. 12–15. The life of Jean de Bueil is surveyed in the introduction to *Le Jouvencel par Jean de Bueil Suivi du Commentaires de Guillaume Tringant*, ed. C. Favre and L. Lecestre, 2 vols. (Paris, 1887–9).

[37] Jorga, *Mézières*, p. 509.

[38] These sentiments are expressed, in part, by the knight in the fourteenth-century *Le Songe du Vergier*, ed. M. Schnerb-Lièvre (Paris, 1982), pp. 39 ff. Alain Chartier does so, but with a lighter touch, in *Le Qadrilogue Invectif*, of 1422, pp. 14 and 29.

second half of the fourteenth century and in the early part of the fifteenth.[39] The
apparatus of the French state, as it struggled to cope with an incapable king, the
rivalries of princes, the Great Schism within the Church, constant war and tax
revolts, spawned a lively political debate during the reign of Charles VI. This reign
witnessed, in the words of Claude Gauvard, "a great debate on the meaning of
justice and on its application . . . . a fever of writing".[40] The ground was prepared
by Charles V whose love of books – especially of translations of the classics – was
well-known. Its full blossoming came during the reign of his unfortunate son,
Charles VI. By the time, in 1392, when the king became incapacitated by mental
instability, there were a dozen or so prominent writers loosely associated with the
French court in Paris with surprisingly similar views about the ills of French
society and their remedies. With one or two exceptions, like the Provençal Honoré
Bouvet and the Italian Christine de Pisan, they came from the north-eastern
quadrant of the kingdom: from Normandy in the north to Champagne in the east.
Many were graduates of the Paris faculties of Arts and Theology and alumni of
the powerful university college of Navarre.[41] All shared in a nostalgia for the reign
of Good King Charles (V) when writers and men of ideas had a ready access to a
king who listened to what they had to say, read what they wrote and showered
them with pensions and positions.[42] Some were excited by prophecies of a more
of less apocalyptic kind which suggested a world-leadership rôle for the manifestly unsuitable young king. All complained in sermons, poetry, letters, political
and legal treatises about the Crown's neglect of its obligations and of the aristocracy's decadence which allowed the fearful exploitation of an innocent peasantry
and the destruction of rich and plentiful land. Not only has this picture of the
men-at-arms of the late Middle Ages struck a strong chord of sympathy in our
more democratic age, but the notion of Good King Charles, which was largely
their creation, has endured. When Raoul Mathei, while carousing in a Paris tavern

---

[39] The centre of this literary renaissance during the reign of Charles V was possibly the College
of Navarre of Paris University. Nicolas Oresme combined the office of its grand master with
that of royal secretary. His pupil and successor as grand master was Pierre d'Ailly whose
spectacular career as royal confessor, university chancellor, bishop and cardinal was an
inspiration to young careerists such as Jean Gerson and Nicolas de Clamanges. Philippe de
Mézières and Eustache Deschamps were also closely associated with Charles V, as was
Christine de Pisan's family. On the Navarre college, see G. Ouy, "Le College de Navarre,
Berceau de l'Humanisme Français", *Actes du 95e Congrès National des Sociétés Savantes;
Philologie et Histoire jusqu'à 1610*, 1 (Reims, 1970), pp. 275–99.

[40] Gauvard, *Grace Especial*, i, p. 54.

[41] D'Ailly was from Compiègne in the Ile-de-France and a Paris Arts graduate. His friend Jean
de Montreuil came from the Pas-de-Calais and proceeded through the College of Navarre
and the Paris Arts faculty. Gerson and Clamanges, both from Champagne, were d'Ailly's
pupils at the college and went on from the Arts to the Theology faculty. Mézières and
Deschamps, though not graduates, were from Picardy and Champagne, respectively.

[42] Christine de Pisan, *Le Livre des Fais et Bonnes Meurs du Sage Roy Charles V*, ed. S. Solente,
2 vols. (Paris, 1936–40), i, p. 39.

in the summer of 1382, was reported to have abused the late king, calling him an avaricious tyrant, his words still ring down the centuries like a blasphemy.[43]

These self-appointed advocates of the public weal who attempted to catch the conscience of the king at the time of Charles VI had a pedigree embedded in centuries of sermon literature quite as ancient as the chivalric genres. They themselves gave inspiration to a new generation of writers such as Alain Chartier, Pierre de Nesson, Jean Juvenal des Ursins. They did not represent the "peasant point of view" (if such a phrase can have any meaning) however passionately they claimed to espouse it and however close some of them were to their peasant roots. Nor, despite their generally clerical status, could they possibly represent that vast and amorphous clerical estate of late medieval France.[44] They are best understood neither as repositories of representative contemporary attitudes, nor as dispassionate observers of their own society, but rather as a reform group whose close attachment to the French royal court and to the University of Paris enlarged their mental horizons and gave depth and subtlety to their analyses of contemporary problems, but at the price of a detachment from the world of ordinary people. Far from treating the Hundred Years War as the stage for the enactment of glorious deeds, they were inspired by the prospect of a final peace between France and England to hold out the hope for a resolution to the other major issues of the day: the schism in the papacy, the menace of the advancing Ottomans and the erosion of French royal power. Responsibility for much of the current crisis was laid squarely at the door of a wicked and rapacious knighthood which had forgotten its obligation to society and which, while failing to repel the English aggressor, had turned its weapons upon its own people.

The sermon tradition of castigating a cowardly and greedy knighthood and of treating the peasantry as their defenceless victim is best represented in the early decades of the Hundred Years War by the Carmelite friar, Jean de Venette. His chronicle of the events of northern France during the period 1340–1368 is rich in detail and enlivened by a sympathy for the class of peasants from which he, himself, had sprung. His analysis of the relationship between soldiers and civilians is illustrated by the parable of the sheepdog who struck up a friendship with a wolf, an arrangement which allowed them comfortably to devour the master's sheep together.[45] This predicatory tradition may also be illustrated from the closing years of the war by the bishop, Jean Juvenal des Ursins, whose interminable treatises were the scourge of the morals of his time. In the intervening years we can see it reappearing in an extraordinary variety of contexts: sermons, of course, by Jean Gerson (also of peasant background); a law book by Honoré Bouvet; treatises on "chivalry" by Christine de Pisan; poetry by Eustache Deschamps; political tracts by humanist men of letters, like Jean de Montreuil; chronicles such as Thomas

---

[43] *Choix de Pièces Inédites Relatives au Règne de Charles V*, ed. L. Douët-d'Arcq, 2 vols. (Paris, 1863), i, pp. 99–100.

[44] J. Barnie, *War in Medieval Society: Social Values and the Hundred Years War, 1337–99* (London, 1974), on the other hand, argues for a certain "representativeness" in literature of social groups such as the regular and secular clergy, the common people, the military élite.

[45] Venette, *Chronicle*, p. 113.

Basin's.[46] If sheer repetition of a theme by contemporary writers may be taken as a guide to its relevance to their own situation, then historians would be well-advised to take it very seriously indeed. But, as with the chivalric literature described earlier, they must be as cautious in the way they use a literature which, for the purpose of moral reform, proposes the knight as a wicked oppressor, as they must be with one which, for altogether different moral purposes, proposes him as hero.

It is sometimes supposed that, while we may be able to understand the mentality and lifestyle of the late medieval knightly warrior through the vast surviving literature of chivalry, through the records of his disputes in the highest courts of law, through the abundant records of the military bureaucracies, and even through the hostile criticism of the preaching clergy, the late medieval peasant must remain either an enigma or a clerical stereotype. This is not entirely true.

It was during the third decade of the last century that a famous director of the historical section of the French national archives claimed to hear the murmur of distant voices in the solitary galleries of his archives. The archivist was Jules Michelet and the voices were those of the fourteenth-century French peasants contained in the old registers of the royal chancery, now catalogued "JJ". "I was not on my guard", wrote Michelet with typical flamboyance, "I expected nothing, when the figure of Jacques [Bonhomme] raised himself from the furrow and barred my way, a figure monstrous and terrible."[47] Michelet's re-creation of the late medieval French peasants in the relevant volumes of his *Histoire de France* will be a recurrent theme of this book: a distorted image, certainly, but one which has infected many historians since his own time.

One of the voices which Michelet may have heard was first heard by Charles V at his castle at Vincennes, near Paris, in the summer of 1373. It belonged to Jehannin Chevalier, known as "Charbonnier".[48] He was a peasant, a "Jacques Bonhomme", of the parish of Marchais-Beton, now in the department of the Yonne, who had travelled a hundred miles of dangerous roads in order to join the crowd of petitioners who daily thronged the royal residences in and around Paris: Saint-Pol, the Louvre, Vincennes. He may have caught the eye of the king himself as he emerged from his morning mass or, more probably, one of the king's officers

46 The best modern edition of Gerson's work is *Jean Gerson: Oeuvres Complètes*, ed. Mgr. Glorieux, 10 vols. (Paris, 1960–73). The French sermons have been analysed by E. Bourret, *Essai Historique et Critique sur les Sermons Français de Gerson* (Paris, 1858). Honoré Bouvet, *L'Arbre des Batailles*. Christine de Pisan, *Le Livre des Fais d'armes et de Chevalerie* must be read in the original ms (Bibliothèque nationale, Paris, fonds français 1243) or in the fifteenth-century translation by W. Caxton, *The Book of Fayttes of Armes and of Chyvalrye*, ed. A. Byles (Oxford, 1932). Eustache Deschamps, *Oeuvres Complètes*, ed. le Marquis de Queux de Saint-Hilaire and G. Raynaud, 9 vols. (Paris, 1878–1903). Jean de Montreuil's political writings have been described by P. Lewis, "War Propaganda and Historiography in Fifteenth-century France and England", *Transactions of the Royal Historical Society*, xv (1965), pp. 1–21. Thomas Basin, *Histoire de Charles VII*, ed. C. Samaran, i (Paris, 1933).
47 Le Goff, *Autre Moyen Age*, p. 28.
48 Archives Nationales, Paris [AN.], JJ 104, no.267.

of the Requests. His story was that, in the year of 1358, the English and other enemies had been lodged in several towns and fortresses of his district. All the people of the open country had been forced to hand over "provisions, ransoms, tools, nails and other things" to the English collectors. One of these collectors was the priest of a neighbouring village whom the people called Sir Peter and who was on very good terms with the English. One day in that year "Sir" Peter, the priest, met Charbonnier, the peasant, in the woods. A violent argument was concluded by the priest "lying there quite dead". The king, either directly or through intermediaries, heard the petition, granted the killer a letter of *rémission*, and ordered him to appear with it before the royal bailiff of Sens.

The orderly, if rather cryptic, summary of evidence which Charbonnier presented in order to obtain a pardon for a homicide committed fifteen years previously is contained in a large register of several hundred pages and classified JJ 104. It is the copy of a royal pardon, called a *lettre de rémission*, emanating from the king in council, drawn-up and sealed in the royal chancery of whose records, these registers form an important part. These famous records, which were started in the early years of the fourteenth century and were terminated, 244 registers later, in the middle of the sixteenth century, contain the texts of about 54,000 letters of remission.[49] Jehannin Chevalier's is not untypical: a man of humble background who had been impelled by desperate circumstances to commit a homicide, now seeking an end to the threat of prosecution by placing himself on the king's mercy. These copies of royal letters must be, and have been since the time of Michelet, an important source for the study of the late medieval peasantry. They are particularly illuminating on the interface between village communities and armed outsiders which bore fruit in the sort of violence which might later require a release from criminal prosecution.

It is, of course, true that Charbonnier and his like presented their case in as favourable a light to themselves as was possible.[50] But there was usually an element of control in the remission procedure which allows us to treat their records as serious sources. When our Jehannin Chevalier received his pardon from the *audencier* of the royal chancery, formally authenticated by the imprint of the great

---

[49] The best short survey of these records is that of M. François, "Note sur les Lettres de Rémission Transcrites dans les Registres du Trésor des Chartes", *BEC*, ciii (1942), pp. 317–24. A much more massive survey of the registers, especially of the Charles VI period, is Gauvard, *Grace Especial*, and her discussion of the remissions as evidence in vol. i, pp. 61–76 is useful. See also B. Guenée, *Tribunaux et Gens de Justice dans le Bailliage de Senlis à la Fin du Moyen Age (vers 1380-vers 1550)* (Paris, 1963), pp. 301–2, and G. Tessier, *Diplomatique Royale Française* (Paris, 1962), chapter 13.

[50] A full discussion of the dangers to historians of JJ evidence in terms of distortion of evidence for reasons of bureaucratic convenience and of special pleading (also because of the costs and dangers for petitioners which would have deterred the very poor and the very distant from Paris) is in Gauvard, *Grace Especial*, i, pp. 64–70. It should also be noted that no petitions were received from the great principalities of Brittany, Aquitaine and Burgundy, and very few from the Languedoc.

seal of Charles V, he was reminded that this was the successful beginning of the process, not its termination. He then had to present the letter to the royal bailiff of his district who would confirm and enregister it only after an investigation of the facts of the case and after having satisfied himself that the relatives of the victim had been duly compensated. Philippe de Mézières, it is true, did complain that this investigation was by-passed in the cases of people with friends at court, but we may assume that peasants such as Charbonnier did not fall within this category. Thus if he, and the others like him, had been at all familiar with the procedures of which the granting of a remission were only a part, they should have been careful to be no worse than economical with the truth. And although the figure of Jacques Bonhomme, rising from the furrow, would require some of Michelet's prodigious imagination to become as familiar a figure to us as Froissart's carefree young noblemen, these records, tantalizingly abbreviated as they so often are, are a useful counterweight to the stereotypes created by the medieval clergy.

Their immediate impact upon historians, however, was to confirm the notion of the peasant as victim. "In this chivalrous war" wrote Michelet of the middle years of the fourteenth century, "which the nobles of France and of England waged, there was, at bottom, only one enemy, one victim of the evils of war, it was the peasant."[51] "The peasants slept no more. Those of the Loire valley spent their nights on islands or in boats anchored in the river. Those of Picardy lived in underground tunnels. The women and children rotted in there for weeks and for months while the men went timidly to the bell-tower to see whether the men-at-arms had left the country."[52] The danger which any social historian of the Hundred Years War faces, especially when confronted by the special pleading of the clerical jeremiahs and that of peasant fugitives from justice, is to exaggerate (as they so often did) the evils of war and the breakdown of systems. Michelet, never fearful of overstatements or contradictions, was also able to discern another image of the late medieval peasantry which contradicted the peasant-victim stereotype and which may be represented by the "Sir Peter" of our story lying in the woods of Marchais Beton "quite dead", with his killer, the peasant, Charbonnier, standing over him. The French peasant could show himself to Michelet, with one blow, strong enough to overcome his "class enemy", the aristocracy and its fellow-travellers, and his "national enemy", the English and theirs. Of course, the very existence and meaning of class-consciousness and national sentiment in the late Middle Ages have been the subjects of intense debate amongst generations of historians, with no agreement likely, but the images of the peasant of the period as class-warrior and as French patriot are, nonetheless, very powerful and not without some meaning. This is why the figure of Jack Goodman, the medieval peasant, was, to Michelet, "monstrous and terrible"; and this is why he embraced him so passionately.

---

[51] J. Michelet, *L'Histoire de France*, iii (Paris, 1837), p. 315.
[52] Ibid., pp. 319–20.

These are Frenchmen, these peasants. Do not blush! Here already is the French people . . . amongst the conflicts of nobles and the elegant jousts where the carefree Froissart promenaded, we have been searching for this poor people.[53]

Michelet's idea that the late medieval French peasantry represents a nascent *patrie* had a profound effect on the writing of history in France during the latter half of the nineteenth century and at the beginning of our own century, and it still exercises an influence. Siméon Luce, who had more excuse than most, as the editor of Froissart's chronicles, to fall under the spell of that heroic version of events, resisted that temptation. He identified a "loyal" peasantry in the fourteenth- century Avranchin and Cotentin: "these humble martyrs of the soil who paid such a price for the honour of remaining loyal to their king".[54] The peasantry of English-occupied Normandy, during the later phase of the Hundred Years War, have also received their apotheosis as neglected national heroes and the debate over the motivation of the Norman brigands, executed by the English military authorities of that period, can still provoke a lively exchange of fire between English- and French-speaking historians.[55] The medieval peasant as "patriot" is not a dead dog.

Nor is Michelet's other notion of the peasant as a class-warrior who had identified the aristocratic man-at-arms, of whatever allegiance, as his class enemy. Luce, already in 1859 very much under Michelet's influence, observed a continuity between that "deadly and regrettable cleavage between the nobility and the people", of the fourteenth century, and the one which culminated four centuries later in the Terror.[56] This idea has since been enlarged upon by Marxist and *Annaliste* historians of the twentieth century who have substantially modified the liberal-romantic image of a peasantry whose normal meek passivity could, in moments of extreme hardship, give way to spontaneous and ferocious violence. Marc Bloch, in a well-known remark delivered to a lecture audience in Oslo in 1929, which was later incorporated into an important study of French rural history, suggested that agrarian revolt might have been as common in the medieval period as strikes are to modern capitalistic enterprise.[57] He showed, moreover, that the consolidation of the village as a corporate entity with the will and the power to act in its own interests against outside interference was a feature of peasant society throughout the medieval period. His relevance to the study of the peasantry in the Hundred Years War period is suggested by the remark that "it was, above all, in dealing with its enemies that the small rural collective not only became conscious of its own identity, but also gradually forced society to accept it as a viable and

---

[53] Ibid., p. 335.

[54] Luce, *Bertrand du Guesclin*, p. 276.

[55] A judicious survey of this debate is C. Allmand, *Lancastrian Normandy, 1415–1450: the History of a Medieval Occupation* (Oxford, 1983), pp. 306–11.

[56] S. Luce, *Histoire de la Jacquerie d'après des Documents Inédits* (Paris, 1859), p. 32.

[57] M. Bloch, *French Rural History: an Essay on its Basic Characteristics*, trans. J. Sondheimer (Berkeley, 1966), p. 170.

living institution".[58] This phenomenon of village solidarity against outsiders has been remarked upon by many French historians since 1929 and Rodney Hilton has observed the same phenomenon in fourteenth-century England where the village communities were quite capable of organising concerted action against "outsiders", including their own lords.[59] The possibility is therefore suggested that the great peasant dramas of late medieval France – the *Jacquerie*, the *Tuchinerie*, the brigandage and rebellion in fifteenth-century Normandy – may have been unusually bloody episodes in an age-old conflict between lords and peasants. The question of allegiances and loyalties of either party to the French or English Crowns is reduced in this scenario to a matter of small significance. In this analysis, the "lord" is represented by the men-at-arms who occupied fortresses and who had established *de facto* lordships throughout the French countryside, the occupants of the upper branches of the tree of war; the "peasant" is the inhabitant of the surrounding villages who had to support them, "lamenting over them that sat on the tree, and that with good reason, for the whole weight of the tree lay upon them".[60]

This present work does not seek to place knights and peasants into the scales of heroism and baseness, patriotism and class-consciousness, because the reality is inevitably more complex. Peter Lewis concludes judiciously, in the context of late medieval peasant rebellion, that both patriotism and social protest were elements "one need not deny" while at the same time acknowledging all sorts of other motives for their actions.[61] Nevertheless, the people who commented upon the war in late medieval France – some of them with happy, some with bitter, experience of it – often did take sides in these matters and tended to group knights either as heroes or oppressors, and peasants either as heroes in the war against the English, rebels against social injustice, or merely as innocent and hopeless victims of a predatory military aristocracy. These classifications, for all their faults, are useful starting-points for our investigation.

This book is a contribution to the study of the soldier-civilian relationship during the Hundred Years War. More precisely, it is a study of the relationship between the professional soldiers who fought in the Hundred Years War and the non-combatant inhabitants of the French villages who were obliged to support them: how each of these groups strove to survive the enormous dangers represented by a continuous state of war and, on occasion, to turn the war to their own advantage. The sudden, spectacular, squalls, represented by famous battles and sieges which captured the attention of chroniclers and poets, are not its subject. Its major concerns are with the slower, but mightier, ocean swells which were generated by longer-lasting and more remote storms within western European society over the previous centuries and which were now breaking in the shallows

---

[58] Ibid., pp. 169–70.
[59] R. Hilton, *Bond Men Made Free: Medieval Peasant Movements and the English Rising of 1381* (London, 1973), p. 60.
[60] *Simplicissimus*, p. 33.
[61] P. Lewis, *Later Medieval France: the Polity* (London, 1968), p. 287.

of French rural society in the fourteenth and fifteenth centuries. The "remote storms" of this metaphor represent the age-old attempts by the nobles to sustain their violent, extravagent and glorious lifestyle out of the profits of lordship, together with the peasants' struggle to limit these lordships by extending their own liberties. The "shallows" represent the intensification of military activity in the Hundred Years War which placed a premium on violence, extravagance and glory just as the profits of lordship were being rapidly eroded.

The focus of the study is on this society as it tried to adjust to the presence of increasing numbers of soldiers in its midst; also on the process by which the military class sought to accommodate the realities of a nasty and brutish war, which was by no means short, and which dragged large numbers of angry and unwilling non-combatants into its net, with the various ideals of the just lord and the just warrior in which non-combatants had no rôle but to be protected and left in peace. These social and ethical problems were by no means unique to the fourteenth and fifteenth centuries in France, but there can be no doubt that, under the pressure of the Hundred Years War, they confronted this society as they had never done before.

1

THE JUST WARRIOR

ALTHOUGH MORE THAN half of the soldiers who fought in the Hundred Years War belonged to the non-noble categories of archer, crossbowman, pikeman, *pillar*, *brigand*, and the large group of armed servants, known as *valets*, the ideal of the just warrior did not apply to them. This is not of course to assert that they were deficient in moral scruple, although the varlets and pillagers, at least, achieved an unparalleled notoriety during this period; nor that they were immune to prosecution when they strayed across that none-too-clear frontier between legitimate acts of war and violent crime. It is because their freedom to make moral choices was severely curtailed by their lowly rank and by their subjection to the men-at-arms. Not all common soldiers could claim with any degree of sincerity, as did Nenelet Agoulant, in 1375, that he had been a man of good reputation "with a great love for the welfare of the realm", but had been forced into service under threat of instant death.[1] On the other hand, all of them could protest, with a fair measure of justice, that they were in no position, once engaged in military service, to pick and choose between one form of warfare and another. Guillaume Jeurbers, a poor labouring man of Perreux (Yonne), who served the French garrison of Ratilly in 1357 as a varlet, made bold to question its captain's intentions when ordered to collect a bale of straw. He refused to set light to it when it had been placed outside the gatehouse of the Moutiers priory.[2] His tiny act of defiance must have been a rarity in the face of a captain's order to obey, or "it would be the worse for him", and it certainly failed to save the gatehouse. It was only when the most successful and ambitious of these common soldiers aspired to the ranks of the warriors who, by tradition, fought on horseback as men-at-arms that they could be judged by the varying standards of the laws of war and of chivalry and could be considered truly to be free men in the moral sense. Like the *parvenus* of any age, they might then be roundly condemned by everybody.

Shakespeare illustrates the point well in the words which he put into the mouths of the common soldiers, Michael Williams and John Bates, on the eve of Agincourt. "Methinks", the disguised Henry V remarks provocatively, "I could not die anywhere so contented as in the king's company, his cause being just and his quarrel honourable." To which Williams replies: "That's more than we know", and Bates: "Ay, or more than we should seek after; for we know enough if we

---

[1] Archives Nationales, Paris (AN), JJ 106, no. 203.
[2] AN, JJ 107, no. 167.

know we are the king's subjects. If his cause be wrong, our obedience to the king wipes the crime of it out of us."[3] It is true that the king makes short work of this breezy disregard for personal moral responsibility, but the points-of-view of Williams and Bates may well be representative of those of common soldiers throughout the Hundred Years War as they deferred to their social superiors. As will be seen, moralists of the period tended to lay the blame for their excesses at the door of their masters.

If loyal service to their lord wiped out the crimes committed in his name by common soldiers, such as Williams and Bates, the knights and squires of the Hundred Years War were expected to exercise more autonomy of judgement. Let us take the example of Jean de Bueil who was the eldest son of Jean IV de Bueil and Margaret, dauphine of the Auvergne. His war-service, on the French side, began as an aristocratic page at the disastrous battle of Verneuil, in 1424, and ended as admiral of France, royal lieutenant on the Gascon frontier, and commander of the army which finally defeated the English at the battle of Castillon in July 1453. His semi-historical, semi-didactic, story of *Le Jouvencel* was written after the end of the Hundred Years War for the benefit of young men-at-arms who might wish to profit by the author's long experience in arms during the latter stages of the Hundred Years War, in order "always to do well and to increase their honour and prowess in the marvellous adventures of war".[4] The story of the Jouvencel's life is a rich mine for the historian of the aristocratic warrior-culture of this period. His success-story as he rose from the position of a threadbare squire in a dilapidated French garrison on the Maine frontier to the status of a military commander in royal service was the dream of tens of thousands of young men of the period with nothing more, and very often rather less, than a tenuously noble pedigree. We see him confronting and mastering the two great traditions to which the late medieval knightly soldier was heir: the tradition of chivalric warfare and the tradition of territorial lordship. Nowhere in the literature of the later Middle Ages is the conflict between these two aristocratic traditions presented more clearly. His first priority and his greatest love is for the life of the warrior: "War! What a joyful thing it is! One hears and sees so many fine things, and learns so much that is good."[5] As he finds himself promoted, however, into positions of authority, he has to assume the functions of lordship without shedding those of the warrior: "I must represent the person of my lord the count of Parvanchières [the royal lieutenant]. So I am a lord."[6] In short, he has to assume the responsibility of a kinglet to preserve justice within his own company of soldiers and within the wider community of his "borrowed lordship".[7] As a warrior, he is "one of the boys", a blithe member of an exclusive caste with its own strange rules and customs. As a lord, albeit of a "borrowed", military, lordship, he belongs to the

---

3   W. Shakespeare, *King Henry V*, Act IV, Scene 1, lines 129–39.
4   *Le Jouvencel*, i, p. 15.
5   Ibid., ii, p. 20.
6   Ibid., ii, p. 14.
7   Ibid.

wider society and must fit in to a seigneurial rather than a specifically chivalric tradition.

De Bueil's is the story of a man who belonged to one of the three important groups of French "chivalry", identified by Philippe de Mézières in the fourteenth century as knights and squires who "continually followed the wars against [their king's] enemies".[8] Mézières knew the type well because he himself had been a man-at-arms of this sort: a cadet of the minor Picard nobility; apprenticed in the wars of northern Italy in the 1340s; serving under Marshal d'Audrehem against the English in the mid-1350s; crusading in North Africa in the 1360s. As a group, they occupied a position in Mézières' military hierarchy between the nobles who responded only to a personal summons from the king, and who were never likely to stray into illegality, and the upstart common soldiers who had assumed the trappings of the knightly warrior without any of its obligations, and were never far from criminality. The apparent assumption that a nobleman was naturally incapable of criminality need not confuse us for long since Mézières believed, along with many other moralists of the age, that noblemen were incapable, by definition, of ignoble deeds. A corrupted nobleman was no noble, just as (as we shall see), for Honoré Bouvet an unjust war was no war. The story shows how a member of the middle group could steer an honest and successful course between, on the one hand, the lofty detachment of the aristocrat whose survival depended neither on wages nor on profits of war and, on the other, the men-at-arms, of whatever social background, whose sole interest was in these rewards.

The Jouvencel's first experience of war was as a member of the French garrison of Luc, since identified as Chateau-l'Hermitage (Sarthe). It was, on the face of it, hardly the stuff of heroic legend. As a ragged and unmounted man-at-arms (the garrison had to share horses), he stole from the clothes-line of the nearby English garrison of Verset and raided its paddocks for goats and milk-cows. His success as a raider was rewarded first with a horse, albeit one which was lame in a hind leg, then with a second-hand cuirass, donated to him by the captain of his garrison. If he had dealings with non-combatants, we hear nothing of them. This was the rough apprenticeship of the majority of men-at-arms at the time of the Hundred Years War who were permanently occupied in the military life, and it may have been the lot of very many of them for their entire careers.

In the Jouvencel's case, however, this age of innocence as a border-raider who serves his king by attacking his enemies across the local frontier, and whose main concern is to prove himself before his companions in arms, "the desire to have honour and worldly praise",[9] slowly gives way to the responsibilities of military lordship. The Jouvencel becomes a royal captain. His obligations as a warrior continue, but his expeditions are no longer conducted in parties of six or seven companions under cover of trees and darkness, but at the head of one hundred

[8] Mézières, *Songe*, i, p. 530.
[9] *Le Jouvencel*, i, p. 21.

lances, each member of which expects from him pay and provisions and the settlement of his disputes over title to ransoms and booty.

The responsibilities of the Jouvencel's "borrowed lordship", as he so aptly calls it, do not end there. Suddenly he is confronted by non-combatants in their rôle as producers of wealth. Their protection from armed enemies becomes his personal responsibility while their wealth is his, and his men's, livelihood. As a young man-at-arms he had scattered all before him in his pursuit of reputation the fate of non-combatants was irrelevant to this quest. Now he has to listen for the occasional pearl of wisdom from the garrulous old captain of Crathor, who, while acknowledging the poverty of many men-at-arms due to the non-payment of their proper wages, explains that to seek compensation by destroying the merchants and the labourers of the surrounding region would be to destroy himself and to impoverish the region which supports him.[10] On another occasion, he attends, with every outward sign of respectful interest, to a royal commissioner, who, with plenty of official pedantry, urges a strict disciplinary control over his men-at-arms so that they do not turn their strength and high spirits against the public weal.[11] He also has to decide for himself what to do with a throng of peasant prisoners, captured in his successful attack on the English-held town of Francheville.[12] These are the responsibilities of borrowed lordship which, in some form or another, all captains of fortresses had to face. Philippe de Mézières, nearly sixty years before, had called them the "fifteen rules of chivalric discipline", which applied to all captains of war, and which included the meting out of justice in the host, the division of the spoils of war, the protection of non-combatants and of merchants coming with provisions.[13] One may only guess at how much Jean de Bueil and his Jouvencel yearned for their youth when the line between friend and enemy seemed more clearly drawn and the rules of the game more simple. Denis Lalande describes the same process in the life of Jean II le Meingre, known as Boucicaut, as he changed in 1391 from the life of "knight errantry" to that of a captain.[14]

The twin responsibilities of late medieval kingship, to preserve justice within the kingdom and to make effective war upon outsiders, and the tensions between these two – often conflicting – responsibilities, have been the subject of a study by Richard Kaeuper.[15] They are different only in degree from the demands made upon the ordinary knightly soldier, such as the Jouvencel, as he advanced up the ladder of royal military service. His ethos of chivalry and his circumstances of lordship often made him into a "kinglet", with considerable local power, and the difficulties of keeping the two demands of war and government in balance could be as acute for the conscientious knight as they were for the French and English

10 Ibid., p. 95.
11 Ibid., ii, pp. 26–7.
12 Ibid., p. 98.
13 Mézières, *Songe*, i, pp. 509–17.
14 Lalande, *Boucicaut*, chapter 2.
15 R. Kaeuper, *War, Justice and Public Order: England and France in the later Middle Ages* (Oxford, 1988).

Crowns. In practical terms, the problem for these captains was a stark one. The effective maintenance of a strong garrison in a state of military preparedness, and the effective prosecution of a war, necessitated the brutal exploitation of non-combatants. Non-existent or insufficient wages had to be substituted by old-fashioned unpaid labour services and dues from the surrounding villages. At the same time, any ordinary sense of justice – indeed any awareness of the wider economic and political context – demanded a protection of the weak by the strong. Was "just warrior", then, almost a contradiction in terms?

An "innocent" warrior is certainly a curious, if not downright contradictory, notion to the modern mind. Fire and sword, the indiscriminate destruction of property and life, are the universal symbols of war: no less appropriate to the Hundred Years War than to any other. Jean de Venette, the Carmelite friar of peasant family, who wistfully surveyed his homeland of the Beauvaisis in 1359 and contemplated the destruction of his own native village, described how houses and churches no longer delighted the eye with newly-repaired roofs, but rather presented the unwholesome spectacle of scattered smoking ruins; how the fields were no longer clothed with the green of growing crops, but were choked with nettles and thistles.[16] A year later, the poet and moral philosopher, Petrarch, on a rare visit to the French capital, expressed surprise that the weed-infested, untilled fields and the ruined and deserted houses belonged to the French kingdom which he had once known. "Everywhere appeared the melancholy vestige of the English passage."[17] The description of the vast plains of Champagne, Beauce, Brie and the Gatinais in the time of Charles VII, written by the Norman lawyer-bishop, Thomas Basin, is now famous: "deserted, uncultivated, abandoned, empty of inhabitants, covered with scrub and brambles", and all because of the greed and indiscipline of men-at-arms.[18] If these were the tracks left by the warrior class in late medieval France, it is hardly surprising that, from that time to this, there have been many variations on the comment that "while he practised the warfare of havoc and pillage, he clung to the image of himself as Sir Lancelot".[19] Was the just warrior merely a creation of romancers?

In order to address this question, an obvious starting-point would be in the medieval ideology of the Just War, but we must not expect either unanimity or consistency in this area. The notion of war as an essentially "good" thing, which could be perverted by "bad" practices, was one which pervaded not only the world of academic theology but also the courts of law, the priestly pulpit and confessional, and – most importantly of all – the world of the men-at-arms themselves. Honoré Bouvet, Benedictine monk of the great abbey of Ile-Barbe, near Lyons, and doctor of Canon law at the University of Avignon in the latter half of the fourteenth century, was at one with the men-at-arms of his own day (whom

---

[16] Venette, *Chronicle*, p. 94.
[17] *Letters from Petrarch*, ed. M. Bishop (London, 1966), p. 196.
[18] Basin, *Charles VII*, pp. 84–8.
[19] B. Tuchman, *A Distant Mirror: the Calamitous Fourteenth Century* (Harmondsworth, 1979), p. 132.

he heartily despised) when he stated that "war is not an evil thing, but is good and virtuous; for war, by its very nature, seeks nothing other than to set wrong right, and to turn dissension to peace".[20] Many of them may have harboured the thought which Sir John Hawkwood was supposed to have uttered that peace would have been their "undoing", but there was little likelihood of that awful eventuality in the late Middle Ages.[21] But, whilst there was agreement on all fronts that military service to one's king and to the crusading papacy was good and virtuous, there were also obvious areas of disagreement. As might be expected, theologians and men-at-arms disagreed over the question of the morality of tournaments and jousts and the high priority which the men-at-arms gave to the praise of the world in general and of attractive ladies in particular. There were disagreements between lawyers and men-at-arms over the legitimacy of private wars by which noblemen in many parts of France had traditionally sought vengeance and compensation for injuries done to them and by which lesser men had found military employment. But the fundamental area of disagreement, and one which encompassed most of these other disagreements, was over the relationship between the military order and the rest of the community: between soldier and non-combatant, knight and peasant. It is here that the smoking tracks of the late medieval man-at-arms, so poignantly described by the chroniclers and poets, must be set against those various ideals of the just warrior which contemporaries would have recognized.

There was a feeling in some quarters that certain categories of non-combatants should be immune from all acts of war. These categories consisted of priests, students, pilgrims, women and children, and peasants engaged in their labour, together with their livestock. Canon lawyers who harked back to the papal decretals inspired by the Peace and Truce of God movements of the eleventh century were often the most emphatic. "Ox-herds and all husbandmen, and ploughmen with their oxen, when they are carrying on their business . . . are secure according to written law . . . since those who cultivate the soil plough and work for all men . . . and all manner of folk live upon their labour."[22] "Everyone knows that in the matter of deciding on war, of declaring it, or of undertaking it, poor men are not concerned at all, for they ask nothing more than to live at peace."[23] Nicholas Upton, who was "not meanly skilled in both laws [canon and civil]" but also had a great deal of military experience in the English armies of the fifteenth century, recognised the "canonical truce" which placed certain groups of people under conditions of permanent truce so long as they were actually occupied in their respective callings.[24] These included husbandmen "commyng to and froo and exercyde in hosebondry", together with their beasts "that tyll and plowghe

---

[20] Bonet, *Tree*, p. 126.
[21] The anecdote was recounted by the Florentine, Franco Sacchetti, and quoted by R. De-lachenal, *Histoire de Charles V*, 5 vols. (Paris, 1909–31), iii, p. 240.
[22] Bonet, *Tree*, p. 188.
[23] Ibid., p. 153.
[24] *The Essential Portions of Nicholas Upton's "De Studio Militari" before 1446*, trans. J. Blount, ed. F. Barnard (Oxford, 1931), pp. 28–9.

and cary corne to the felde". He was, no doubt, familiar with the English military ordinances which gave an absolute protection to churches and ecclesiastical property; to unarmed women and to non-noble children under the age of fourteen, to unarmed clergy and, on occasion, to peasants engaged in their labours.[25] We must also note Upton's grim rider that "this was not observyd in my time in Fraunce".[26]

Nevertheless, before we dismiss these "blanket" safeguards as nothing more than the pious hopes of antiquarian dreamers, we must acknowledge that such sentiments were widely dispersed throughout late medieval society, and that men-at-arms themselves were not immune to a nostalgia for an imagined past when warfare was, in the words of that veteran soldier, Sir John Fastolf, "betwixt menne of werre and menne of werre".[27] Philippe de Mézières, who had commanded soldiers on the Calais frontier during the early years of the Hundred Years War, believed that the "laws of true chivalry" prescribed for the military order the task of fighting for "those who are oppressed and cannot defend themselves",[28] and no less a person than the English constable, Sir John Cornwall, was converted to pacifism by his bitter experiences of the war between Christians in 1421.[29] The French captain, Jean de Beaumanoir, according to a mid-fourteenth-century poet, roundly condemned his English opposite number, Richard Bamborough, for tormenting "the poor people who sow the corn, who tend the beasts and the vines, so that we can have plenty".[30] And although the twenty-six garrisons of English-occupied northern France between 1420 and 1444 whose accounts have been analysed by Philippe Contamine appear to have shown little mercy to peasant non-combatants, they rarely took women prisoners and never took clerics.[31]

However desirable one might have felt the blanket immunity of non-combatants to be, the notion of the just warrior, the chivalrous knight, could never be tied to such a standard. As Christopher Allmand pointed out, Sir John Fastolf may have yearned for an exclusively soldierly war but, in the real world of 1435, he advocated a most brutal and systematic form of scorched-earth policy in enemy territory: "brennyng and distruynge alle the lande as thei pas, both hous, corne,

[25] *The Black Book of the Admiralty*, ed. T. Twiss, i (London, 1871), pp. 453, 460, 467 and 469. These are the ordinances of war of Richard II (1385) and of Henry V (1419).

[26] Upton, *Studio Militari*, p. 29.

[27] *Society at War: the Experience of England and France during the Hundred Years War*, ed. C. Allmand (Edinburgh, 1973), p. 35. A fuller analysis of Fastolf's report to Henry VI's Great Council in France (1435) may be found in T. Meron, *Henry's Wars and Shakespeare's Laws: Perspectives on the Law of War in the later Middle Ages* (Oxford, 1993), pp. 196–8.

[28] Mézières, *Songe*, i, pp. 531–2.

[29] P. Contamine, "La Théologie de la Guerre à la Fin du Moyen Age: la Guerre de Cent Ans fut-elle une Guerre Juste?", *Jeanne d'Arc: une Epoque, un Rayonnement: Colloque d'Histoire Médiévale, Orléans 1979* (Paris, 1982), p. 18.

[30] *Le Combat de Trente Bretons contre Trente Anglois*, ed. G. Crapelet (Paris, 1827), p. 15.

[31] P. Contamine, "Rançons et Butins dans la Normandie Anglaise, 1424–1444", *Actes du 101e Congrès National des Sociétés Savantes, Lille, 1976, Philologie et Histoire* (Paris, 1978), p. 257.

veignes and all treis that beren fruyte for mannys sustenance, and all bestaile that may not be dryven, to be distroiede".[32] The reasons for this are largely practical ones, related to the war policies of the sovereigns as they attempted to terrorize "rebels" into submission; also to the material interests of the men-at-arms. But they did have a theoretical basis which must briefly be examined.

The academic lawyers of the late medieval law schools of Italy and of France, the so-called post-glossators, were severely compromised by their recognition of the legitimacy of *marque* and reprisal which allowed innocent parties to suffer for the guilt of a compatriot.[33] The law of *marque* has been defined as "the right granted to an individual by his sovereign lord to recover, by force if necessary, his own property, or its equivalent, from a foreigner or a fellow-citizen of that foreigner, when he is not able to recover his property by normal means".[34] It is but a short step from this idea of collective responsibility for an injury to the notion that the "enemy" of a sovereign prince, such as the king of England, was not merely the king of France and his military following, but included the rest of the body politic: the body of which he was the head and all of his subjects, combatant and non-combatant, the members. The concept of total war is not an invention of the twentieth century and even Honoré Bouvet, who quite clearly hated himself for saying it, had to admit that, "if on both sides war is decided upon . . . the soldiery may take spoil from the enemy kingdom at will, and make war freely; and if sometimes the humble and innocent suffer harm and lose their goods, it cannot be otherwise".[35]

Much of the French nobility recognized this Germanic concept of collective responsibility in the rather different context of their cherished right to engage in private war: a right which no self-respecting academic lawyer, like Bouvet, would ever accept. The private war which took place during the third quarter of the fourteenth century between the count of Saint Pol and the Bofremont family may be taken as typical of many others. The count's men "raided, plundered and despoiled many of the lands and villages of the aforesaid Philibert and Jehan de Bofremont . . . along with those of their friends, their family, their allies, counsellors, supporters and comforters, and of their men, officers and subjects".[36] More detail of what might have been meant by the raiding and despoiling of villages was provided by the royal procurator in the Paris *parlement* in December 1395,

---

[32] C. Allmand, "The War and the Non-combatant", *The Hundred Years War*, ed. K. Fowler (London, 1971), p. 180.

[33] On the post-glossators, see W. Ullmann, *The Medieval Idea of Law as Represented by Lucas da Penna* (London, 1946), and the introduction by H. Hazeltine. On the subject of *marque* see M.-C. Chavarot, "La Pratique des Lettres de Marque d'après les Arrêts du Parlement, XIIIe–début XVe Siècle", *BEC*, cxlix (1991), pp. 51–89.

[34] R. de Mas Latrie, "Du Droit de Marque au Droit de Représailles au Moyen Age", *BEC*, 6th series, ii (1866), p. 530.

[35] Bonet, *Tree*, p. 154. On the connection between Bouvet and the post-glossators, see N. Wright, "The Tree of Battles and the Laws of War", *War, Literature and Politics in the Late Middle Ages*, ed. C. Allmand (Liverpool, 1976), pp. 24–6.

[36] AN, JJ 106, no. 176.

as he prosecuted Geraud de Pardiac for his war against the count of Armagnac. According to his deposition, Pardiac had, along with unspecified other crimes, captured 130 head of cattle, fifty sheep, 157 goats, together with thirty-one men who had to ransom themselves for a total of more than 300 florins. One prisoner, called John, was castrated and his wife was also mutilated. Pardiac burned down a total of seventy-three houses.[37] If the whole issue of private war, engaged without the authorisation and control of a sovereign, was utterly abhorrent to many (though not of course to Pardiac who insisted that this was common practice in his part of the world), there can be little doubt that the idea of a peasantry as a member of the body politic, as an aider and comforter of its lord, as an "enemy", was much more widely accepted. The immunities of non-combatants made little sense, as Philippe Contamine has remarked, in a society in which all able-bodied males were potential combatants and in which all the resources of a territory were drawn into the war-effort by "the expedient of taxation".[38] We come closer now, on the purely theoretical level, to an understanding of how the medieval man-at-arms might emerge from the smoke of the burning villages, so poignantly described by Jean de Venette and others, with his reputation as a just warrior unsullied.

The idea of entering "enemy" territory was very much in the minds of the thousand men-at-arms accompanied by a similar number of mounted archers who rode out along the Garonne valley in October 1355 and who were led by the flower of English chivalry: the Black Prince, eldest son of the English king; the earls of Suffolk, Warwick, Oxford and Salisbury; Sir James Audeley; Sir John Chandos; Sir Richard Stafford.[39] While in the territory of the count of Armagnac, who was the French commander in the Languedoc, the army moved through the country-side in three divisions. The herald of Sir John Chandos describes how, as the Black Prince "rode towards Toulouse; not a town remained that he did not utterly lay waste; he took Carcassonne and Béziers and Narbonne and all the country was ravaged and harried by him . . . whereat the enemies in Gascony made no great rejoicing".[40] Sir John Wengfeld, "governor of the prince's affairs", did rejoice, however. "Since the war began, there was never such loss nor destruction as hath been on this raid." The taxes which this area paid the French Crown, as Wengfeld well knew from captured account-books, had supported a great part of its army.[41] Denifle, at the end of last century, indignantly described the raid as "more of an invasion of a strong army of brigands, pillaging a defenceless countryside and seeking as much booty as possible, than a proper military campaign".[42] He echoes the complaint of "The People" in Alain Chartier's fifteenth-century poem. "This

---

[37] P. Durrieu, *Documents Relatifs à la Chute de la Maison d'Armagnac-Fezensaguet et à la Mort du Comte de Pardiac* (Paris, 1883), pp. 14–15.

[38] Contamine, "Rançons", p. 243.

[39] H. Hewitt, *The Black Prince's Expedition of 1355–1357* (Manchester, 1958).

[40] Ibid., p. 140.

[41] Ibid., p. 73.

[42] Denifle, *Désolation*, ii, p. 85.

isn't war which is fought in this kingdom. Lacking order and justice it is mere brigandage and public violence. There are calls to arms and standards are raised against the enemy, but these exploits are conducted against me, destroying my poor substance and miserable life."[43] This raid in force, however, was not essentially different from a dozen other such *chevauchées* organised by the English Crown during the course of the fourteenth century; always with the same purpose of displaying power, ruining the enemy and enriching the participants with booty. The Prince's father had described one of his very first campaigns in similar terms. "We began to burn in the Cambrésis so that that country is clean laid waste as of corn and cattle and other goods."[44] In fact, as Malcolm Vale has observed, there was little to distinguish these raids, except in the matter of royal involvement, from the multitude of raids on private enemies with which the turbulent Gascon nobility, of which Pardiac himself was a member, was only too familiar.[45] There was no difficulty in identifying "enemies" who could be killed, held for ransom, and plundered at will, because, with some few exceptions, everyone and everything in enemy territory was fair game. The captains who were discharged by the Black Prince after the Spanish campaign of 1367 expressed the idea well when they called the whole of France "their chamber".[46]

When the army of the Black Prince crossed back into English Gascony, on 28 November 1355, laden with booty from the rich lands of the Languedoc, a substantial nucleus was not disbanded but went into the great fortresses which defended the frontier. The Black Prince established his headquarters at Libourne while his other commanders, English and Gascon, set themselves up in the garrisons of Cognac, Rochefort, Tournay, Taillebourg and elsewhere in the middle Garonne valley. This was the core of the army which was to march north during the following year to the famous victory at Poitiers, but its duties during that winter were similar to those of any army of occupation of a frontier area: keeping alive and raiding enemy territory. Now a much more careful distinction had to be made between, on the one hand, the non-combatants of English territory who had the right to protection by, and from, these garrisons in their midst; and, on the other, the inhabitants of enemy territory who might be killed and robbed at will. These men-at-arms were not only on the physical borderland between English and French territory, but also on the moral and legal borderland between the just warrior and the armed criminal. When they had ridden in the company of the Black Prince into the plains of the Languedoc, burning and plundering as they went, "pillaging a defenceless countryside", they had been the equivalent, on a

---

43 Alain Chartier, *Quadrilogue Invectif*, cited by M. Mollat, *La Guerre de Cent Ans Vue par Ceux qui l'ont Vécue* (Paris, 1992), p. 132.

44 *Robertus de Avesbury, De Gestis Mirabilibus Regis Edwardi Tertii*, ed. E. Thompson (Rolls series, 1889), p. 306.

45 M. Vale, "The Gascon Nobility and the Anglo-French war, 1294–98", *War and Government in the Middle Ages: Essays in Honour of J.O. Prestwich*, ed. J. Gillingham and J. Holt (Woodbridge, 1984), p. 141.

46 Froissart, *Chroniques*, ed. Luce, vii, p. 65.

much grander scale, of the Jouvencel in his age of innocence. When in garrison on English territory, they had some of the obligations which went with his borrowed lordship, and their captains had the responsibility of enforcing them.

When a soldier moved out of a field army into the garrison of a fortified place, his status as a just warrior was not inevitably compromised. He might continue to see himself, as did the Jouvencel, fighting the king's enemies across the frontier while at the same time defending the king's loyal subjects in the surrounding territory. Indeed, the ill-paid garrison soldier who fought for his king in circumstances of desperate hardship was something of an ideal type in this period. The young Boucicaut, who later in the fourteenth century was to become a marshal of France, was praised for not taking flight from hardship as did many "tender novices", but desirous "at all costs to remain in garrison".[47] The Jouvencel, himself, was a model of the fifteenth-century type, who consciously chose the hard garrison life in preference to the easy life at court.[48] But the disciplinary ordinances which regulated the conduct of field armies, and were enforced by a regular chain of command, were not so easily maintained in these new conditions, and the temptation by both captains and their men to make a personal profit from local power often became irresistible. This was particularly the case when the garrison was not in receipt of regular and sufficient wages.

The complaints of the Italian agents in Avignon of the Datini business empire during the 1380s may stand for innumerable others of the same kind by non-combatants. "It seems that their soldiers do more harm to their subjects than to those who are not in their obedience because they cannot get hold of their wages."[49] "The men-at-arms who are wintering in the fortresses of Provence, which they have captured, attack friends and enemies alike, to keep alive. At present, they take more livestock and victuals from their friends than they ever did from their enemies, and all because they lack money and cannot get any."[50] "The troops of the seneschal [of Beaucaire] rob and plunder friends and enemies so that their ransoms will allow them to survive."[51]

It is clear, therefore, that a garrison soldier could maintain his status in the eyes of the non-military world as a just warrior if he could demonstrate that he attacked only the king's enemies and protected only the king's loyal subjects. His first priority as a soldier was service to the Crown in the exercise of its responsibilities to its people of leadership in war and as fount of justice. Poverty and hardship were, at one and the same time, a test of his chivalry and a spur to action against the enemy. If he failed the test, but remained in arms, he would slip into the vast

---

[47] Contamine, *Guerre, Etat*, p. 210.
[48] *Le Jouvencel*, i, pp. 39–56.
[49] "Annales Avignonaises de 1382 à 1410: Extraites des Archives de Datini", ed. R. Brun, *Mémoires de l'Institut Historique de Provence*, xii (1935), pp. 17–142; xiii (1936), pp. 58–105; xiv (1937), pp. 5–57; xv (1938), pp. 21–52 and 154–92. This quotation is from xii, p. 47.
[50] Ibid., p. 49.
[51] Ibid., pp. 57–8.

throng of men-at-arms who were, in Philippe de Mézière's snobbish analysis, upstarts and *parvenus*: they may have looked like knights but were really low-born people, worse than any Saracen.[52] They were freebooters, *routiers*, men of the Companies.

The most careful working-out of the proper relationship between soldiers and "friendly" non-combatants was undoubtedly in English-occupied northern France during the time of Henry V and his brother, the duke of Bedford, as the English attempted to win the hearts and minds of their subjects in the occupied territories. It should not surprise us, in circumstances when the Crown was most anxious to demonstrate the justice of its own war, and to reclaim its rights to the French Crown and to its duchy of Normandy, that it should demonstrate this concern by insisting that the warriors in its service should be "just" ones. They were, at least for a while, just warriors in a sense which would have been recognized by the lawyer, Honoré Bouvet, half a century earlier: subject to a strict chain of command; content with their wages; fully occupied only with the king's wars and not about their own private business; living apart from the community in garrisons.[53] But this was only an unusually thorough implementation of policies which the kings of France and of England had attempted, rather fitfully and erratically perhaps, to enforce upon their soldiers throughout the entire war.

For kings minded to ignore their obligations to the common weal, there were always fearless and outspoken preachers, and other "ghostly counsellors", who were licensed to remind them in the most forceful of terms. The ageing Edward III and his grandson, Richard II, along with the men-at-arms who served them, were verbally bludgeoned from the pulpit at Rochester until the death of its bishop, Thomas Brinton, in 1389, brought Richard some relief. "Armies go to war" Brinton had noted sourly, " not with the prayers of the people behind them but with the curses of many; for they march not at the king's expense or their own, but at the expense of churches and the poor, whom they spoil in their path. And if they do happen to buy anything, they give nothing but tallies in payment. Christ fed five thousand on five loaves. These men do a greater miracle, for they feed ten thousand on little tallies . . ."[54] Charles VI of France suffered, with apparent equanimity, the same kind of verbal lashing from the Augustinian court preacher, Jacques Legrand, and from the Paris University chancellor, Jean Gerson. These priests reminded kings, and knights, of their obligation not only to fight and win wars against their enemies, but also to preserve justice at home by protecting their non-combatant subjects. We can see their message re-appearing in the preambles

---

52 Mézières, *Songe*, i, p. 531.

53 The obligation of soldiers in Lancastrian service to live in garrison and not to involve themselves in private business has been described recently by R. Massey, "Lancastrian Rouen: Military Service and Property-holding, 1419–49", *England and Normandy in the Middle Ages*, ed. D. Bates and A. Curry (London, 1994), pp. 275–7.

54 G. Owst, *Literature and Pulpit in Medieval England* (Cambridge, 1933), p. 338. For a general survey of preaching at this time, see H. Leith Spencer, *English Preaching in the Late Middle Ages* (Oxford, 1993)

to royal ordinances: "Charles [VI], by the grace of God, king of France, to all those who read these letters, greetings. Amongst all the cares and solicitudes which we have continually for the good government of our kingdom, our pricipal desire and one which we have constantly, by day and by night, is that the people of our said kingdom should be able to live under us in peace and tranquility, that they should be guarded and ruled by good justice and preserved and defended from all acts of violence . . ."[55] His father had made the point, but rather more succinctly, as he addressed the officers of his supreme court, the *parlement*, in 1360: "Justice is more necessary and must be done more rigorously and diligently in time of war than in time of peace."[56]

This ideal of royal justice was spread widely in French society, even in the darkest days of the war when there was no obvious sign either of the king's power or of any sort of justice. It is hinted at in the words of a desperate woman, called La Wyette, who lived with her children in the wasteland around Précy-sur-Oise in 1358, when she declared that, in these bad-lands, "justice dared not reign".[57] It is suggested in the cataloguing of injuries committed by men-at-arms of the surrounding fortresses against the common people of the castellany of Bergerac between 20 February 1379 and 15 June 1382. The purpose of this list of atrocities, in the words of its authors, the *jurats* of Bergerac, was that "later,when the time is ripe, these wrongdoers may be punished by good justice".[58] This ideal of justice to be had in this world, as well as in the next, was the one which prevented society from disintegrating into the sort of chaos and anarchy so beloved of science-fiction writers today who contemplate the world after the nuclear holocaust. It centred upon kings who were often woefully inadequate to the task, or indifferent to it. But, just occasionally, the shaky apparatus of late medieval government rewarded the faithful.

The Crowns of France and of England sometimes went further than the mouthing of mere platitudes about justice, although there was no lack of posturing for the sake of effect. In the early years of the war, the English garrisons in Brittany were forbidden by Edward III (though without any serious effort at enforcement) to pillage and to requisition goods from "people living in the king's obedience", and their captains were commanded to leave the people who wished to live in such obedience in peace and tranquility.[59] The French Crown, during the fourteenth century, had repeatedly been reminded by regional Estates which voted taxes for its war of its duty to prevent the pillaging of "corn, wine, victuals and other things which belong to the king's subjects" and the royal ordinances which were so often

---

[55] *Ordonnances des Rois de France de la Troisième Race*, various editors, 21 vols. (Paris, 1723–1849), viii, p. 62.

[56] Ibid., iv, p. 726.

[57] AN, JJ 105, no. 362.

[58] *Le Livre de Vie: les Seigneurs et les Capitaines de Périgord Blanc au XIVe Siècle*, ed. E. Labroue (Bordeaux, 1891), p. 404.

[59] "Mémoire Présenté à Edouard III par Gauthier de Bentley sur les Affaires de Bretagne, 1352", *Oeuvres de Froissart*, ed. K. de Lettenhove, xviii, p. 340.

the product of such meetings were forever banning unauthorised *prises* of corn, wine, victuals, or insisting that they be paid for at the market rate.[60] It made captains personally responsible for the misdeeds of soldiers under their command. It even authorised peasants to resist such depredations in any way which they thought fit, even, though with obvious misgivings on the part of the authorities, by associations of neighbouring villages summoned to collective action by the sound of church bells.[61] Prohibitions against plundering the king's subjects were incorporated into military contracts as early as 1367 when Charles V contracted the service of Jean, count of Armagnac, against the Free Companies. His soldiers were forbidden, in territory subject to the king, to "set fires, take or imprison people or working animals for their own victualling or private profit".[62]

Undoubtedly the most spectacular development of this initiative by the Crown to control the activities of its soldiers in "friendly" territory was, as mentioned above, in English-occupied Normandy during the third decade of the fifteenth century.[63] Even that doughty champion of Valois legitimacy, Jean Juvenal des Ursins, had to admit that the English soldiers and administrators were often a great deal more disciplined than the French at this time.[64] As early as 1418 Henry V had encouraged people in the English-occupied territories to bring complaints against soldiers before civilian *vicomtes* and he had, at the same time, insisted that his soldiers must pay for everything they took. When his brother, the duke of Bedford, took over from him in France, in 1422, commissions were sent into the provinces to see that the royal ordinances were observed and to hear complaints about breaches of them. Clauses against the pillaging of "friendly" non-combatants were introduced into captains' indentures and provision was made for deductions from wages for all infringements of this rule. "Because certain captains, men-at-arms, archers and others have frequently attempted to capture for ransom peasants and other village people resident in the open country on the pretext that they are brigands or Armagnacs . . . we . . . have forbidden and do forbid the aforesaid and any others to be so bold as to take, ransom or imprison any merchant, peasant, craftsman or other resident of the open country on pain of punishment as criminals."[65] The powers of civilian, and largely French, officials, notably the *vicomtes*, over the affairs of garrison soldiers were enormously enhanced. The

---

[60] *Ordonnances*, iii, p. 139. The connection between French royal ordinances and the bargaining process between Crown and people in the regional Estates has been explored by R. Cazelles, "La Réglementation Royale de la Guerre Privée de Saint Louis à Charles V et la Précarité des Ordonnances", *Revue Historique du Droit Français et Etranger*, 4th series, xxxviii (1960), pp. 530–48.

[61] *Ordonnances*, v, p. 658 and viii, p. 63.

[62] M. Verrier, "Le Duché de Bourgogne et les Compagnies dans la Second Moitié du XIVe Siècle", *Académie des Sciences, Arts et Belles-lettres, Mémoires*, 4th series, viii (1901–2), p. 316.

[63] Allmand, *Lancastrian Normandy*. Also B. Rowe, "Discipline in the Norman Garrisons under Bedford, 1422–35", *English Historical Review (EHR)*, xlvi (1931), pp. 194–208.

[64] Ursins, *Ecrits Politiques*, iii, p. 110.

[65] Rowe, "Discipline", p. 204, citing a disciplinary ordinance published at Caen, December 1423.

system began to break down after Bedford's death in 1435, but it had achieved a remarkable measure of success to that point, as the reports by these very *vicomtes* testify of soldiers living "like simple persons of the country, paying their way".[66] For a brief moment in the history of the Hundred Years War, the distinction, in the context of garrison warfare, between just warrior and armed criminal had a practical meaning for ordinary people. The all-too-familiar figure of the *routier* captain, like Richard Venables, whose company made war on everybody from its base in the fortified monastery of Savigny, had not disappeared. However, in the name of the English Crown, he was pursued by the duke of Bedford as a "robber and plunderer", and spectacularly eliminated.[67] Just at the time when this fragile system was beginning to collapse in English territory during the late 1430s, Charles VII promulgated what has been described as an "extraordinarily detailed and enlightened set of rules for protecting the population from the excesses of soldiery".[68] This was the *Ordonnance* of 1439.

It would be quite misleading, however, to present the kings of France and of England as consistent in their attempts to protect their own non-combatant subjects from their own soldiers. They themselves were knights, surrounded by noble advisers, and brought up on a culture of chivalric heroism which urged upon them a close involvement in military activity and a desire to be "one of the boys". Charles V's well-known reluctance in this area was exceptional, and his father, who allowed himself to be captured fighting at Poitiers, was much more in the mould of medieval kingship. Richard II was described by Philippe de Mézières, in the late 1380s, as a young king surrounded and virtually imprisoned by bristling black boars, the warrior progeny of Edward III.[69] "Far from being antipathetic, monarchical values and aristocratic values were complementary."[70]

Moreover, and on a more practical level, kings were expected to pay their garrison soldiers, and to pay them out of taxes which came from the very categories of non-combatants which required protection by these garrisons: peasants and traders. It was a short and logical step for the Crown, in times of national emergency, to allow its soldiers to take these taxes directly, "at source", in place of wages which might in easier times have been distributed to them by the treasurers of wars. The principle of "beneficiary pays" was a clear one. The most obvious example of this dangerous tendency was during the troubled regency of the future Charles V after the capture of his father at Poitiers when he could ill afford to pay his garrisons in the region of Paris. The captain of Etampes, for example, "because [he] had no wages from us [the regent], we authorised him in

---

[66] Ibid., p. 201.
[67] B. Rowe, "John, Duke of Bedford, and the Norman 'Brigands' ", *EHR*, xlvii (1932), pp. 598–9.
[68] Meron, *Henry's Wars*, p. 129.
[69] Mézières, *Songe*, i, p. 395.
[70] P. Contamine, "L'Etat et les Aristocraties", *L'Etat et les Aristocraties (France, Angleterre, Ecosse) XIIe–XVIIe Siècle; Actes de la Table Ronde Organisée par le Centre National de la Recherche Scientifique, Maison Française d'Oxford, 26–27 Septembre 1986*, ed. P. Contamine (Paris, 1989), p. 20.

our aforesaid letters and gave him licence to take from the countryside . . . all manner of victuals necessary for men-at-arms".[71] His lieutenant, and future constable, Bertrand du Guesclin, did the same in 1363 for the captain of Brée (Mayenne), allowing him to "make suitable financial arrangements" with parishes as far as the Breton frontier for the benefit of the "war effort".[72]

However logical and necessary this step might have seemed at the time, it created a troubling precedent. It eroded the distinction which had been so carefully worked out in the various just war doctrines between protection of the king's subjects and assault upon the king's enemies. A soldier could now reasonably claim that his service to the Crown was not incompatible with the plundering of its subjects, and non-combatants might find themselves attacked by "just warriors" from all sides. Du Guesclin's captain on the Breton frontier, the squire Jean Dorenge, took prisoners for ransom, set fire to houses, robbed, raped and otherwise assaulted people – all within the territory which he was supposed to protect.[73] Euphemisms could never disguise the fact, at least from its victims. The Jouvencel of Jean de Bueil, who delighted, as we have seen, in talk of the justice of the French king's cause and of the noble calling of arms, listened attentively and approvingly to an old captain as he advised the taking of "tribute" from the king's subjects of the region, "from which we are assigned our proper wages". Lest there be any doubt about the exact meaning of this reference to wages in the form of tribute, the captain quickly dispels all ambiguity.

> If it please the king, our lord, to supply us with victuals and money to sustain us, we will serve him in all his enterprises and obey all his orders – as indeed we must do – without levying or exacting anything from the inhabitants of the countryside here. If, however, other affairs, or false counsel, prevent him from provisioning us or paying us, we ourselves must raise victuals and finance both from persons in our own obedience and from enemies, as reasonably as we can. From those of our own side we will demand as modest a collection as we can, telling them that their contributions will guarantee them against everybody.[74]

There were many other forms of "tribute" which could be taken from "friendly" non-combatants without formally compromising one's status as a just warrior. The persons who lived in the *réssort* of a castle or walled town were expected to contribute to its defence: to the maintenance of its walls and to the patrolling of its battlements. Such services could usually be commuted for cash, but were never popular because they always seemed disproportionate to the protection which was offered in return. In 1367, for example, the inhabitants of Saint-Mard complained that they were being forced by the royal castellan of Passavant to perform sentry duty on a castle which was never used by them as a refuge.[75] Soldiers had also,

---

[71] Cazelles, "Jacquerie", p. 664.
[72] Luce, *Du Guesclin*, p. 582.
[73] Ibid., pp. 582–3.
[74] *Le Jouvencel*, i, pp. 95–6 and ii, p. 83.
[75] *La Guerre de Cent Ans Vue à Travers les Registres de Parlement, 1337–1369*, ed. P. Timbal *et al.* (Paris, 1961), p. 153.

traditionally, been entitled to requisition goods necessary for the effective prosecution of the war and, although this *droit de prise* prescribed due payment at the market price, it is clear that payment was more often in worthless promissory notes and tallies than it ever was in hard cash.[76] Perhaps the most common excuse of all for the taking of tribute by garrison soldiers was the command by the king, in times of imminent military threat, that all moveable property held by individuals in the open country should be withdrawn into the safekeeping of loyal garrisons lest it fall into the hands of enemies. When the owners of this property showed an understandable reluctance to remove their beasts and moveable wealth from a hypothetical enemy to a very real and hungry garrison, then soldiers felt themselves at liberty to take whatever they were able to find outside the fortress walls. This excuse was used by the squire, Jean le Prevost, as a member, "without wages or profits", of the garrison of Domart-en-Ponthieu in 1359, to take livestock and provisions from the surrounding countryside. The royal lieutenant, the count of Saint-Pol, had announced that "whosoever had victuals and provisions in the open country should place them in a fortress within a certain time" in order that the enemies of the kingdom should not enjoy them. He also added, with admirable frankness, that "the aforesaid fortresses might be supplied and provisioned by them".[77]

We have now reached an area of soldierly activity which was the daily experience of garrison soldiers and which could not be accommodated easily with the pristine theories of theologians and lawyers about the Just War. Soldiers could attack fellow subjects without necessarily placing themselves outside the law, as criminals. The distinction between the just and the unjust was now as much a moral one as a legal one: were the armed men using their rights over noncombatant subjects in a genuine way, to further the king's wars, or merely as a pretext to enrich themselves? What moral principle which overrode all casuistry could be appealed to?

"The laws of true chivalry", as Philippe de Mézières interpreted them, offered protection to "those who are oppressed and cannot defend themselves".[78] Certain myths which surrounded the origins of the knightly class supported this view. Ramon Lull had established the classic formulation of the legend in the late thirteenth century when he wrote that the French *chevalier* was the Roman *miles* of old and that, in times past, each knight was elected by a thousand citizens who provided him with a castle and with rents to support himself. In return, the knight publicly swore "to guard peace and passage, and to rule all in tranquility so that peasants may labour in the fields and merchants may travel safely".[79] The legend was transported to the French court by Christine de Pisan, the polymath daughter

[76] Ibid., pp. 90–96.
[77] AN, JJ 108, no. 208.
[78] Mézières, *Songe*, i, p. 532.
[79] Ramon Lul, *Le Livre de l'Ordre de Chevalerie*, Bibliothèque nationale, Paris (BN) MS Fonds Français 1971, fos. 7–8. This is a late medieval French version of his *Libre del Ordre de Cavayleria*.

of Charles V's astrologer, and by the Paris theologian and university chancellor, Jean Gerson. They modified it only to the extent of what they considered more appropriate to the pretensions, if not the capacity, of the Valois monarchy. They insisted that it was the prince in ancient times, not the people, who chose "one portion of the people to be set aside for his own company, to protect his own person, the common people, the clergy, women, the labourers and the country".[80] These were interpretations of chivalry which attempted to strike a balance between the duties of knights as professional warriors and their duties as lords exercising authority over subjects. They were based on the manifestly false assumption that war and justice, knighthood and responsible lordship, were compatible objectives. Inevitably, when measured against the standards of this golden age of chivalry in an imagined past, the men-at-arms of the later Middle Ages were bound to fail. It was a concept of chivalry which laid too great a stress on *noblesse oblige* and not enough on survival: too much on the exercise of responsible lordship and not enough on war. The clerk in the anonymous *Songe du Vergier* of the time of Charles V may stand for all who measured by this standard when he remarked how soldiers, whose duty it was "to guard and defend the whole country against all oppression", now do "exactly the opposite".[81]

The aristocratic interpretation of what categories of weak and defenceless people could appeal to an aristocratic sense of chivalry inevitably was more limited. It tended to favour either widows and orphans, or captive men-at-arms, all of their own, noble, class. It did not encompass the peasantry. Indeed, one of the most famous deeds of "chivalry", in Froissart's catalogue of feats of arms, was the rescue at Meaux of the duchesses of Normandy and Orleans and other noble ladies from the hands of the rebellious peasants. The count of Foix, the Captal de Buch, and others "went on killing [the peasants] until they were stiff and weary and they flung many into the River Marne".[82] A rebellious peasant was the moral equivalent of the monsters of legend over whose demise no-one shed any tears.

The law of arms was not only respected by men-at-arms, but was also much more precise and practical than the general code of chivalry which meant so many different and incompatible things. The law of arms regulated the day-to-day conduct of men-at-arms and was based upon the customs and traditions of their profession. It had nothing whatsoever to tell them about their relationships with other classes within the wider society.[83] The matter of the law of arms was drawn almost entirely from the areas of potential dispute between men-at-arms concerning the taking of knightly prisoners, the ransoms which could be demanded of them, the distribution of the profits of war between companions in arms, the organisation of tournaments and jousts, coats of arms, and the loss and gain of

---

[80] Pisan, *Charles V*, ii, pp. 5–6. Bourret, *Essai*, pp. 117–18.

[81] *Songe du Vergier*, p. 15.

[82] Froissart, *Chroniques*, ed. Luce, v, p. 106. It must be acknowledged, of course, that this counter-jacquerie was an exceptional circumstance.

[83] Wright, "Tree of Battles", pp. 19–21.

reputation. Its rules could be enforced in law courts, up to the very highest in the land, but its penalties were as much in terms of loss of honour within the noble peer group as they were of fines and imprisonments. It was, in short, a professional code of knightly soldiers with no points of reference outside that noble group. These were the "laws of true chivalry" as they were understood by the mass of men-at-arms who fought in the Hundred Years War, and which were felt to have any relevance to their situation. Geoffrey Charny addressed over one hundred questions on just such matters to the knights of King John's Order of the Star, and we may assume that he wanted answers to them.[84] Not one of them from this most serious-minded of men-at-arms was about "those who are oppressed and cannot defend themselves", at least in the wide sense that Mézières intended. The sense of responsible lordship and of *noblesse oblige,* which insisted upon the knight's obligations to that wider community which included peasants, was an ideal which did not come naturally to men-at-arms and it had to be instilled into the hearts of military captains by the guardians of the public weal and imposed upon the mass of soldiers by their strict discipline. It could be expected to do so only if this did not conflict with their first priority which, as the Jouvencel admitted, was to be an effective warrior, esteemed by their peers.

It is clear, then, that the ideal of the just warrior, the chivalrous knight, was not in the least moribund in the conditions of late medieval France. Geoffrey Charny, the knight of the fourteenth-century wars, knew that in wars which were properly initiated and properly conducted, participants might expect rewards of honour in this life and eternal ones in the next.[85] The Jouvencel of Jean de Bueil, flushed, nearly a century later, with the success of a raid on the English, and with good wine, was in no doubt that war "when it is undertaken in a just cause, to defend the right, is justice itself . . . a fine calling and a good one for young men".[86] It is clear, too, that there was general agreement between all who commented and interpreted "chivalry", at this time, that the ideal of the just warrior was not in the least compromised by the pillaging of enemy non-combatants and the destruction of their property. This may not have been a particularly honourable form of warfare in which the reputation of a man-at-arms for prowess might be acquired but it was a fact of life: perhaps a regrettable one. Froissart, reporting the robberies, burnings and murders which were committed by the English army at Caen, in 1346, felt that such things were inevitable in an army of this size which contained plenty of common soldiers "of little conscience".[87]

Where important disagreements, or at least different emphases, on this subject of "chivalry" were evident was when knights relinquished their rôle as warriors beyond the frontier, and assumed a policing function within their own society: when the functions of occupation and control took precedence over those of

---

[84] G. de Charny, *Demandes,* Bibliothèque Nationale, Paris [BN] MS Nouvelles Acquisitions Françaises 4736.

[85] G. de Charny, "Le Livre de Chevalerie", *Oeuvres de Froissart,* ed. Lettenhove, i, p. 512.

[86] *Le Jouvencel,* ii, p. 20.

[87] Froissart, *Chroniques,* ed. Luce, iii, pp. 146–7.

fighting. The concept of chivalry which the knights themselves were prepared to recognize had little or nothing to offer as guidance in this area beyond a general injunction to keep themselves ready, by constant practice in arms, for the next military adventure. Conventional, "peace-time", lordships had evolved over centuries of bargaining and conflict and were regulated by a host of individual charters of liberties; but these military lordships of the Hundred Years War were not regulated by custom in the same way. Military necessity had forced the Crowns of France and of England into a multitude of compromises over the entitlement of its own non-combatant subjects to live and work free of harassment by its own soldiers. In circumstances where it could not pay the several thousand soldiers which it required on a continuous basis for the effective prosecution of its wars, it had no choice in the matter. Others, usually outside the ranks of the knightly class, adhered to high principle. They insisted upon a tight military discipline (worthy of the supposedly Roman progenitors of chivalry) under the Crown and its officers and in the service of the common good. They stressed the rôle of the knight in the wider community: a rôle which knights had traditionally ignored, and they continued to insist on an absolute duty of soldiers to be content with their wages and to offer an unconditional protection to their people. Their attachment to such high principle in the teeth of such obvious practical difficulties condemned them to a great deal of dissatisfaction and to the firm conviction that they lived in an immoral age. The fourteenth-century Tree of Battles which was to Jean Froissart, that champion of the warrior ideal of chivalry, a tree in its glorious summer foliage, was to Honoré Bouvet, guardian of the ideal of the public weal, a "Tree of Mourning".[88]

---

[88] Bonet, *Tree*, p. 79.

2

WARLORDS

THE UNWILLINGNESS OF the men-at-arms who fought in the wars of the fourteenth and fifteenth centuries to give serious consideration in their code of honour to their relationship with the other, non-combatant, classes of society was eventually to lead to the collapse of their proudly independent lifestyle. In the shorter term, however, it gave them great strength to preserve a lofty detachment from the miseries of the wider community in wartime. Contemporary critics condemned them on two fronts: firstly, with the accusation that their way of life was "dishonourable", in that it made victims of the weak and harmless ("what honour and valour [is there] in attacking a poor innocent?"[1]); secondly, by describing their way of life as "un-lordly", in that they "took no thought for the mutual usefulness of lord and men" and failed to protect their subjects from the enemy.[2] These were good and solid grounds for criticism which appealed both to the knightly and to the aristocratic aspirations of all men-at-arms, but they were arguments rooted in an idealized landscape of the past which was far removed from the real world of later medieval France. In this real world, soldiers had to make a precarious living from the country and in conditions where the so-called "mutuality" of lord and man had been reduced, as never before, to a bitter cycle of rebellion and repression.

The clerical appeal to a code of chivalry which was founded in classical ideas of military discipline and on Christian ideals of love and sacrifice could be dismissed as irrelevant by the man-at-arms who recognized another, more exclusive, form of "chivalry". The appeal to a sense of lordliness in the men-at-arms of the Hundred Years War was easily rejected by them, at least in the sense that Venette and Mézières intended, the one which stressed the public service rôle of knighthood. Lordship, however, was susceptible to other interpretations. It must not be forgotten that the man-at-arms was a lord, or he aspired to be one, and that even that most famous of knights-errant, Don Quixote, whose head had been turned completely by the romances of chivalry, "fancied himself crowned by the valour of his arms at least with the empire of Trebizond", while his more hard-headed squire sustained himself with the vision of "some isle".[3] Although

---

[1] Bonet, *Tree*, p. 154.
[2] Venette, *Chronicle*, p. 66.
[3] M. de Cervantes Saavedra, *The Adventures of Don Quixote*, trans. J. Cohen (Harmondsworth, 1970), pp. 33 and 66.

"immovable property" in land and castles, when captured in war, legally became the property of the sovereign head of the war and not of the individual captor, the practice was often rather different and it was frequently treated by soldiers like any other form of booty. The heads which filled the massive helms and bacinets which are now in the armoury of the Tower of London and in the Musée de l'Armée in Paris were as crammed with ideas of lordships to be won or protected as they were with ambitions to serve their ladies or unhorse their opponents, and the examples of the *condottiere* princes of fifteenth-century Italy, like the Sforza dukes of Milan, were not wasted on such young French men-at-arms as the Jouvencel.[4] But this desire to win land and castles, as well as more moveable property, did not, for the most part, include a sense of *noblesse oblige* towards the non-combatants who lived and worked within these borrowed or assumed lordships. It did, however, involve the assumption of other "lordly" values which were not at all compatible.

Lords not only needed the support of the local people in goods and services, but they expected it as a right. Theirs was an expensive style of life. As men-at-arms they were expected to possess the mount, the lance and sword, and the body-armour of the knight, even if their equipment at times more closely resembled Don Quixote's scavengings than the splendid examples of the modern museums. In addition to these bare necessities, however, they aspired to live in a certain style which went far beyond the strictly necessary. "They wore pearls on their hoods or on their gilded and silver girdles", wrote the horrified Jean de Venette in 1356, "and elaborately adorned themselves from head to foot with gems and precious stones. So assiduously did all [nobles and knights], from the least to the greatest, cover themselves with these luxuries that pearls and other precious stones were sold for high prices and could hardly be found at all in Paris."[5] Although the knights who rode the streets of Paris in the tightly-fitting tunics and the pointed shoes which so scandalized this monk were not typical of their comrades in the provinces, they may be taken as representative of a general desire amongst this class for a lordly and conspicuous consumption. A squire serving in some remote and forgotten theatre of war may not have found such easy access to precious stones, but his war-gains as a garrison soldier might be quickly translated into the trappings of an aristocratic household. The English squire, Jack Spore, who found himself in possession of a ten-year-old boy after a raid on the village of Saint-Julien-du-Sault, with no-one to pay his ransom, "had him mounted upon a horse, charged with his lance and bacinet, and made him his page".[6] It is true that the lordly desire for lavish display and a sumptuous life-style sometimes conflicted with the warrior culture which Geoffrey Charny and Jean de Bueil so well represented: one which exulted in the hardships of the honest man-at-arms

---

[4] "Si que vous-meisme serez prince et tendrés la principauté que vous aurez conquestée à l'espée, comme ont fait plusieurs vaillans hommes ou temps passé, et encores de present le conte Francisque [Sforza]." *Le Jouvencel*, i, p. 45.

[5] Venette, *Chronicle*, p. 63.

[6] AN, JJ 111, no. 355.

and which lionized the knights who did not pander to their bodies with those luxuries (such as the white sheets and soft beds which Charny dreamed of) which were suspected of undermining the fighting spirit.[7] This puritanism of the "poor companion", however, has something in it of the making of a virtue out of necessity. Wealth, and the conspicuous consumption of it, far from being a bar to lordship, was almost its precondition.

Leaving aside, for the moment, the benefits which came to soldiers directly from their position as "masters of the soil", the profits which came to men-at-arms from their specifically warrior activities were often spectacular. The booty which could be acquired legitimately, for example after the successful assault upon a town, could enrich all ranks in an invading army down to the very humblest. After the capture of Barfleur, in 1346, the town was "plundered of its gold, silver and precious jewels. [Edward III's army] found so much of it there that the very servants of the army turned up their noses at fur-lined gowns."[8] Robert Knolles' capture of Auxerre, in March 1359, earned him 500,000 gold *moutons* in booty alone, and if we add to this the ransoms of prisoners and the forty thousand *moutons* and forty thousand pearls which were the agreed price of his evacuation of the place, the profits for an army of two or three thousand men may easily be calculated.[9] In addition to the profits from booty, men-at-arms could also win small fortunes by receiving the surrender of enemy men-at-arms and by negotiating ransom agreements with them. To pluck one example from thousands, the ransom of Guillaume, lord of Chateauvillain, may be mentioned. This Burgundian nobleman was captured by four French captains at Marigny, in 1430, and a ransom of twenty thousand *saluts d'or* was agreed.[10] This represented the promise of a little less than twenty kilograms of gold coin for each of the four captors. The frenzied excitement of the dozen English knights and squires who attempted to receive the surrender of the king of France after the battle of Poitiers can easily be imagined. The ransom agreed for him, at the first treaty of London, was four million gold crowns, weighing (if it had ever come to that) many tons. Neither ransom was paid in full, and a great deal of the captor's rights in any ransom had to be shared with more senior military officers. Nevertheless, large sums of money changed hands as a result of these encounters. In addition to the ransoms of individuals, a man-at-arms on campaign, especially if he were of some rank and significance, could be offered protection-money by persons who wished to release their property from the threat of capture or destruction. Two captains in the army of John of Gaunt, Walter Hewet and Thomas Caon, were instrumental in negotiating several agreements of this nature with the anxious owners of houses in the

7 Charny, "Livre de chevalerie", p. 487.
8 Froissart, *Chroniques*, ed. Luce, iii, p. 134.
9 Delachenal, *Charles V*, ii, p. 34. The international trade of France was carried on with the gold *chaise* or *agnel* (commonly called the *mouton*), which weighed about 3.58 grams. P. Spufford, "Coinage and Currency", *Cambridge Economic History*, iii (1963), pp. 576–602.
10 A. Bossuat, "Les Prisonniers de Guerre au XVe Siècle: la Rançon de Guillaume, Seigneur de Chateauvillain", *Annales de Bourgogne*, xxiii (1951), pp. 7–35. The *salut d'or* of 1421 weighed 3.884 grams. J. Lafavrie, *Les Monnaies des Rois de France*, i (Paris, 1951), p. 83.

Pays de Caux, in October 1369.[11] They had sufficient standing in this English army to ensure that at least some of these manors were spared from the flames of the withdrawing soldiers.

It must be appreciated, however, that such windfall profits for certain men-at-arms almost always involved corresponding losses for other men-at-arms in terms of ransoms paid and property lost, and, although the balance of opportunity may have favoured the English aggressors over the French defenders, the equation is not a neat one. From the very beginning of the war, there was English territory in France which had to be defended by soldiers in the English allegiance: firstly, in Gascony, then in Brittany, the Calais district and Normandy. For much of the first half of the fifteenth century, there was a huge area of English occupation in northern France, in addition to Gascony, which few of the English landowners before about 1436 imagined to be merely temporary. English men-at-arms were captured for ransom quite as often as were French ones. The wheel of fortune turned quickly in wartime. The four captors of William of Chateauvillain, mentioned above, were soon themselves victims of a Burgundian offensive, with ransoms of their own to pay. The balance of profit and loss could only be tipped firmly in favour of the men-at-arms as a group, rather than as lucky individuals, if they could take advantage of revenues derived from taxation. When receipts from "extraordinary" taxation were redistributed for the benefit of nobles in the form of pensions and wages, the budget of the State became "to some extent the budget of noble assistance".[12]

The most obvious way in which taxation brought revenue to soldiers was in the form of wages disbursed by treasurers of wars or by other royal officials. All combatants who served in royal armies could expect wages according to a sliding scale of rank, even if, as we have noticed above, they were rarely paid regularly. In 1351, daily wages in the French armies were set at forty *sous tournois* for a banneret, twenty for a simple knight, ten for a squire and five for an armed varlet.[13] Soldiers in English armies could expect to be paid similarly until they entered enemy territory at which point they were expected at least to supplement their wages by plunder, if not entirely to live off the countryside.[14] Where wages were paid on a regular basis, for example to the French garrison of Bayeux on the Normandy frontier during the 1370s, the benefits were not inconsiderable. Rogier le Masnier was its castellain from 1371 until 1378. We know that he received three hundred gold francs in 1371; four hundred *livres* (each approximately equal in value to the gold franc) in 1372; three hundred *livres* in 1373; two hundred gold francs and one hundred *livres* in each of the years from 1375 until 1377.[15] He

11 AN, JJ 108, no. 382.
12 Contamine, "French Nobility", p. 151.
13 *Ordonnances*, iv, p. 67.
14 K. Fowler, "Les Finances et la Discipline dans les Armées Anglaises en France au XIVe Siècle", *Cahiers Vernonnais*, iv (1964), pp. 66–67.
15 *Gallia Regia, ou Etat des Officiers Royaux des Bailliages et des Sénéchaussées de 1328 à 1515*, ed. G. Dupont-Ferrier, 6 vols. (Paris, 1942–61), i, pp. 516–17.

boosted this income with gifts from the king of about one thousand francs, fines on watch-keeping defaulters, and with supplementary wages for his involvement in the inspection of fortresses within the bailiwick of Caen.[16] Here was a knight who lived in some style as a paid employee of the Crown, although he insisted that these payments had not made him rich.

On the other side of the frontier from Bayeux were the great English fortresses of the Cotentin peninsula centred upon Saint-Sauveur-le-Vicomte until 1374 and on Cherbourg from 1377. Sir John Chandos, a major figure in the entourage of the Black Prince, had made himself rich as captain of Saint Sauveur. It is true that not all of his captain's income, as we shall see, derived from the English Exchequer, but the wages of the nearby Cherbourg garrison in 1378 weighed so heavily upon the English taxpayers that a complaint was made about them in the House of Commons.[17] By 1378, English garrisons were scattered along the northern coast of France, from Brest, in the far west (whose captain, Robert Knolles, was another major figure in the wars of the fourteenth century), to Calais and its dozen or so satellite fortresses in the east. Regular wages, especially on this latter frontier, were an important source of garrison income during the fourteenth century, and the English garrisons in Normandy during Bedford's regency between 1422 and 1435 were substantially financed from the Norman taxpayers. Nevertheless, however loud were the complaints of taxpayers on both sides of the Channel – and the peasant in a fifteenth-century work by Alain Chartier complained that money wasted in soldiers' wages could have bought England outright[18] – wages were not enough to sustain the thousands of men-at-arms and other soldiers who made their living from this war. Some did not even expect any.

In addition to their desire for lordly display and an income to accommodate it, the men-at-arms of the Hundred Years War also inherited from their connections with lordship an attitude to the peasantry which can only be described as a suspicion, sometimes bordering on outright hatred. Lords on both sides of the Channel harboured a certain bitterness bred of an ancient, and, by-and-large, a losing struggle to sustain their fortunes in the face of peasant solidarity and passive resistance. The story of the economic decline of the landed nobility in western Europe during the late Middle Ages and the relative progress of their peasantries towards an end to arbitrary taxation and labour services is well beyond the scope of this present work.[19] It left a legacy of bitterness amongst landlords for which the conditions of war afforded some solace. In fact, men-at-arms were often found to be treating the peasants in their area of military occupation with a ruthlessness

---

[16] AN, JJ 112, no. 14.
[17] Fowler, "Finances", p. 57.
[18] A. Thomas, "Une Oeuvre Patriotique Inconnue d'Alain Chartier", *Journal des Savants* (Sept.–Nov. 1914), p. 447.
[19] For its effect on France, see G. Bois, "Noblesse et Crise des Revenus Seigneuriaux en France au XIVe et XVe Siècles: Essai d'Interpretation", *La Noblesse au Moyen Age, XIe au XVe Siècle*, ed. P. Contamine (Paris, 1976), pp. 219–33. On England, see R. Hilton, "Y eut-il une Crise Générale de la Féodalité?", *Annales* (1951), pp. 23–30.

which was difficult to understand and which seemed to go well beyond reasonable self-interest. It seemed to have nothing to do with feelings that these peasants were "political" enemies, in the sense that they were loyal to a rival sovereign. It appeared to be a more fundamental antagonism. Jean de Venette thought that men-at-arms took a malicious delight in the sufferings of innocent non-combatants[20] and it is not unduly fanciful to suppose that it was, indeed, an exquisite pleasure for some lords to exercise a "pure" form of lordship, uncomplicated by ancient and undesirable customs; to be able to respond to the usual signs of peasant resistance with that massive show of force which they were incapable of mobilizing in time of peace; to tear up charters of liberties in the name of military necessity. The average man-at-arms, who was not a landed proprietor, took his cue from his fellow men-at-arms who were part of the landed aristocracy. Very often, the latter were both the military as well as the social superiors of the former.

All but the most privileged captains in royal service lived off the tribute paid to them by non-combatants. "Friendly" non-combatants had to pay for their own safety, whether they liked it or not. "Enemy" non-combatants, who had acquired the status of enemy by paying protection-money to the wrong people, were forced to ransom themselves, either collectively or individually, in a system known as *appatisation*. However carefully the captain of Crathor, in *Le Jouvencel,* may have attempted to distinguish between the contributions demanded of friends and the *appatissemens* extracted from enemies, there was, very often, no meaningful distinction between the two. Fortresses occupied by soldiers of the French, English, or other allegiances very quickly assumed the features of warlordships. These were lordships in that very primitive sense which was more closely akin to the anarchic conditions of western Europe in the tenth and eleventh centuries, described by Marc Bloch as the "first" age of feudalism, than it was to the more recent and more orderly period of centralizing monarchies under Edward I and Saint Louis.[21] They maintained themselves, to a greater or lesser extent, by selling safeconducts to travellers on the nearby roads and bridges and by forced contributions from the neighbouring villages. Huge profits could be made from the sale of safeconducts, especially by garrison soldiers who controlled vital land and sea routes. John Fotheringay's garrison at Creil which controlled the road between Paris and Compiègne in the late 1350s was reported to have made 100, 000 francs from the sale of safeconducts alone.[22] Their loyalties to a warring sovereign (Fotheringay fought in the name of the king of Navarre), though always vigorously asserted, usually came a poor second to considerations of material self-interest. They had become robber barons.

The most notorious of these robber barons were the captains of freebooting companies like Fotheringay, known as *routiers,* men of the Companies, *écorcheurs.* The Gascon squire who had the good fortune to make a stylish entry into

---

[20] Venette, *Chronicle*, p. 111: "rather did the burdens which bore so heavily upon the people seem to please the lords and princes . . .".

[21] M. Bloch, *Feudal Society*, trans. L. Manyon, 2 vols. (London, 1965), i, pp. 59–69.

[22] Denifle, *Désolation*, p. 219.

Orthez under the very eye of the great chronicler, Jean Froissart, arrived with a mule train of possessions "like a great baron".[23] He had made his fortune in the French wars, fighting where possible for the English Crown; and, although he had had his share of rich ransoms and booty, his conspicuous wealth (he dined off silver plate) was derived largely from the occupation of land which he had won for himself in the French kingdom. In Picardy, for example, he had been one of a number of adventurers in the service of the king of Navarre who "were, for a time, lords of the fields and the rivers [where he] and his friends won a great deal of wealth". Some time later, he and his friends captured the town of La Charité-sur-Loire and, for a year and a half "everything was ours along the Loire as far as Le Puy in the Vélay". Even in that very year of 1388 when he had attracted the admiring attention of Froissart, he claimed to be drawing such a substantial yearly income from the castle and lordship of Thurie, in the Tarn, that he boasted himself to be unwilling to exchange it for Orthez itself where the count of Foix and Béarn held his lavish court. His concern at that particular moment was whether to sell the place to agents of the French Crown in the Auvergne, or to enjoy it for a while longer. The name of this otherwise obscure bastard of a minor noble house was the Bascot de Mauléon. He is typical of a large group of independently-minded, professional, men-at-arms who made a good, if risky, living out of the war. Had it not been for a few idle hours before a fire in the Hostelry of the Moon at Orthez, where chronicler and captain enjoyed the hospitality of Ernauton de Pin, he would have been forgotten like most of the others.

At least from the time of the battle of Poitiers, in 1356, onwards, there were always castles, fortified churches and manor houses within the kingdom of France occupied by men-at-arms like the Bascot. These fortresses were the centres of "borrowed" lordships which provided for their occupants in the long intervals between the grander military adventures organised at an official level: the crusades against the heathens and the Turks, the *chevauchées*, the sieges. The professional soldiers who occupied them were identifiable as freebooters not because they denied allegiance to the king of France, the king of England, or to some other warring sovereign. Indeed, the Bascot insisted (and there is no reason to doubt him) that he had always been loyal to the kings of England because his family estate was in the district of Bordeaux.[24] It was rather because they made a living out of soldiering without depending upon wages paid to them by their sovereign. Paid service in a royal army or garrison was an occasional and unexpected bonus, and they lived almost entirely out of the profits of "borrowed lordship".

The Bretons of unknown loyalty who occupied three miserable fortresses in the Nièvre during the late 1350s were receiving money, "fat, cheeses, eggs and other victuals and necessities" from the local people who paid "in order to be able to

---

[23] The Bascot de Mauléon's story may be read in *Jean Froissart, Voyage en Béarn*, ed. A. Diverres (Manchester, 1953), pp. 88–111. A good English translation is *Froissart, Chronicles*, ed. Brereton, pp. 280–94.

[24] Ibid., p. 288.

live peacefully in their homes and to go about their work without the constant threat and fear of the aforesaid enemies".[25] The immediate threat to the lives and property of these local people was from the Bretons themselves and when the Mignart family entertained members of the garrison of Corvol-l'Orgueilleux in their home, they claimed that they did so "for fear that they might otherwise be killed and their buildings and goods burned and destroyed". It was possible, indeed it was a frequent complaint, that villages often had to pay *patis* simultaneously to several different garrisons, but we may assume that the garrison of Corvol did attempt to offer some very temporary security to the Mignart family against other outsiders. The freebooters had a powerful interest in guarding the people who provided their material support. Criminal protection-rackets are not unfamiliar phenomena in the urbanized, developed, world of today, and the conditions of superficial order and harmony, even genuine security, which they can produce in neighbourhoods which are subjected to them can surprise those who equate crime with disorder. No doubt, like others in similar positions, our Breton freebooters of the fourteenth century demanded heavy financial compensation for being pressed to evacuate their precious borrowed lordships in accordance with the treaty of Brétigny in 1360.[26]

During periods of prolonged truce between England and France, as occurred after the Brétigny agreement in 1360, military entrepreneurs, such as these Breton adventurers, could combine into formidable armies of occupation and campaign. They defeated the army of the royal lieutenant, Jean, count of Tancarville, at the battle of Brignais in April 1362. The freebooter, Seguin de Badefol's, safeconducts were respected throughout the Mâconnais, Forez, Vélay and lower Burgundy during much of the 1360s, and were drawn up in princely style. "Let it be known to all that I, Seguin de Badefol, captain of Anse for the king of Navarre, have given good, safe and sure conduct and special safeguard to masters. . . . Given at Anse under my seal, the fifth day of August in the year of grace 1365."[27] The centre of this extensive temporary lordship, from November 1364, was the town and castle of Anse, "borrowed" from the cathedral chapter of Lyon and controlling traffic along the Saône valley between Burgundy and Lyon. According to one of Seguin's officers, there was no knight, squire, or rich man in this territory who dared to come out of his own house "unless he was *appatised* to us".[28] He was bought out, in July 1365, for forty thousand florins and a papal absolution.[29] A little later, Geoffrey Tête-Noire, whom Philippe de Mézières dismissed as a low-born upstart, was granting similar letters commencing "Joffroy Teste-Noire, duke of Ventadour and count of the Limousin, lord and sovereign of all the

25 AN, JJ 104, no. 231.
26 An attempt to secure the evacuation of Brouillamenon in 1360 is described in *Hundred Years War*, ed. Fowler, pp. 191–2.
27 G. Guigue, *Récits de la Guerre de Cent Ans: les Tards-venus en Lyonnais, Forez et Beaujolais, 1356–1369* (Lyon, 1886), p. 108.
28 Ibid., p. 107.
29 Delachenal, *Charles V*, iii, p. 234.

captains of the Auvergne, of Rouergue and of the Limousin ...".[30] We may safely assume that in an area of France where even knights and squires feared to tread without insuring themselves with safeconducts signed by these captains of companies, the inhabitants of the villages enjoyed no greater security.

Although the activities of men of the Companies, such as Seguin de Badefol and Tête-Noire, were condemned by lawyers and moralists as not war but brigandage; and although lawyers and other writers insisted that the freebooters were not true knights, but pillagers, robbers and low-born upstarts, the lines of demarcation between war and brigandage, and between chivalrous knights and highway robbers, were not at all clear in practice. Captains of the Free Companies, who had acquired their wealth and reputation as freebooters, moved in and out of princely service with an ease which suggested no sense of impropriety: they married into the traditional aristocracy, acquired titles of nobility and offices of high command within the armies of the rival kings, and they achieved immortality alongside the Black Prince and Sir John Chandos in the pages of Froissart's chronicles. Charles V's famous constable, Bertrand du Guesclin, had begun his spectacular military career as a freebooter in the Breton wars and he never lost a taste for such company. His conversation while sitting down to dinner in the company of a group of *routier* captains is revealing of the man. When Du Guesclin remarked upon the excellent quality of the wine he was drinking, and asked about its cost, his host reported himself unable to comment on the price as "the vendor was not alive at the time when we acquired it".[31] Some of his rivals on the English side, such as Robert Knolles, or Hugh Calverley, had pasts which were no less murky. In Knolles' case, it may have been non-noble to boot.[32] Their way of life, as professional knightly soldiers, allowed them to explore the furthest avenues of the knight's adventurous calling. They were, as the Bascot de Mauléon declared to Froissart, "as skilled and trained in war as any people could be; as much in preparing for battle and in turning it to their advantage as in scaling and assaulting towns".[33] The count of Armagnac wanted the service of Mérigot Marchès on his planned crusade, in 1390, not only to rid the Auvergne of an appalling freebooter, but also because "in all deeds of arms he knew [Marchès] to be skilled and subtle in the taking by assault of towns and able to advise in all matters of war that one might need".[34] It was impossible either to exclude them from a profession which placed such a high value on these capabilities or from the service of princes who needed these skills so much in their wars. The army of Charles VII, under Poton de Xantrailles, Antoine de Chabannes, La Hire, Ambroise de Loré, was a veritable army of freebooters.[35] And when it came to the occupation of territory and the

---

[30] Froissart, *Chroniques*, ed. Luce, xiv, p. 141. Mézières' reference to him is in Mézières, *Songe*, i, p. 530.
[31] Keen, *Chivalry*, p. 232.
[32] Delachenal, *Charles V*, ii, p. 32.
[33] *Froissart*, ed. Diverres, p. 91.
[34] Froissart, *Chroniques*, ed. Luce, xiv, p. 162.
[35] C. Allmand, *The Hundred Years War: England and France at War c.1300–c.1450* (Cambridge, 1988), p. 76.

exploitation of the profits of local power, there was really very little to choose between the methods of the Companies and those of soldiers in more regular service to a sovereign prince.

If we turn our attention from freebooters like the Bascot de Mauléon and Seguin de Badefol to a French captain like Enguerrand d'Eudin, whom no-one would have dared call a freebooter, the scenery is not so very different. Enguerrand, like his fellow-Picard, Philippe de Mézières, made his reputation as a warrior in the retinue of Arnoul d'Audrehem, who became a marshal of France, and Enguerrand himself was to end his days as royal governor of the Dauphiné.[36] Yet, while he was captain of the important royal garrison of Loches, between 1358 and 1364, a complaint of abuse of power was brought against him by the lord of Montrésor. He was accused of treating the castle of Loches (jokingly known as "Picardy" though it was in the heart of Touraine) as his own personal property; of boasting that the kings of France and of England could "boil their pots" for sixty years before the gates of Loches before he would allow them entry; of holding a royal sergeant and several burgesses for ransom and of having extorted money with menaces from parishes in the castellany. It is not necessary to believe all of the charges laid against him to recognise in this captain of Loches a familiar kind of borrowed lordship, even if legitimated, as the *routiers'* were not, by official letters of commission. The captaincy of Bayeux which brought such handsome rewards in wages to Rogier le Masnier in the 1370s, as we have already noted, was not always so well provided. The Norman knight Henri de Coulombières, who was an important captain in French royal service between 1357 and 1381, had become captain of the place on 27 December 1357. He received no wages whatsoever for the first nine months of his captaincy making it inevitable, as he later declared, that many things such as corn, beverages, and beasts should be taken from the local people without compensation, just as he had done when defending his own fortified house of Coulombières in the Calvados.[37] The *routier* captain and the royal captain were not so very different.

Henri de Coulombières' experience as a captain in the service of three kings of France is also a useful reminder that not all captains of fortresses were foreigners to their area of military control. If the traditional lord of a castle or fortified manor was capable of organising its defence, as was clearly the case at Coulombières, he was not likely to be replaced by a royally-appointed outsider. One might expect a traditional lordship of this kind to have been less oppressive for the local people than a borrowed lordship of the *routier*-type. Perhaps Henri de Coulombières was more likely to have thoughts of posterity than was the Bascot de Mauléon at Thurie or Sir John Chandos at Saint-Sauveur: more anxious to maintain the value of his inheritance and less concerned with quick profits. Perhaps the lord of Montrésor's protest against the high-handed actions of Enguerrand d'Eudin at

---

[36] H. Martin, "Enguerrand d'Eudin, Capitaine Royale de Loches, Sénéchal de Beaucaire, Gouverneur de Dauphiné, 13. – 1391", *Bulletin Trimestriel de la Société Archéologique de Touraine*, xxxii (1958), pp. 131–59.

[37] AN, JJ 108, no. 303. Contamine, *Guerre, Etat*, pp. 605–6.

Loches represented the voice of traditional local power against an alien military élite. Possibly so. There is certainly a danger to the historian in considering only the breakdown of a system of rural defence: a system which naturally involved the close co-operation between local lords and their dependent peasantries. An appreciation of mutual self-interest may often have got the better of those more traditional social animosities which have been described above. Gabriel Fournier's studies of the "sociology" of medieval French castles have provided us with many examples from this period of a system of mutual co-operation working smoothly. The castle of Montaillou, for example, which had in the early fourteenth century been the home of Beatrice de Planissoles during that great purge of Cathar heretics now made famous by Emmanuel le Roy Ladurie, was, in the following century, equipped with lodges in its bailey which the inhabitants rented for the protection of themselves and their livestock in times of local emergency.[38]

The traditional landed aristocracy, however, as Coulombières' own experience demonstrates, was also being converted into warlordism by the constant threat of attack by enemy soldiers and by the pressing demands of royal officials to maintain a state of war-readiness: officials who had the rights to destroy, to confiscate, and to order repairs at the owner's expense of any indefensible stone building. The knight Robert de Bicher, for example, had seen his castle taken over by sergeants of the royal bailiff of Mâcon, in 1364, and then by soldiers in the service of the royal lieutenant, the count of Armagnac. In the course of regaining his property, Robert's captain assaulted royal sergeants and, when safely in possession, took to robbing merchants on the road to Marcigny-les-Nonnains (Saône-et-Loire): no doubt in order to help recoup his losses and to pay for the necessary repairs to the walls.[39] Of the 108 fortified places which were officially inspected by Rogier le Masnier and his two companions in the bailiwick of Caen during the winter of 1372, all of the fortified abbeys, priories and churches had a professional captain, as did many of the secular lordships.[40] A large majority of both the ecclesiastical and secular lords were given orders by the inspectors, on the authority of the royal bailiff, to carry out expensive modifications in order to bring their fortresses into a state of defensibility. The costs of a professional captain and the upkeep of walls and gates bore heavily upon a property-owning class which was already weakened by declining rents, war-damage to mills and barns, and, very often, by heavy ransom demands upon themselves or on members of their families. In such circumstances, a soft form of lordship which respected the traditional rights of the local communities may not have been a realistic option.

---

[38] G. Fournier, *Le Château dans la France Médiévale: Essai de Sociologie Monumentale* (Paris, 1978), p. 237. Also, E. Le Roy Ladurie, *Montaillou: Cathars and Catholics in a French Village, 1294–1324*, trans. B. Bray (Harmondsworth, 1978).

[39] AN, JJ 108, no. 372.

[40] "Relation de la Visite des Forteresses du Bailliage de Caen", ed. A. de Caumont, *Société des Antiquaires de Normandie, Mémoires*, series 2, i (1840), pp. 185–204. The professional captains were probably appointed jointly by the proprietors and the royal *baillis*, but the cost was the former's.

The more vigorous forms of warlordship were more likely: those which compelled non-combatants to contribute to the maintenance of their "protector", and to the upkeep and patrolling of his castle walls, whatever their precious charters of liberties might have said to the contrary, and whatever doubts may have been expressed as to the quality of this protection. "Every misery increased on every hand", runs the jeremiad of Jean de Venette, "especially among the rural population, the peasants, for their lords bore hard upon them, extorting from them all their substance and poor means of livelihood."[41]

It is very likely that the spark which ignited that brief but bloody peasants' revolt in the spring of 1358, known as the *Jacquerie,* was the breach of local customs by the traditional lords of the Beauvaisis as they attempted to serve the Crown against the rebellious city of Paris.[42] The licences to plunder which the regent had issued to his captains in place of wages, together with the ruthless exploitation of the local *taille,* the seigneurial revenues from tolls and from justice, and the revival of forced labour to repair castle-walls and of watch-services on their battlements, all attracted the murderous wrath of the common people. It seemed to them to be a return to the dark days of serfdom, and it was a particularly bitter irony when the warlords who demanded these services were the French king's friends not his enemies, traditional lords not foreign captains. The spokesman for the Fourth Hierarchy, the common people, in Philippe de Mézières' *Dream of the Old Pilgrim,* complained that when war came to the French kingdom, it "made us serfs instead of freemen. We were afflicted not only by the sword of our English enemies, but by our own lords too. We were all oppressed by *gabelles, tailles,* taxes, watch-duties; by pillage and servitude."[43] Jean de Venette, ever to the fore with complaints of this sort, wrote that when the English enemies made the villages of central and western France "tributary to them", the "natural lords of the villages" wished to do the same. "The only desire of the nobles was to ruin the peasants and to work them to death."[44] Jean Juvenal des Ursins took up the theme in the fifteenth century: "the way the king's men made war was to make themselves into tyrants and alienate their own people".[45] The return to an arbitrary form of lordship by the very families who had, in an earlier period, negotiated charters of liberties with the villages clearly was more foul and unnatural to the local people than the more predictable depredations of public enemies. They were certainly complained of more bitterly.

The process by which soldiers in occupation of a fortress exploited the villages by "pillage and servitude", and by making them "tributary", was not as straightforward as may at first be imagined. In many cases, these soldiers were foreigners to the territory *appatised*; they did not know the local geography, nor the rich families of the district who were capable of paying substantial ransoms. They did

---

41 Venette, *Chronicle,* p. 94.
42 See below, pp. 84–5.
43 Mézières, *Songe,* i, p. 455.
44 Venette, *Chronicle,* p. 95.
45 Juvenal des Ursins, *Écrits Politiques,* iii, pp. 109–11.

not know the secret places in the forests and caves where peasants were accustomed to seek refuge in times of trouble and where they hid their treasures and their beasts. They were vulnerable to ambush. The dangerous tasks of ferreting-out such valuable, indeed essential, intelligence and of negotiating deals with the local peasantry did not, as a rule, belong to the men-at-arms. It was the function of the common soldiers in their personal retinues, usually known as *valets* or *pillars*.[46] Some of these common soldiers were (as we shall see in the following chapter) recruited in the district and either seduced by promised rewards, or bullied by threats, into this form of service. Their foraging activities on behalf of their masters, the knights and squires, at one and the same time kept these latter supplied with the necessities and luxuries of life, and spared them some tasks which would certainly have demeaned them.[47]

In December 1373, according to the testimony of ten "poor labourers" of the parish of Saint-Romain-sur-Cher (Loir-et-Cher), two men armed with swords and heavy jackets, and who were not known in the community, rode into their village with the clear intention of taking property without payment, of extracting ransoms from the people, and of raping women.[48] They were called *pillars* and were assumed to be associated with the much larger companies of men-at-arms who were then terrorizing the district. Such was the panic which this couple of lightly-armed soldiers inspired in the village that the whole population of the village fled into the nearby woods, where they remained for many days. The story, as told by this group of peasants, which ended in the death by drowning of three *pillars,* is not unlike many others. They all show that non-combatants were able easily to distinguish between the knightly soldiers, the men-at-arms, who were the employers of pillagers and varlets, and the *pillars* and *valets* themselves, who did their dirty work. In some cases, they knew these armed servants personally because they had been recruited locally. The stories describe the multifarious activities of this ubiquitous low-life of the contemporary military world as they brought plunder, livestock and prisoners back to their masters in the occupied fortresses; as they tortured prisoners in order to extract ransoms, and as, tensely, they negotiated *patis* agreements with village leaders, and collected it when it came due. It is a pity that we know so little about these soldiers who were so important to the effective functioning of warlordism. The fact that to call a man a *pillar*, in those days, was a serious insult which often led to bloodshed, is sufficient indication of their reputation in the wider community.[49] Bishop Thomas Basin of Lisieux knew the type well and observed that, while the men-at-arms in the latter

---

[46] Wright, "Pillagers", pp. 16–19 and 22–23.

[47] The stratification of warfare on social lines was obviously an important feature of the Hundred Years War. Even at the battle of Agincourt the attack on Henry V's baggage, which was guarded by varlets and boys, was by "a body of armed peasants, led by three mounted knights". J. Keegan, *The Face of Battle* (Harmondsworth, 1978), p. 84.

[48] AN, JJ 106, no. 77.

[49] Guille Adam, " qui estoit pillart de tresmauvaise conversacion", was murdered in 1368. AN, JJ 106, no. 45.

stages of the Hundred Years War might be honest enough, their varlets (*famulos*) were so insolent as to be intolerable: of vile character and rotten with vice.[50]

When garrisons, whether they consisted of the swollen households of traditional lords or the retinues of royal captains, became self-supporting in this manner, they did not necessarily lose their strategic function of frontier defence or of defence of the kingdom in depth, but they became more like independent lordships than outposts of royal power. The Crown often viewed them as both useful and cheap repositories of soldiers who could be called upon when needed; also as symbols of royal authority, even when the substance of royal control had largely disappeared. Enguerrand d'Eudin boasted of his independence and was accused of making comfortable arrangements with the English garrison of Cormery in order more effectively to fleece the local people.[51] Here, at least from the point-of-view of the "sheep", if not of their royal "shepherd", was a real-life example of Jean de Venette's parable of the sheep-dog running with the wolf. The teeming English garrison of Saint-Sauveur-le-Vicomte in the Cotentin, during the 1360s, was eminently self-sufficient as it lived off the ransoms of no less than 263 parishes which were dependent upon it, and it, too, had agreements with neighbouring French garrisons to divide between them the market in protection.[52]

It may be supposed that the strategy of conquest by the English Crown during the period after the battle of Agincourt, in 1415, altered the pattern fundamentally, at least on the English side of the lines. Instead of the borrowed lordships usurped by freebooters or assumed on a temporary basis by the captains of royal garrisons, as was the situation during much of the fourteenth century, the territory of the English occupation now consisted of real lordships granted to a new landowning class, with every prospect of permanence. In the heartland of Normandy, far removed from the frontier of war as it extended during the 1420s towards the Loire, the land settlement of Henry V and his brother, the duke of Bedford, consisted of "what were essentially non-military occupations".[53] Captains of castles within this hinterland, secure in their receipt of regular wages, could contemplate the investigation of civilian *vicomtes* into the activities of their garrisons with great equanimity. The *vicomte* of Gisors, for example, made an enquiry amongst merchants and labourers of the open country around the castle of Gaillard, in March 1429. He reported that there were no complaints, and that the captain and his retinue "lived like simple persons of the country, paying their way without seizing or exacting anything from the people".[54] But, in the early stages of the conquest, Henry V described his captains in typically warlord terms: "Whereas many captains of towns and fortresses, and their lieutenants in the duchy of Normandy, usurp greater powers than the king has invested them with,

50 Basin, *Charles VII*, ii, pp. 32–3.
51 Martin, "D'Eudin", p. 139.
52 AN, JJ 107, no. 221.
53 Allmand, *Hundred Years War*, p. 32.
54 Rowe, "Discipline", pp. 199 and 201.

or that is proper, oppressing and plundering his subjects both of money and provisions".[55]

As the English warlords were being tamed, to an extent, by the civilian administration of Normandy, the real warlords of this period were the captains in the service of Charles VII, such as La Hire, Xantrailles and La Trémouille, and the freebooting captains in "French" France, such as Rodrigo de Villandrando.[56] La Trémouille, for example, who had captured and garrisoned several fortresses in the early 1420s with orders not to allow pillage but to make their soldiers live on their wages, nevertheless did pillage, "very gently", as he claimed, and only in the "customary" things, such as beds, sheets and cows. A priest was also ransomed.[57] Nevertheless, as the tide of war moved northwards once again, to Dieppe and Harfleur in 1435, into Maine from 1446, and into Normandy proper from 1449, the revenues available for English soldiers' wages dwindled just as the need for them had enormously expanded. The familiar pattern re-emerged of independent warlordships, precariously maintained by forced contributions and services from non-combatants. Thomas Basin described how, in these latter years of the war, the French and English armies were largely composed of unpaid irregulars under self-appointed leaders, who plundered foes by preference, but everyone by necessity.[58] "Royal garrisons, now the only effective military force in the duchy, were left to work out their own action under the command of their captains, with little, if any, central directive. . . . Defeat, like the initial conquest, was conducted in purely personal terms."[59]

In a period when wages were such a precarious commodity and the profits of war in ransoms and booty even more so, knights who had to make their living from war were impelled by necessity as well as by their own cupidity and assumptions of social superiority to become involved in the exercise of lordship over land. The profits which came to them from *patis*, otherwise known as "collective ransoms", "tribute", "contributions", together with the sale of safeconducts, had the great virtue, as far as soldiers were concerned, of regularity. The tribute from villages continued to be paid even during periods of official truce when no other source of income might be available. The terms of the treaty which ended the war between the kings of France and of Navarre in 1365 were fairly typical. During the period of truce, it declared, no-one was to "make any . . . act of war, save only that the people of the fortresses of either party may continue to collect and to impose the ransoms from those who have already agreed them, without raising them or making new ones".[60] And, although there was always the chance that these temporary lordships might be terminated suddenly by a successful siege and

55 Cited by Meron, *Henry's Wars*, p. 145.
56 Perroy, *Hundred Years War*, p. 303.
57 AN, X2a 18.
58 Basin, *Charles VII*, pp. 196–7.
59 A. Curry, "The First English Standing Army? Military Organization in Lancastrian Normandy, 1420–1450", *Patronage, Pedigree and Power in later Medieval England*, ed. C. Ross (Gloucester, 1979), p. 208.
60 *Mandements et Actes Divers de Charles V, 1364–1380*, ed. L. Delisle (Paris, 1874), p. 109.

assault, the chances were very healthy that they would be concluded by an evacuation treaty. In which case, substantial compensation might be expected for the garrison in occupation, collected, as always, from the local people.

The social and economic conditions of France during the fourteenth and fifteenth centuries hardly represent a logical continuation of what Marc Bloch called the "second" feudal age in which the nobility's political independence and arbitrary authority were being eroded from above by a powerful and assertive Capetian monarchy, and from below by a self-confident peasantry and bourgeoisie. They look more like a reversion to some of the conditions which gave birth to the Middle Ages in the "first" feudal age of the ninth and tenth centuries. Bloch's first feudal age was characterized by a "great and universal decline in population".[61] So, too, was France in the later Middle Ages. In eastern Normandy, according to Guy Bois, the drop in population between 1347 and 1442 meant that "where about ten people had once lived, there were now only three",[62] and there are comparable figures for other areas of France.[63] During the first feudal age, in Bloch's famous analysis, the general insecurity of life "induced men to draw nearer to each other", into "aggregations" of people living "cheek by jowl" but separated from others by vast empty spaces. The wilderness enveloped and encroached upon them.[64] Jean de Venette in the fourteenth century, and Thomas Basin in the fifteenth, might well have been describing this very phenomenon. "The eye of man was no longer rejoiced by the accustomed sight of green pastures and fields charmingly coloured with the growing grain, but rather saddened by the looks of the nettles and thistles springing up on every side."[65] We know too that the dramatic fall in population was not reflected in a proportional abandonment of villages: a very strong indication that the general insecurity of life then, as in the first age, had induced men to draw nearer to each other and to abandon the peripheral areas of cultivation.[66]

Above all, the reduction "to insignificance" of the social function of wages during the first feudal age, which obliged employers either to take men into their own households or "to grant [them], in return for [their] services, estates which, if exploited directly or in the form of dues levied on the cultivators of the soil, would enable [them] to provide for themselves",[67] has unexpected parallels in the

---

[61] Bloch, *Feudal Society*, i, p. 60.

[62] Bois, *Crise*, p. 62.

[63] E.g. E. Baratier, *La Démographie Provençale du XIIIe au XVIe Siècle* (Paris, 1961). R. Germain, *Les Campagnes Bourbonnais à la Fin du Moyen Age, 1370–1530* (Clermont-Ferrand, 1987).

[64] Bloch, *Feudal Society*, i, p. 61.

[65] Venette, *Chronicle*, p. 94.

[66] G. Duby, *Hommes et Structures du Moyen Age* (Paris, 1973), chapter 18. G. Fourquin, *Histoire Economique de l'Occident Médiévale* (Paris, 1969), p. 333. The ideas in this paragraph were first presented by the author, in "Feudalism and the Hundred Years War", at a conference at the University of Sydney, in March, 1984, and published in *Feudalism: Comparative Studies*, ed. E. Leach, S. Mukherjee and J. Ward (Sydney, 1985), pp. 105–23.

[67] Bloch, *Feudal Society*, i, p. 68.

conditions of garrisons during the Hundred Years War. No-one could describe the wages paid to soldiers in this period as "insignificant", but there can be no doubt that the great employers of soldiers, the kings of France and of England, were obliged to grant to their captains "estates" in lieu of wages, or at least to tolerate the appropriation of such estates by men in their service. If the first feudal age was characterized by the abrogation of royal rights of justice and taxation by private individuals, so too was French society in the later Middle Ages. If the collapse of central government in Charlemagne's empire after his death took the form of local potentates claiming regal powers in return for their "protection" of the district, so too did the collapse of royal authority in France under the Valois kings. It is only prudent to acknowledge that this "feudalisation" of late medieval France was a short-lived and patchy phenomenon by the standards of the western Europe of an earlier age, as was the failure of royal power. It did not even match the so-called "second serfdom" which was being imposed by the landowners in much of eastern Europe during this very period, who were profiting from their own military might and from "the delegation of power that a rump state had accorded them".[68] Nevertheless, the warlordism of garrison captains during this period must have seemed to many at the time to be a disastrous reversion to an age of barbarism and anarchy, of arbitrary lordship and abject serfdom, and it would be wrong of us, with our greater hindsight, to discount that sentiment.

---

[68] E. Le Roy Ladurie, *The French Peasantry 1450–1660*, trans. A. Sheridan (Aldershot, 1987), p. 65.

3

THE PEASANT AS VICTIM

SO OFTEN HAS it been said that peasants in pre-industrial societies were, and in Thirld World societies still are, the innocent victims of war, that such statements about the Hundred Years War should not take us by surprise. A Norman clerk of the early thirteenth century had written that when kings make war on each other the peasant pays so dearly for it that he has nowhere to sleep at night, "nay, even the cottage that he had, low and small, is burned and his oxen and sheep are seized, his sons and daughters bound, and he himself led away a wretched prisoner so that he is sorry to be alive".[1] Honoré Bouvet wrote, in a book presented to Charles VI of France and to several of the royal dukes, that "in these days all wars are directed against the poor labouring people and against their goods and chattels",[2] and his younger but more eminent contemporary, Jean Gerson, preached a sermon before the royal court at the Louvre palace in 1405 which left little to the imagination. The court preacher described a poor man, his wife, and his "four or six" children, made destitute by frequent taxation, screaming with hunger, huddled around a hearth which "with luck" might be warm, and then confronted by pillagers who threaten to beat them and to burn their house if they did not pay a ransom.[3]

Nearly five centuries later, Jules Michelet, who did so much to stamp his imprint upon Hundred Years War studies in the modern era, declared that "in this chivalrous war ... which the nobles of France and of England waged, there was, at bottom, only one enemy, one victim of the evils of war: it was the peasant".[4] His generous heart was stirred by their suffering. "When we now stroll beneath the walls of Taillebourg or of Tancarville ... when we contemplate the slanting, squinting windows over our heads which watch our passing, the heart becomes tight as we experience something of the sufferings of those who, for many centuries, languished at the feet of these towers. It's not even necessary to have read the old stories. The souls of our fathers still shout within us for their forgotten sorrows." Emile Zola has described how the misfortunes of *Jacques Bonhomme* in the late medieval period were put to polemical purpose in Bonapartist propaganda, and how some nineteenth-century peasants thrilled to these overheated accounts of "centuries of blood, centuries during which our flatlands, as they were

---

1   M. Wood, *The Spirit of Protest in Old French Literature* (New York, 1966), p. 19.
2   Bonet, *Tree*, p. 189.
3   Gerson, *Oeuvres Complètes*, vii, pp. 1170–71.
4   Michelet, *Histoire*, iii, p. 315.

called, resounded with one, single, massive cry of pain, of raped women, battered children and hanged men".[5] The modern historian of the Hundred Years War may have reservations about the "centuries of blood", but none at all about the identification of the French peasant of this period as the worst victim of the war.

To quibble with such a consensus risks being an exercise in bad taste although it is by no means certain that the French peasants were the war's worst victims, nor indeed is it clear what such a statement might mean. For purposes of analysis, it is possible to divide the mass of people who experienced the Hundred Years War into the three categories proposed by Michel Mollat du Jourdin. There were those who decided upon it (the princes); those who waged it (the soldiers); and those who suffered it (largely the peasants). But, in this latter category has to be included "ruined lords and ruined clerks".[6] In the allegorical literature which was so popular at this time, War is an all-consuming monster which destroys everything it touches and there can be no doubt that, in the final analysis, it was no great respecter of persons. Warlords, as described in the previous chapter, were not always dining off silver plate like the Bascot of Mauléon in 1388, and they very often came to violent ends. Hardly a year after the services of Mérigot Marchès were so earnestly being solicited by the count of Armagnac, in 1390, he had his head on the executioner's block at Les Halles in Paris.[7] The hardships of the military calling were not the inventions of stern moralists, or the products of the special pleading and self-justification of nobles, but were the common experience of most of its practitioners. We must not be too quick to discount the testimony of those such as Philippe de Mézières who praised the "valiant" knights and squires, defrauded of their wages by corrupt officials: poorly-dressed and poorly-mounted in marked contrast to the military leaders and their retinues.[8] Gutierre Diez de Gámez, standard-bearer of the "Unconquered Knight" Don Pero Niño, even insisted, in 1431, that the life of commoners was much more luxurious than that of a knight such as his master.[9] It might also be noted that the peasants who, in Michelet's imagination, trembled beneath the walls of Tancarville, would have been faced, in May 1438, by a tiny and desperate English garrison of the place. It had not been paid or provisioned for a long time. Its members left every day without the captain's knowledge or authorization in order to find subsistence in the surrounding countryside which, as the captain described it, "is entirely destroyed and uncultivated".[10] Whose situation was hardest?

The notion that the knightly soldiers, encased in their plate armour and in their codes of honourable warfare, did not run the same level of risk as the "defenceless" peasants may also be a misconception. "In this war between gentlemen",

---

5 E. Zola, *The Earth*, trans. D. Parmée (Harmondsworth, 1980), p. 90.
6 Mollat, *Guerre de Cent Ans*, pp. 141–44.
7 Keen, *Laws of War*, pp. 97–99.
8 Mézières, *Songe*, i, p. 521.
9 Gutierre Diez de Gámez, *The Unconquered Knight: Chronicle of the Deeds of Don Pero Niño*, ed. and trans. J. Evans (London, 1928), p. 12.
10 Bois, *Crise*, p. 299.

Michelet wrote of the aftermath of the battle of Poitiers, "the worst that could befall the vanquished was to go and take part in the feasts of the victors; to hunt and to joust in England; to enjoy the insolent courtesy of the English."[11] But Jean Froissart was more realistic when he wrote that "there died [that day at Poitiers] . . . the full flower of French chivalry".[12] After contemplating the horrific casualty-figures amongst the French nobility in the great battles of Edward III, the Black Prince and Henry V — even after the skirmish in Brittany in 1353 in which 89 members of the élite Order of the Star were killed because of their oath never to retreat — there can be few who are unable to sympathise a little with the military men who admitted to the occasional "great martyrdom" of their way of life.[13] Geoffrey Charny, a surviving member of the Order, in a little poem written some time before his death at Poitiers, describes the fear of the man-at-arms "when you see your enemies in front of you, coming towards you with lances lowered to run you through, and swords ready for when they miss", arrows and crossbow bolts raining down, the bodies of friends lying dead on the ground, and oneself unable to take flight for fear of dishonour.[14] *The Vows of the Heron*, which purports to describe a banquet which took place at the very beginning of the Hundred Years War, in 1338, shows Edward III's military captains making all sorts of preposterous or distasteful boasts about the parts which they are to play in the coming war. While the chivalrous earl of Salisbury promises to keep one eye permanently closed until he has fought the French, and the more sinister Jean de Fauquemont vows to set fire to the Cambrésis and to spare "neither church nor altar; neither pregnant woman nor any child that I can find", the hard-headed Jean de Beaumont makes a frank admission of fear. "When we are on campaign on our trotting chargers, our bucklers round our necks and our lances lowered, and the great cold congealing us all together, and our limbs are crushed before and behind and our enemies are approaching us, then we would wish to be in a cellar so large that we might never be seen . . ."[15]

In the light of this, and of the frequent stories of genuine hardship and destitution of nobles whose estates had been reduced to wildernesses and whose reserves had been consumed by huge ransoms, Michelet's more memorable pronouncements appear over-stated, as is his idea that the noble's experience of captivity was a matter merely of an enforced idleness away from home. Another side to the case may be represented by a story told to the judges of the Paris *parlement* in 1440. The nobleman, Henriet Gentian, described to them his sufferings as a prisoner of François de la Palu.[16] As inducement to pay his ransom of

---

11 Michelet, *Histoire*, iii, p. 291.
12 Froissart, *Chroniques*, ed. Luce, v, p. 60.
13 The story of the catastrophe which overwhelmed the Order of the Star is told in Froissart, *Chroniques*, ed. Luce, iv, p. lxxii.
14 "Le Livre Messire Geffroi de Charny", ed. A. Piaget, *Romania*, xxvi (1897), pp. 394–411, pp. 401–2.
15 Cited by Keen, *Chivalry*, p. 223. On the satirical meaning of this poem, see B. Whiting, "The Vows of the Heron", *Speculum*, xx (1945), pp. 261–78.
16 AN, X1a 4798.

six thousand crowns, all his teeth were knocked out with a hammer and some of them were sent to his lord, the duke of Bourbon. He was placed in a dungeon, where he counted sixteen snakes and other "venomous creatures"; he was stripped and beaten several times; he was drenched with scalding water; he was suspended by his thumbs; he had to spend nights, chained, with a sack of corn on his head. In case he was inclined to shrug off these discomforts, his captor threatened to lead him through the countryside with a ring through his nose, "like a bull". An exceptional case, certainly, but there are enough stories of noble prisoners chained hand and foot in deep dungeons to remind us that the prospect of captivity was not one which men-at-arms could contemplate with complete equanimity.[17]

Nor should we ignore the difficulties faced by the country clergy, whose parishes and remote priories, as well as their own persons, were often as vulnerable to predatory soldiers as everything else in the open country. Henri Denifle's two volumes entitled *The Devastation of Churches, Monasteries and Hospitals during the Hundred Years War*, published at the end of the last century, should discourage any underestimation of the church's losses during this period. The capture and ransoming of priests, and the robbing of churches, were not approved-of in the best-regulated armies, but they certainly took place. The priest Berthelemi Gernet had been captured by soldiers of the Beseram garrison and set a ransom of 1,300 francs,[18] and the *curé* of Comblisy was set such an "excessive" ransom by the Navarrese in the post-Poitiers period that he had to serve as their chaplain and was forced to "sing masses" in their fortress.[19] Honoré Bouvet grudgingly admitted that the English of Gascony, although an "evil and proud race", did not "willingly lay hands on clerks",[20] but there are plenty of stories, not to mention the boast of Fauquemont in the *Vows of the Heron*, which suggest that the English were not always so restrained. The English knight Sir John Harleston used to sit with a group of fellow captains drinking from silver chalices which had been looted from churches,[21] and Froissart reported an English squire entering a church during high mass, seizing the chalice from the priest at the moment of consecration, and knocking the priest to the ground.[22] Mérigot Marchès, the *routier* captain who occasionally fought under the English colours and who was eventually executed for his crimes, recalled the good old days when "we rode out on adventure and might find a rich abbot or a rich prior",[23] and at least two country priors wrote movingly about their own misfortunes at this time. Honoré Bouvet had fled his native Provence and abandoned his priory of Selonnet because of the wars of Raymond of Turenne. He remarked bitterly that "the

---

[17] Contamine, "Rançons", p. 257.
[18] AN, JJ 110, no. 361.
[19] AN, JJ 90, no. 435.
[20] Bonet, *Tree*, p. 187.
[21] Keen, *Chivalry*, p. 232.
[22] Froissart, *Chroniques*, ed. Luce, v, p. 175.
[23] Ibid., xiv, p. 164.

man who does not know how to set places on fire, to rob churches and usurp their rights and to imprison the priests, is not [deemed] fit to carry on war".[24] Hugh of Montgeron, prior of Brailet in the diocese of Sens, who ran, clothed only in a monk's habit, from his hiding-place in the woods on an October night in 1358 when the English of the Chantecocq garrison came upon it unexpectedly, clearly felt himself also to be a victim of the war.[25] Witnessing his property consumed by soldiers and his resources wasted upon useless safeconducts and ransoms, the desperate conclusion to Prior Hugh's hurried account of his misfortunes, written on the inside cover of his prayer-book, has often struck a chord of fellow-feeling. "I am writing this out behind our barn on Wednesday, the festival of St Martin, 1359, because I dare not write elsewhere. Do you who live in cities and castles ever see trouble equal to my trouble? Farewell. Hugh."

The idea of the peasant as the chief victim of this war is, however, very firmly rooted in a natural sympathy for a class of people who belonged, more than any other, to the open countryside: the areas so often abandoned to their own devices by the public authority. The well-off peasants might seek refuge from soldiers either in a walled-town or in a castle whose bailey was equipped to receive them along with their livestock, and whose captain was willing to accommodate them. The majority had no security save in flight to their parish church or to the forests and caves. The widow, known as "La Wyette", who lived at Précy-sur-Oise (Oise) in 1358 was left, on the death of her husband, with two small children under the age of five years. She had no trade which would allow her to establish herself in a "good town" and she had to make a living by tending her neighbours' vines. Because of the frequent attacks of "enemies and other persons", and because "it was being said that [the king] had abandoned all property in the open country to the power of [his] enemies", she was often forced to hide with her children in bushes and hedges, "living there like wild beasts".[26] Hugh of Montgeron's plight is not to be underestimated as he lay in his hiding place in the Bois des Queues on that October night when the English soldiers came to find him, but he subsequently found accommodation with a fellow priest in the town of Sens and he still had money enough, along with stocks of wine, oats, cloth and pigeons, to buy safeconducts from the English. His peasant neighbours who shared the hide-out in the woods may have had fewer options.

It is significant that, despite the loss of his priory in the highlands of Provence, Bouvet's chief sympathy was not for his own clerical estate. It was for the peasants, for the "poor innocent who has nothing more in mind than to eat his dry

24 Bonet, *Tree*, p. 189. For Raymond de Turenne's responsibility for Bouvet's departure from Provence, see *L'Apparicion Maistre Jehan de Meun et le Somnium Super Materia Scismatis d'Honoré Bonet*, ed. I. Arnold (Strasbourg, 1926), p. 62.
25 J. Quicherat, "Récit des Tribulations d'un Religieux du Diocèse de Sens Pendant l'Invasion Anglaise de 1358", *BEC*, xviii (1857), pp. 357–60. An English translation may be found in Venette, *Chronicle*, pp. 253–54.
26 AN, JJ 105, no. 362.

bread alongside his sheep in the fields, or under a hedge or thicket".[27] When he described all wars as directed against peasants, he did not mean that there were no other victims; nor did he mean that soldiers no longer fought against soldiers. He meant that the warfare to which he was the reluctant witness was not confined to warriors and inevitably drew peasants into its embrace, and that it was his moral duty as a priest to represent their interests in high places. Soldiers may have had some choice in the matter of whether to fight or to go home, and the clergy had some protection of the cloth, but peasants had no choice but to struggle on in the hope of better times to come. Peasants produced food, which the man-at-arms did not; they had possessions, especially in metal tools and livestock, which could be transformed for military uses; they had, or were thought to have, hidden reserves of cash which could be converted into protection-money. The menfolk represented a source of free labour and other services; their wives and daughters afforded sexual gratification; their young sons made useful servants. It was inevitable that soldiers when they found themselves in a position of local strength should have used that power by appropriating these goods and services. Some of this property and service could be taken with every show of official justification. Their captains might appeal, as we have seen, to royal ordinances which ordered the withdrawal, during an emergency, of moveable property into the security of fortresses, and which allowed captains to confiscate property in lieu of wages. They might appeal to local custom which required service from the local communities in the repair of walls and in the watch-keeping patrols.

None of these goods and services, however, necessitated killings and destruction – certainly no "centuries of blood" – and most of them required the exact opposite: a healthy and prospering peasantry. It is very likely that the most brutal encounters between large numbers of men-at-arms and peasants, which involved widespread death and destruction, were not acts of war at all, in the strict sense. The brigandage of peasant outlaws and the occasional peasant rebellion which will be described in the following chapter were important features of this great period of instability, and were intimately connected with the war. Their repression by men-at-arms, usually of the same nominal allegiance as the rebels, were always very bloody. Leaving these phenomena aside, however, it can be seen that the killing of peasants and destruction of their property normally only took place in two specific sets of circumstance. Either it happened during those raids on enemy territory, called *chevauchées,* in which destruction of property was a principal objective, or it happened when reprisals were being taken on non-combatants for the non-payment of their ransoms and *patis.*

The lumbering advance of a large army, like that of Edward III, the smoking evidence of which could be seen from the walls of Paris during the winter of 1359, usually gave sufficient warning of its approach: time enough for the village children who kept watch from the church towers to sound the alarm so that an orderly evacuation could be organized. There were occasions, however, as during

[27] Bonet, *Tree,* p. 154.

this campaign, when peasants placed too much confidence in the strength of their fortified parish church, and they were caught, with catastrophic consequences to themselves, in the deadly embrace of an army equipped for larger prey. In the single Easter week of 1360, according to the testimony of Jean de Venette, one hundred inhabitants of the village of Orly were slaughtered by the English and no less than nine hundred other peasants were burned to death or slaughtered at Châtres as their church-refuges were reduced to smouldering rubble.[28] The church at Orly was taken by storm on Good Friday 1360, after the destruction of its walls. That of Châtres, the lower windows and doorways of which had been firmly blocked up, was bombarded by stone missiles from the nearby hill but was eventually lost because of disagreements between the captain of the place and the peasant refugees. As the flames took hold so that even the tower and the bells were consumed, the peasants tried to let themselves down from the windows by ropes, but were "brutally slaughtered" by the English who jeered at their self-inflicted catastrophe. It may be doubted, however, if the attackers benefited much from the "large supply of food", the "household goods and utensils and tools", the "crossbows, lead, stones and other instruments of war" which had been crammed into the fortress.[29]

By the 1380s, the French high command had learned its lesson, and Froissart reports the advice given by certain French veterans to the king of Castile as they assisted him against the invading army of John of Gaunt.

> We have been told that the people of your kingdom fortify churches and bell-towers and use them as refuges for themselves and their goods. You must know that this will be to the great loss and injury of your kingdom, for, when the English ride out, these little fortresses in churches and bell-towers will not hold out against them. Rather will they be sustained and nourished by what they find within them.[30]

The *chevauchée* strategy, employed by the English Crown during much of the fourteenth century, was different only in scale from the strategies operating in the multitude of private wars which were waged, usually by nobles, throughout this period in the teeth of frequent royal prohibitions.[31] The objectives of punishing the enemy in "head and members" for his denial of justice, of compensating oneself for perceived injuries, and of demonstrating one's power were very much to the fore. Both kinds of war were likely to have peasants as important targets. In January 1375, two knights, Gilles of Verlette and his son, acknowledged their part in one of the many private wars which straddled the Franco-imperial border, and which, as they admitted, involved the burning and destruction of houses, the capture of men, women and children for ransom, the killing of men and the

---

[28] Venette, *Chronicle*, pp. 99–100.
[29] Ibid., p. 100.
[30] Froissart, *Chroniques*, ed. Luce, xii, p. 321.
[31] The royal prohibitions of the thirteenth and fourteenth centuries have been interestingly analysed in Cazelles, "Réglementation Royale".

plundering of their property, and "all other acts of war".[32] One of their opponents was Pierre de Bar, son of the lord of Pierrefont. He had learned well from his association with such notorious captains of the Companies as Arnaud de Cervole, known as the "Archpriest", and Yvain de Galles, and he, too, admitted to his part in the killing of people, the destruction of houses by fire, the raping of women, and the taking of all manner of goods "by way of vengeance and act of war".[33] No-one doubted that this litany of atrocities described proper acts of war. The only question was whether these were proper wars.

The killing of large numbers of peasants, as an act of war, and the systematic destruction of their property only took place, as a rule, within those restricted areas which had the misfortune to come within the range of one of these marauding armies. It is true that an army of this sort, which could be several thousands strong, and divided into two or three battle-groups each surrounded by its own busy cloud of foragers, could have a devastating effect upon a wide area. Such an army, minute though it may have been by the standards of more modern ones, had the logistical requirements of a medium-sized town and depended almost entirely on its foragers. Edward III reported that his army moving through the Cambrésis in the winter of 1339 burned and destroyed "commonly" a track of between "twelve or fourteen leagues" (up to fifty kilometres) in width.[34] The armies of Edward III, with captains such as Jean de Fauquemont and comprising anything from 2% to 12% of convicted criminals, many of them murderers seeking royal pardons in return for military service, never lacked soldiers unsqueamish enough for this sort of work.[35] Robert Knolles, about to embark in 1370 on a march from Calais into the Ile-de-France, requested and received royal pardons for fifty-five named criminals who had contracted to serve him. Forty-three of these were murderers and the rest were rapists and thieves.[36] Nevertheless, campaigns on this scale were rare during the Hundred Years War. Of the sixty-three years between 1337 and 1400, there were major campaigns in only eighteen.[37] More frequent were the private wars conducted on a smaller scale by an aristocracy which was largely untamed by the endless royal prohibitions against this tradition; also by the passage of companies of freebooters in search of opportunities to exercise their talents. Even when we include these, usually minor, military enterprises, it must have been a rare catastrophe for a French peasant to find himself caught in their paths.

The killing of peasants by soldiers and the destruction of their property were much more "normal" in situations of reprisal and terrorization, where soldiers

---

[32] AN, JJ 106, no. 176.

[33] AN, JJ 107, no. 118.

[34] Avesbury, *Edward III*, pp. 306–8. Rogers, "By Fire and Sword", pp. 8–9, argues convincingly for a typical radius of destruction of five leagues (i.e. about twenty kilometres) either side of the main track of the army. On this scale, the Black Prince's 68-day *chevauchée* in 1355 would have devastated 18,000 square kilometres of the Languedoc.

[35] H. Hewitt, *The Organization of War under Edward III* (Manchester, 1966), p. 30.

[36] *Calendar of Patent Rolls*, preserved in the PRO, Edward III, 16 vols (1891–1916) vol. 14, pp. 392–454.

[37] K. Fowler, "Truces", *Hundred Years War*, ed. Fowler, p. 184.

were attempting to negotiate collective and individual ransoms and were encountering resistance. Indeed the activities of entire armies on campaign in enemy territory cannot be treated as an entirely separate category from those of garrison soldiers attempting to secure their sources of supply. Both were enmeshed in the trade of protection in return for payments. Henry V, who struggled vigorously to protect his own peasant subjects, was not at all merciful to those of his enemy who failed to offer provisions to his armies and he routinely used the threat of fire to enforce contributions.[38] The rigours experienced by the nobleman Henri Gentian during his captivity were altogether exceptional and quite contrary to those customs of knightly warfare which were embodied in the law of arms. Indeed, maltreatment of noble prisoners in order to obtain a ransom from them annulled their obligation to pay it and entitled them to escape if they could.[39] On the other hand, protection against such tortures which the law of arms usually afforded to the captive man-at-arms was certainly not available to the peasant, and Jean Juvenal des Ursins was not the first to complain about the "new kinds of torment used to extract money from poor people".[40] The discharged soldiers of the Black Prince had a fearful reputation for the "injuries and inhuman tortures" which they were known to use against their prisoners.[41] Those who refused to pay *patis* to the garrison of Pierre Perthuis in Burgundy during the late 1360s had their houses burned down and their ears chopped off.[42] Raymond of Turenne, whose wars in the county of Provence had forced Honoré Bouvet to abandon his priory in Selonnet for the relative security of the royal court in Paris, was accused in the Paris *parlement* of having imprisoned "poor labourers"; of having killed some of them directly and of having left others to starve in obscure dungeons.[43] The Bourgeois de Paris, in the following century, described some of the refinements of torture which the *Ecorcheurs* employed against peasant victims, including the incarceration of men in locked bins while their wives were raped above their heads, on the lids.[44]

Long periods of imprisonment awaiting ransom were not as common for non-noble as for noble prisoners. A nobleman might survive ten or more years of close imprisonment, as did Louis de Chalon after he had been captured at the battle of Auray in 1364.[45] Peasants, on the other hand, either paid up or perished, and Thomas Basin describes how the peasants of Lower Normandy who were captured by French and English soldiers in the aftermath of the 1435 rebellion either paid their ransoms on the spot or were strangled or drowned.[46] It is true that these

---

38 Meron, *Henry's Wars*, pp. 117–18.
39 *Guerre de Cent Ans*, ed. Timbal, pp. 322–29.
40 Juvenal des Ursins, *Ecrits Politiques*, i, p. 56.
41 AN, JJ 104, no. 211.
42 E. Petit, *Ducs de Bourgogne de la Maison de Valois: Philippe le Hardi, 1363–1380* (Dijon, 1909), pp. 263–64.
43 AN, X2a 12.
44 *Journal d'un Bourgeois de Paris, 1405–1449*, ed. A. Tuetey (Paris, 1881), p. 356.
45 AN, JJ 105, no. 273.
46 Basin, *Charles VII*, pp. 220–21.

actions were part of the general repression of peasant revolt which, as we have already noted, always prompted the most brutal treatment. Such conduct was not, however, unique to those circumstances. In the catalogue of acts of war committed by members of the garrisons which surrounded the town of Bergerac, between February 1379 and May 1382,[47] 168 non-combatants were taken prisoner and forced to pay ransoms in gold coin and in goods. Their average value was pitifully small; ten thousand times less than the sixty thousand gold francs demanded of Louis de Chalon; yet the pressure placed upon them to pay was at least as great. No less than sixteen of them were described as having been tortured "with great blows", and some died under this treatment. A wretched individual who was captured by a pillager of the Bourc d'Espagne in 1382, and taken to the castle of Bouglon (Lot-et-Garonne), was later retrieved, presumably by relatives, "quite dead".[48] Some nine years later, a varlet who had been in the service of the English knight, Robert Chesnel, was captured by Jean le Mercier. When questioned by officers of the Châtelet court in Paris, he admitted that his job had been to beat prisoners either until he was exhausted or until they had agreed to a ransom which his master felt to be adequate. He confessed to having been party to the deaths of no less than sixty Frenchmen, by close imprisonment, by starvation, and by beating them "too much".[49] The threat of such treatment and of the burning of houses in reprisal raids, known as *courses*, was usually enough to persuade the persuadable; and there were always alternatives to ransoms in hard cash for those who had none of this commodity.

Pierre de Nesson, poet and official at the court of John, duke of Bourbon, during the first half of the fifteenth century, was well-enough known for his hatred of war to be teased by his friend Alain Chartier for admitting a preference for the long life of the peasant to the short one of the noble.[50] In his *Lay de Guerre*, written probably in 1429, the great She-devil, "War", "goddess of the infernal regions" who "reigns in the climate of France", prides herself in having brought labour in France to an end. Of the labouring population, in this grim reckoning, all the women and girls are raped; the old men are ransomed to their last penny; the able-bodied men become thieves and brigands; and the boys all become "pages".[51] All of these fates which the Hundred Years War brought to peasant households will be examined in more detail in this chapter and the next, but the most curious one is the last: "And in order to bring all labouring to an end, the children of labourers I will make into pages", on lines 301–2. The career of the unsavoury Jean le Gastelier, who was Robert Chesnel's torturer and who died a traitor's death at Les Halles, is not untypical of a form of ransom-payment, in service, which involved the exchange of no cash or goods. He had been captured by Chesnel

[47] Labroue, *Livre de Vie*, see p. 37, n. 58.
[48] Archives Départementales (AD) Pyrenées-Atlantiques, Pau, E 49, fo. 4r.
[49] *Registre Criminel du Châtelet de Paris du 6 Septembre 1389 au 18 Mai 1392*, ed. H. Duplès-Agier, 2 vols. (Paris, 1861–64), ii, pp. 94–95.
[50] A. Piaget and E. Droz, *Pierre de Nesson et Ses Oeuvres* (Paris, 1925), pp. 18–19.
[51] Ibid., pp. 47–69.

when only about twelve years old and "for the doubt and fear which he had of the English, who were very strong in the region and in the whole kingdom of France, he dared not depart from them without their leave, because, if he had been recaptured by these English, he knew well enough that he was a dead man".[52]

The number of boys and youths captured in the villages and then assuming the functions of "pages" to men-at-arms must have been very substantial indeed, and the formula "liberated as a page without any payment" was one which may have been regularly used in fifteenth-century Normandy.[53] The extraordinary adventures of these teenagers, who were swept into the peripheral riff-raff of the warrior fraternity, firstly as pages, then, if they were fortunate enough to attain maturity, as varlets, would provide ample material for the picaresque novelist and they must have constituted a well-known, and much-hated, social type in late medieval France. Grimmelshausen could have been describing them, but in the context of the wars of a later century, when he wrote: "Insolent and swaggering and, for the most part, godless folk . . . In a word, hurting and harming and, in turn, being hurt and harmed, this was their whole life". Most of them, he continued, died in battles and in sieges, but those who survived, "unless they had been right thrifty reivers and robbers, do furnish us with the best of all beggars and vagabonds".[54] Many of these auxiliary soldiers and servants must have begun their careers, like le Gastelier, as child-slaves, in a form of self-ransom.

The French Chancery registers are full of their stories. Jean Baudier, a thirteen-year-old from Châlon-sur-Saône, was taken into the service of Rifflard, bastard of Flanders, who had made his name during the 1360s as an adventurer in the north-eastern borderlands of France. He was Rifflard's page until his master abandoned him at Bruges. Here, as a sixteen-year-old war veteran, he was taken into the service of some English knights returning from the crusade in Prussia, and he served them as a page for a further ten years. He even took part in John of Gaunt's "Great March" across France, in 1373.[55] Jehannin Doncet from the village of Beine, in the Yonne, began his service at the even younger age of eleven when he was captured by the English of the Regennes garrison in 1359.[56] He served them both at Regennes and in England. Another boy, this one aged only nine, who was captured by the Englishman, Jack Spore, and who could not pay his ransom, described himself at first as a "page" whose tasks included the carrying of his master's equipment, and later as a "poor varlet".[57] The seventeen-year-old Guillaume Vaudin, who had been captured by a member of the Saint-Sauveur garrison in the previous year, also described his service as "in the office of

---

[52] *Registre Criminel*, p. 98.

[53] Contamine, "Rançons", p. 257.

[54] *Simplicissimus*, pp. 33–34. It is worth noting that in the statistics of criminals and of the victims of crime in Gauvard's survey (*Grace Especial*) 'valets' constituted a very high proportion of both categories (i, p. 413).

[55] The seneschal of Hainault's prosecution of Rifflard before the *parlement* in 1367 is recorded in AN, X2a 7, fos. 336–38v. Baudier's story is in AN, JJ 111, no. 115.

[56] AN, JJ 112, no. 109.

[57] AN, JJ 111, no. 355.

page and as his [master's] varlet".[58] It is true that boys as young as fourteen were able to exercise some choice in these matters, and Pierre Chays was a lad who made no excuse but "the folly of youth", for joining the Companies at that age.[59] Nevertheless, it is difficult to imagine even the most precocious of nine- and eleven-year-olds engaging in this form of service without some element of compulsion

Gilles de Rais' confessions, in 1440, to pederasty on a spectacular scale suggests the very real likelihood that some of the services performed by these boys were of a sexual nature, but these are never mentioned. The capture of women for such purposes, on the contrary, is mentioned so often in the remission records that it has been reduced to a bland formula. Nesson's she-devil, "War", boasts that "there will be neither old or young woman who is not taken, raped and dishonoured".[60] Many soldiers admitted to "raping women and deflowering virgins", to the "violation of women", to the "raping of married and unmarried women". Martial Sobout, who had served during the early 1360s under the *routier* captain, Guiot de Pin, admitted that such acts were customary amongst the "men of the Companies",[61] and although the details of these cases are often obscure, the scale of the problem is clear enough. Some women were assaulted in their own homes, and Jean le Comt, who was a member of the French garrison of Falaise in 1372, seems to have made a practice of evicting a husband to spend nights with his wife.[62] More often they were taken into fortresses and forced to stay there, anything from "all night", as was the fate of a woman-prisoner in the fortress of Puy-de-Chalus in 1379,[63] to the week which Jehanne, Thevenin Billart's wife, was forced to spend with the squire, Robert de Varigny, in his castle of Chassy (Nièvre).[64] "Borlaine's" daughter, of the parish of Saint-Colombe-sur-Loing, spent five years between 1358 and 1363 in the castle of Saint Fargeau.[65] Boys and women were not usually ransomed for cash or goods, but they were spared little suffering on that account.

The adult males who were captured in the villages often faced ransoms of a more recognizable sort, but they, too, sometimes paid them off in non-monetary ways. Their enforced service to men-at-arms is often described in the remission texts as that of "pillager", which may have been similar to, perhaps indistinguishable from, that performed by the servant-varlet. The prime function of this

---

[58] AN, JJ 108, no. 266.

[59] AN, JJ 109, no. 174.

[60] Piaget and Droz, *Pierre de Nesson*, lines 307–8. The stereotypes of 'la grande criminalité' which attached themselves to soldiers are analysed in Gauvard, *Grace especial*, i, p. 205. Without underestimating the violation of women as an act of war, it must be acknowledged that the litanies of atrocities which surface in JJ evidence may have been as closely tied to the humanist literature of political debate as to the realities of the particular situations.

[61] AN, JJ 112, no. 40.

[62] AN, JJ 111, no. 72.

[63] *Livre de Vie*, p. 406.

[64] Luce, *Du Guesclin*, pp. 609–11.

[65] AN, JJ 107, no. 167.

ominously-named auxiliary was to keep his master supplied with the necessities,
occasionally the luxuries, of life, and no-one could have been better chosen for
such a task than someone who knew the local communities well. The English and
their allies in the garrisons of Oissery and La Ferté-sous-Jouarre (Seine-et-Marne)
had, in 1359, recruited Robin Gonel, an inhabitant of the village of Charny, to help
them.[66] His erstwhile neighbours later accused him of having guided the English
on their expeditions to capture the "good men" of the district. They said that
when the prisoners were brought into the fortress of Oissery, Gonel would reveal
how much each of them was worth, and, thanks to his "wickedness and treason",
many were forced to pay ransoms and others died in captivity. It is impossible to
say what precipitated this man into such a dangerous form of service which led to
his violent death at the hands of his betrayed neighbours, but many who lived long
enough to justify themselves insisted on their lack of choice in the matter. Jehannin
Perrart had time enough after he had been "jokingly" questioned by a group of
peasants about his activities as a collaborator with the men-at-arms of the region
to insist that he had been captured and forced to accompany the soldiers.[67] Anyone
familiar with the remission texts is not deceived into thinking such "jokes" were
made in a spirit of good humour and Perrart died, soon after this exchange of
pleasantries, of the kicks which he received.

All these forms of compulsory service to men-at-arms were ransoms, of a sort,
in that they purchased a measure of temporary security and a promise of freedom
to come. Nevertheless, we are constantly reminded by these stories of what Marc
Bloch once called the meaninglessness of the term "free will" as applied to the
poor and the weak in society.[68] The girl, Borlaine's daughter, who spent five years
in the castle of Saint-Fargeau between 1358 and 1363 owed her arrival there to
the "poor labourer", Guillaume Jeurbers, who belonged to a neighbouring parish.
Jeurbers had been recruited into the garrison of Saint-Fargeau in order to escape
English soldiers in the service of Robert Knolles who were then at Malicorne, and
no doubt the provision of suitable girls was one of the many services he was forced
to offer the men-at-arms of the garrison.[69] His was hardly a ransom in any
generally-acceptable meaning of that word, but he probably had as little choice in
the matter of service to the French garrison of Saint-Fargeau as he would have had
to the English one of Malicorne had these enemies of the kingdom managed to
capture him.

Service ransoms were probably more common for peasant-prisoners than for
nobles, merchants and priests because of their relative poverty, although all of
these other classes had plenty of experience of them. The squire Beraud de Caillat,
who had the misfortune to be captured by the freebooting garrison of Carlat in
1375, discharged part of his ransom by arranging *patis* for them amongst his own
people, by bringing a surgeon to treat wounded members of the garrison, and by

---

[66] AN, JJ 106, nos. 155 and 166.
[67] AN, JJ 107, no. 251.
[68] Bloch, *Feudal Society*, i, p. 256.
[69] AN, JJ 107, no. 167

making himself useful to them in a variety of other ways.[70] The *curé* of Comblisy, as we have already noted, paid off his ransom to his Anglo-Navarrese captors in the religious services which these ruffians still craved. The bulk of all ransoms, however, those of the peasants included, were in cash and in goods. They were imposed on peasants as collective ransoms on entire parishes, in the form of *patis*, and on individuals for the purchase of their own liberty or for the return of captured livestock.

That peasants were taken prisoner for ransom in a distorted image of the chivalric practice was common knowledge, although rarely boasted about. Honoré Bouvet denounced the soldiery of his day for taking from their prisoners "great and excessive ransoms . . . and this especially from the poor labourers who cultivate lands and vineyards and, under God, give sustenance to all by their toil".[71] One of the English garrisons in Brittany, in 1350, was accused of rounding up peasants "like cattle" in order to force ransoms from them, at leisure, in the dungeons of Ploërmel[72] and even the heroic Jouvencel found himself in reluctant possession of large numbers of peasant captives. We may assume, however, that this indiscriminate capture of peasants was not common. Soldiers in occupation of land made haste to recruit local people as collaborators, who could identify for them the rich men of the district, capable of paying worth-while ransoms. Robin Gonel's service to the garrison of Oissery in 1359 has already been noted. A woman called Jehanne appears to have provided similar services in 1359 to the garrison of La Ferté, to whom she came on a daily basis to advise them where to find the prosperous households.[73] It was rare for the ransom of a peasant to amount to more than about a dozen gold francs in value, but these sums could mount up into sizeable profits for their recipients. Of the 168 persons captured in the Bergerac castellany between 1379 and 1382, each of those who survived the ordeal paid ransoms in gold coin and in goods which included iron nails, wine, salt, wheat, hens, wax, pepper, cloth, boots, shoes, jackets, shirts, saddles, axes, rope and ginger.[74] The average value of these payments was about five or six gold francs. In the twelve parishes of the Casteljaloux castellany which suffered periodic raids, mainly in 1382, at least thirty-seven people were taken prisoner to the fortresses of Bouglon, Captieux and Montagut. If we exclude one exceptionally large ransom of 157 francs, the average cost of redeeming a live prisoner was 21 francs and a dead one, twelve.[75] Even larger ransoms were obtained from non-combatant prisoners, including peasants, in Normandy during the English occupation of the fifteenth century.[76]

The ransoms of nobles were debts of honour which were honoured by the prisoner as much out of fear of being reputed a liar and a cheat as from any

---

[70] AN, JJ 111, no. 121.
[71] Bonet, *Tree*, p. 153.
[72] *Combat*, ed. Crapelet, p. 14.
[73] AN, JJ 109, no. 12.
[74] Labroue, *Livre de Vie*, pp. 10–11 provides a partial analysis.
[75] AD Pyrénées Atlantiques, Pau, E 49.
[76] Contamine, "Rançons", p. 259.

misgivings about his eventual prosecution through the courts. Prudent captors insured their risk of allowing their prisoner a temporary liberty in order to collect his ransom by securing pledges who would guarantee against default. Most noble prisoners who failed to find their ransom, however, would return, like King John of France did in 1364, to captivity. Such behaviour could not be expected of peasants and it was usually left to their relatives to buy them out of imprisonment before they were starved or tortured to death. When Matiot du Pont was a prisoner in chains of the garrison of Saint-Sauveur-le-Vicomte, in 1371, it was his sixteen-year-old son-in-law, Guillaume Vaudin, who was sent by his relatives and friends to negotiate the ransom.[77]

Captured livestock was also ransomed. We may be sure that the enormous numbers of livestock lost by the inhabitants of the open country around Bergerac in the Dordogne and Casteljaloux in the Lot-et-Garonne in the early 1380s could not all be used or consumed by their captors in the nearby fortresses.[78] Seventy-two oxen and the same number of donkeys and asses, together with hundreds of horses, mules, goats, cows and hens, were taken from the former district in a little over three years. These losses represented both a capital loss to their owners and a loss of livelihood, and their recovery was often a matter of life or death. When, in 1370, five peasants of the village of Morgues (Eure-et-Loir) confronted five pillagers who had taken their draught animals, they "politely" (as they later claimed) asked for their return, "so that they could gain their livelihood by working their lands".[79] "Politeness" was as short-lived as jocularity in these circumstances and four of the robbers were soon dead and the fifth put to flight. The desperate need of peasants to get back to work meant that plunder was often sold back to its original owners. The men-at-arms and their servants who pillaged in Aizier and Vatteville (Eure) in 1368, and took off thirty or more horses and mules, reappeared in front of the gates of Vatteville demanding fifty gold francs for the return of the stolen property.[80] Peasants were naturally anxious not to lose these indispensable beasts and we know that "harsh and ugly words" were exchanged in 1363 between the captain of the fortified church of Bazoches-les-Gallerandes and one of the peasant refugees in his safekeeping who wanted to buy back stolen livestock in defiance of the captain's orders.[81]

The vital part which the collective ransoms of whole parishes, known some-times as *patis*, played in the economy of war has already been discussed. A meeting of the Estates at Senlis in 1432 discussed "the provision of *patis* for the sustenance . . . of men-at-arms",[82] and this protection-money was treated by such soldiers as a valuable property-right which could be bought and sold, passed on to heirs and squabbled over in courts of law. We know that they were a huge

---

77 AN, JJ 108, no. 266.
78 AD Pyrénées Atlantiques, Pau, E 49.
79 AN, JJ 108, no. 157.
80 AN, JJ 106, no. 45.
81 AN, JJ 107, no. 309.
82 Keen, *Laws of War*, p. 252.

burden upon the peasantry who often had to pay, simultaneously, to several different "protectors" as Jean Juvenal des Ursins readily testified. He declared at a meeting of the Estates at Blois, in 1433, that "villages were so *appatised* that one poor village was paying *patis* to eight or ten places, and if they did not pay-up the villages and churches were set on fire".[83]

The scale of the *appatisation* of the French countryside as a whole may be illustrated from the case of the English occupation in Brittany during the fourteenth century. The occupation had begun in 1342 and, by 1359, the three principal English fortresses on Vannes, Bécherel and Ploërmel were, between them, sharing the *patis* of 124 parishes.[84] The receipts from these ransoms paid for 85% of the costs of the garrisons, together with the expenses of the English royal lieutenant in the duchy and his headquarters staff. The smaller garrisons financed themselves completely out of these collective ransoms in a way which was angrily denounced in a memorandum of Walter Bentley, English lieutenant of the duchy, in 1352. These garrisons, he complained, "make gross profits in divers ways, namely by pillaging poor people and others on their borders . . . rapidly destroying the poor people and Holy Church, to the great detriment of the war-effort of our lord the king".[85] Although the ransoming of the Breton countryside by the English was brought to an end at the treaty of Guérande, in 1365, the respite was short-lived, and a new occupation began in 1371. By 1384, 120 parishes of West Finisterre were paying ransoms to the English garrison of Brest, which supplemented this income by levying tolls on sea-borne commerce including that of pilgrims to Saint James of Compostela. On the French side of the frontier there were fortresses which, in 1371, came under the control of Olivier de Clisson, who was later to become constable of France. In that year he had been authorized by royal letters to allow his captains to continue to take "all ransoms and compositions which he and his captains and the people who were living in the said fortresses had taken in and on the land in the obedience of our said enemies . . .".[86] Their effect, of course, was to allow the wretched Bretons to be ransomed by both sides.

We can obtain a reasonable idea of the scale of this problem when we appreciate that this was only one of half a dozen major frontiers between English and French control within the French kingdom in the fourteenth century, and that, although these frontiers certainly attracted the bulk of military activity, there were castles, walled towns and villages, fortified churches, fortified farmhouses scattered all over the kingdom, each with its own complement of soldiers. In every place that soldiers, however disreputable and unacknowledged by higher authority, had set themselves up in a fortified place, there a "frontier" was created, inviting opposition by soldiers of different allegiances. Only a tiny proportion of these soldiers at any one time were paid wages sufficient to allow them to buy what they needed to survive, let alone to prosper in the manner to which they felt entitled.

---

[83] Juvenal des Ursins, *Ecrits Politiques*, i, p. 57.
[84] Fowler, "Finances".
[85] Bentley, "Mémoire", p. 340.
[86] A. Lefranc, *Olivier de Clisson, Connétable de France* (Paris, 1898), p. 436.

Many of them had no expectation of such rewards. They relied upon the protection-payments of the non-combatants who came within their range, and had to be compensated handsomely for the loss of this income in the evacuation treaties which (more often than force) brought an end to their temporary lordships. In 1390, for example, when the Hundred Years War was in a period of prolonged truce, no less than 250,000 francs was agreed by the Estates of the Languedoc in compensation for *routier* captains such as Mérigot Marchès, Ramonnet de Sor, Guillaume de Caupène and Chopin de Badefol who had agreed to vacate their castles.[87] Even in the relatively well-regulated area of English occupation during the fifteenth-century regency of Bedford, the garrisons on the Maine frontier were deriving an annual income of 25,000 *livres* from *patis*, enforced by punitive expeditions against recalcitrant villages in enemy territory.[88]

It is hardly surprising, then, that there are many cases of peasants destroying the very fortresses which should have offered them refuge in time of need, and of preventing the creation of new ones. The "good people" of Entre-Deux-Mers, in the Bordelais, had helped to capture the castle of Camarsac from the French in 1378, and for thirty years it had lain in the (presumably dilapidated) condition in which the last garrison had left it.[89] When, at the end of this period, Raymond de Chanteloup and his brothers wanted to restore the place, their intention was opposed vigorously by the town council of Bordeaux acting on behalf of the "public weal". The place, it argued, was not situated on a frontier and therefore could not support itself by "living off the enemies"; so it was inevitable that its occupants, "when they do not find enough to eat and drink, will be obliged to pillage the goodman, to take his corn, his wine, his horses, his calves, his hay, and to beat people". Their argument did not prevail, but their concern is under-standable. When, in 1370, the fortified parish church of Berthegon (Vienne) was evacuated by a small company of French men-at-arms who had been accustomed, during their occupation, to take "victuals and necessities from [the king's] subjects in the open country around the said fortress", the place was immediately "knocked down by the people of the district. That is to say that all which had been done to fortify and make the church secure was destroyed, and there is, at present, no fortress there."[90] Since the local people not only had to sustain the garrison by tribute, but also very often had to pay for its evacuation if it was held illegally, it is hardly surprising that when they eventually gained control of a castle like La Roche-de-Vendaix, which had been Mérigot Marchès' base of operations in the late 1380s, they left "not one stone upon another".[91] Mérigot had claimed that his previous headquarters, at Aloise, had netted him "more than twenty thousand francs per annum" in *patis*.[92] The castle of Poix, situated where the Paris to Calais

---

[87] J. Monicat, *Les Grandes Compagnies en Velay, 1358–1392* (Paris, 1928), pp. 83–84.
[88] Contamine, "Rançons", p. 250.
[89] Boutruche, *Crise*, p. 174.
[90] AN, JJ 109, no. 116.
[91] Froissart, *Chroniques*, ed. Luce, xiv, p. 203.
[92] Ibid., p. 163.

and Rouen to Valenciennes roads crossed, had fallen into the hands of some English soldiers in August 1358. The people of the good towns of the district, together with those of the open countryside, agreed to pay the fifteen thousand gold *moutons* which were demanded for its evacuation only on the condition that the castle should afterwards be destroyed.[93] Although owned by Jean Tyrel, who fought loyally in the king's wars, it had been captured three times and the countryside had been ravaged by each set of occupants.

Although we may assume that Christian principles and the ideal of an old-fashioned Christian chivalry exercised a faint restraint upon the activities of some of these scattered garrisons, there are few signs of it. More obvious are the signs of a knightly class which cared little for the sufferings of non-combatants because they had troubles and dangers enough of their own. They were supported by armed servants who were recruited for their unscrupulousness, or terrorized into it. In such circumstances we can understand the comment of Honoré Bouvet, without endorsing it unequivocally, that "in these days all wars are directed against the poor labouring people and against their goods and chattels",[94] and, in the similar circumstances of the German countryside during the Thirty Years War, why Simplicissimus the Vagabond, who had just witnessed the flaying alive of some peasants by musketeers, "pondered . . . upon the enmity which there is ever between soldiers and peasants".[95]

[93] *Guerre de Cent Ans*, ed. Timbal, pp. 283–302.
[94] Bonet, *Tree*, p. 189.
[95] *Simplicissimus*, p. 32.

4

PEASANT RESISTANCE: REBELS AND BRIGANDS

THE METAPHOR OF war as a tree of battles clearly tapped great depths of meaning in the fourteenth and fifteenth centuries. Certainly a grim hierarchy of conflict and rapacity was in evidence during the Hundred Years War: one in which the military chiefs, whilst warring against their king's enemy, preyed upon the ordinary men-at-arms under their command by pocketing the lion's share of wages and third shares of all war-gains.[1] The men-at-arms, in their turn, lived off the foraging labours of their *pillars* and *valets*, who, in turn, robbed the peasants at the bottom of this chain. The metaphor implied, moreover, that although war sustained all of these multitudes of combatants, it had a life of its own which none of them could master. Pierre de Nesson's great she-devil, War, it should be remembered, also presented war as an impersonal force of nature, too powerful for mere human contrivance to direct, let alone bring to a conclusion. The manuscript of Bouvet's *Tree of Battles*, which was presented to the king's brother, John, duke of Berry, in the early years of the fifteenth century, is illustrated, as are several other manuscripts of this work, with a tree of battles. This one, however, is surmounted by Lady Fortune with her wheel.[2] Although the tree metaphor was suggestive of the fixed "feudal" hierarchies in which peasants were permanently in subjection to the men of war in the branches, and all linked together by the bonds of lordship, Lady Fortune presented a different perspective. She might be expected, on occasion, to offer a brief ride on her wheel to anyone bold enough to take the place of those whom she had casually thrown off.

Just as there is a danger in presenting the peasants as the *only* victims of war, there is also a danger in suggesting that in their contacts with soldiers they were *always* the losers. The relationship between soldiers and non-combatants in late medieval France was more complex and by no means as one-sided as the previous chapter might suggest. Even the sort of people who have been described there as "victims" may not have been as passive and unwilling as they might, later, have claimed to be. Jehan le Petit, of the parish of Gréville (Manche), was known to his neighbours as a man of unsavoury reputation without any employment or trade.[3] His collaboration with the English garrison of Saint-Sauveur-le-Vicomte, in the

---

[1] D. Hay, "The Division of the Spoils of War in 14th-Century England", *Transactions of the Royal Historical Society*, 5th series, iv (1954), pp. 91–109.

[2] British Library MS, Royal 20 C viii.

[3] AN, JJ 109, no. 287.

early 1370s, however, allowed him to swagger through his village armed with sword and buckler; to threaten his neighbours "in open church"; to boast that, if he so willed it, the garrison would leave no house standing and no property fit for cultivation. To cap it all, he enjoyed a "great and excessive salary". Here, one might guess, was a man who had been of no importance in local society and who, for an all-too-brief moment, was able to break free of the traditional power-structure of the Norman village. This enabled him to exercise a mastery over the peasant oligarchs, often known officially as "the better and wiser part" of the community, who had hitherto ordered his life. His was a service-ransom of sorts, but it was also a dramatic step-up for him. The service ransoms, as pages and varlets, which have been described in the previous chapter, were often dangerous and unpleasant. But they also opened up new vistas of opportunity and adventure for impoverished youths. Service of this sort took the "poor man", Jean Baudier of Châlon-sur-Saône, to Bruges, to England, and on several of the English campaigns in France, eventually finding him employment as a varlet of the duke of Burgundy's chamberlain, Jean de Mornay.[4] Young Thenein Flamendeau of Saint-Julian-du-Sault who, as a boy of "nine or ten", had entered the service of the Englishman Jack Spore, spent ten years with his master in Burgundy, Brittany, Spain and "elsewhere both inside and outside the kingdom". When he returned with the "men of the Companies" to his birthplace, in 1368, he had to be told that this was his home, for he remembered nothing of it.[5]

Peasants could become soldiers, if only in a very lowly capacity, and take their chances with the men-at-arms on that wheel of fortune which had been set in motion by the engine of war. The general call to arms, known as the *arrière-ban*, which the French Crown occasionally made to its subjects at times of great national emergency appealed to all able-bodied adult males and did not exempt peasants. Peasants were also recruited in the armed retinues of men-at-arms as pillagers and armed varlets. If they attempted, as Flamendeau attempted, to return to honest labour at the end of their service, they had plenty of tales to tell their friends whom they had left behind. If, however (as was his experience in 1377), suspicions had been aroused against them for some of their military activities, they might be forced, like him, into the life of an outlaw. This was a particularly dangerous kind of outlaw who knew how to handle weapons, mount an ambush, and kill. Pierre de Nesson's she-devil of War, who turned all able-bodied peasants into brigands of the woods, would now have him in thrall.

It has often been noted that peasants are not always as passive and long-suffering as they are so often portrayed in sentimental literature. The peasants who were flayed over a log by soldiers in front of the shepherd-boy, Simplicissimus, in Grimmelshausen's seventeenth-century tale, had just mutilated and buried one of these soldiers' companions alive and gruesomely murdered several others.[6] "The peasants of the Spessart and the Vogelsberg are as little wont as are the

---

4 AN, JJ 111, no. 115.
5 AN, JJ 111, no. 355.
6 *Simplicissimus*, p. 30.

Hessians and men of the Sauerland and the Black Forest to let themselves be crowed over on their own dunghill."[7] Emile Zola's story of the peasants of the nineteenth-century Chartrain, in which the "centuries of blood" leaflet was read in the Fouans' cow-shed, is not a story about a meek and submissive peasantry. On the contrary, its theme is the durability of a class, represented in this novel by the Fouan family which had bought its freedom in the early fourteenth century and had been fighting "with savage passion" ever since over "a property of derisory proportions, constantly in jeopardy".[8] Zola's contemporary, Victor Hugo, describing the peasant rebellion of the *Vendée* in his *Quatrevingt-treize*, was thrilled by the capacity of thousands of rebels to conceal themselves in the silent Breton forests, ready to launch surprise attacks on their enemies.[9] "The peasant", he wrote, "has two great strengths: the field which feeds him, the wood which hides him."

Michelet himself, who did so much to arouse our sympathies for the peasants who "trembled" beneath the shadows of Taillebourg and Tancarville, and for Joan of Arc who was, for him, the perfect example of a peasant fallen victim to a brutal soldiery, was not in the least unaware of the awful strength of "Jacques Bonhomme" when stirred into common action. Like Jean de Venette, five hundred years before him, he delighted in the account of the peasant-hero, Grandferré. "This affair was valiantly conducted by the peasants, by Jacques Bonhomme."[10] The huge Grandferré was one of a number of peasants who had fortified a farmhouse belonging to the monastery of Saint-Corneille at Compiègne. In 1359, according to Venette's account, this man was single-handedly responsible for the wounding and death of no less than eighty-three members of the Creil garrison who had come to attack the place. "One of his blows, aimed straight, never failed to cleave a man's helmet and to leave him prostrate, his brain pouring out of his skull."[11] No doubt the story was wildly exaggerated by Venette's wishful thinking, but it demonstrated to Michelet how the "trembling" peasant could be transformed by a mysterious chemistry into a figure "monstrous and terrible".

The chemistry may be less mysterious if the involvement of discharged common soldiers on the side of the peasants may be postulated. Guillaume l'Aloue, who was captain of the Longueil peasants and Grandferré's master until his death in the first encounter with the English, may well have had some military experience in the service of Bertrand du Guesclin,[12] and Sir Thomas Gray's unheroic account of the skirmishes in his *Scalacronica* suggests that l'Aloue's company consisted of *brigauntz* as well as "common folk of the band of Jacques Bonhomme".[13] As will be explained more fully below, the word "brigand" at this time

7 Ibid., p. 28.
8 Zola, *The Earth*, p. 48.
9 V. Hugo, *Quatre-vingt-treize* (Paris, 1880), pp. 252–61.
10 Venette, *Chronicle*, p. 90.
11 Ibid., p. 91.
12 S. Luce, *La France Pendant la Guerre de Cent Ans: Episodes Historiques et Vie Privée aux XIVe et XVe Siècles* (Paris, 1890), pp. 61–82.
13 *Scalacronica*, p. 141.

could signify not "bandit" (as was Pierre de Nesson's fifteenth-century meaning), but "common soldier", and we may be dealing here as much with a fruitful co-operation between returning peasant-soldiers and their friends and relatives who had stayed behind as with the deeds of one heroic individual. The involvement of these common soldiers, called *briganz*, in the resistance of peasants to garrison soldiers is also a feature of events at Charny (Seine-et-Marne) which took place two years later, in 1361.[14] When Robin Gonel, who was suspected of working for the garrison of nearby Oissery, came into the village of Charny, pretending to be fleeing from the Oissery men but secretly planning their assault upon the village tower, he was captured by a group of people who had been sheltering in this tower. It consisted of local residents and "briganz", and he was soon stabbed to death.

Armed violence was not the monopoly of men-at-arms or of the common soldiers who served them. It was a feature of medieval society at almost every level, including that of the peasant. The professional expertise of common soldiers, returned from the wars, may have made it more effective, but they worked within an environment in which violent criminality was always close to the surface. John Bellamy has remarked, in the context of contemporary English society, that, because men of lower rank carried knives as a matter of course, and the gentry, swords, any quarrel was likely to end in bloodshed, "especially since society viewed martial deeds and a willingness to engage in them as a valuable quality in any man".[15] Not all labourers, it may be remembered, even in Pierre de Nesson's pessimistic *Le Lay de Guerre*, were robbed, raped or enslaved by the great she-devil of War. The able-bodied males, she had declared, "who are of middle age, I will make into brigands and will set to pillaging".[16] Although Marc Bloch claimed that peasant revolt was endemic to medieval society generally, and although "brigands of the woods" preyed upon travellers on the roads, and upon law-abiding peasants, in all ages up to our own, the later Middle Ages in western Europe, dominated by the Hundred Years War, witnessed an unprecedented development. "Peasant disorder," as Peter Lewis remarked, "was endemic wherever there was military disorder."[17] "To this rude life [of brigandage] Jacques Bonhomme had grown hardened", wrote Roland Delachenal in 1916, "as often as not pillager on his own account, conscious of his strength, feared by pillagers and stragglers, capable even of concerting a common action, he was as used to striking blows as to receiving them."[18]

---

[14] AN, JJ 106, nos. 155 and 161.
[15] J. Bellamy, *Crime and Public Order in England in the Later Middle Ages* (London, 1973), p. 25.
[16] Lines 303–4.
[17] Lewis, *Later Medieval France*, p. 286.
[18] Delachenal, *Charles V*, ii, p. 31.

Rebellion

The late Middle Ages was the great time of peasant revolts, and those which took place on French soil were intimately connected with the activities of soldiers and often announced by the ringing of the same church bells which in other circumstances warned the communities of their coming. It is curious that the *Jacquerie*, the affair of a mere fortnight of late May and early June in 1358, should have attracted so much attention from the chroniclers of the period and have marked itself so effectively upon the minds of contemporary Frenchmen that "jacquerie" is now part of the vocabulary.[19] The proximity to Paris of Saint-Leu-d'Esserent, where the revolt started, and of the provinces of Champagne, the Beauvaisis, Brie and Picardy into which it spread, may claim some of the credit for its notoriety. The precise rôle of Paris in the rebellion, and that of its famous provost, Etienne Marcel, is still hotly debated, but there can be no doubt that the inhabitants of the capital gave encouragement and support when their interests coincided with the peasant rebels: especially in their actions against the fortresses which were strangling the city's supplies and communications. It does however require more than mere encouragement from townsmen to bring peasants into open rebellion, especially during a busy time of the agricultural year, and we must direct our attention more closely to the conditions of the open country to the north and east of Paris in order to discover the true source of the *Jacquerie*. In this plentiful region there appears to have been no grievance at this time of a purely economic nature which might be connected to cereal, or any other, prices. On the other hand, there can be little doubt that it was the presence of large numbers of soldiers, most of whom were in the service of the French Crown and attempting to live off the countryside, which was the spark of revolt.[20]

The opening act of the *Jacquerie,* on 28 May at Saint-Leu, is filled with significance. Here, a number of peasants reinforced, no doubt, by the tough and independent quarrymen of the district, attacked a group of men-at-arms in the regent's service, killing four knights and five squires. It appears that the men-at-arms, led by Raoul de Clermont, were attempting to carry out the regent's orders by installing themselves in garrison of the fortified abbey of Saint-Leu which commanded an important bridge over the Oise. In doing so, and as they made haste to bring the building into a state of defensibility and to ensure the sustenance of

---

[19] The *Jacquerie* of 1358 has been well studied. The most recent studies of the revolt focus upon the involvement of non-peasants, e.g. Cazelles, "Jacquerie"; P. Durvin, "Les Origines de la Jacquerie à Saint-Leu-d'Esserent en 1358", *Actes du 101e Congrès National des Sociétés Savantes, Philologie et Histoire jusqu'à 1610* (Paris, 1978), pp. 365–74; D. Bessen, "The Jacquerie: Class War or Co-opted Rebellion?", *Journal of Medieval History,* xi (1985), pp. 43–59. The analysis of J. Flammermont, "La Jacquerie en Beauvaisis", *Revue Historique,* ix (1879), pp. 123–43, has survived remarkably well, however, and is the basis of Leguai's interpretation in his useful "Revoltes Rurales". See also M.-Th. de Madeiros, *Jacques et Chroniquers: une Etude Comparée de Recits Contemporains Relatant la Jacquerie de 1358* (Paris, 1879).

[20] Delachenal, *Charles V,* i, pp. 398–9.

the new and enlarged garrison, they must have made light of the ancient liberties of the local people some of which were enshrined in their precious charter of 1176. The people of Saint-Leu were roused to action by the high-handed rejection of local custom and emboldened by the various royal ordinances (most recently in March 1357) which permitted armed resistance against soldiers who requisitioned property without payment. "We [the regent] have commanded and do command . . . that no soldier . . . take, pillage or rob our subjects of corn, wine or any other victuals . . . and if they do the contrary, we wish and command that anyone may resist them by any method which seems best to them, and to call for help from neighbouring villages by the sound of bells."[21] What made this region so volatile was this combination of particular grievances against soldiers who rejected local custom in favour of arbitrary power, combined with a general sense of outrage that men-at-arms who were supposed to offer the country-people protection were actually behaving like their enemies. As we know, the regent who was to become Charles V was, at one and the same time, and depending upon the audience he was addressing, allowing and forbidding his soldiers to provision themselves from the people. Peasants who resorted to violence against the king's men, therefore, could claim some legal justification. This was a revolt which André Leguai has described as that of a property-owning peasantry against their oppressors: the nobles of the region and the men-at-arms who had arrived "from everywhere".[22] The symbols of this oppression, and the targets of peasant fury, were the castles and other fortresses of the region. The men-at-arms who had been so taken by surprise, whether they were supporters of Charles of Navarre, at Mello, or English supporters, like the Captal de Buch, at the Market of Meaux, or loyal subjects of the French Crown, like the Norman and Picard knights and squires in the region of Amiens, massacred the peasants with a will.

Superficially, there are few points of similarity between the short-lived and apparently spontaneous violence of relatively prosperous peasants in the *Jacquerie* and the other peasant revolts of late medieval France which seem to have been little more than occasions when the perennial phenomenon of low-level banditry reached the critical and explosive mass of insurrection. The *Tuchinerie* of the southern provinces of France, which began during the late 1360s in the upper Auvergne, in the diocese of Saint-Flour, and which spread out into the Languedoc during the early 1380s, only to be confined once again to the Auvergne, is fairly typical of this type of revolt, at least in its opening and closing stages.[23] This is hardly surprising from a phenomenon which takes its name from a word which probably meant neither more nor less than "brigandage". Criminal bandits known as *tuchins* were reported from Normandy several years before the *Tuchinerie*, and in the Nivernais long after its termination. The *Tuchinerie* of the

---

[21] Durvin, "Origines", p. 369.
[22] Leguai, "Revoltes Rurales", p. 55.
[23] C. Portal, "Les Insurrections de Tuchins dans la Pays de Langue d'Oc, vers 1382–1384", *Annales du Midi*, xvi (1892), pp. 433–74. M. Boudet, *La Jacquerie des Tuchins, 1363–1384* (Riom, 1895).

Auvergne, as distinct from the wider rebellion in the Languedoc which was linked
to the tax-revolt of several of the great southern towns, can confidently be located
in the context of military oppression and of peasant resistance to it. The upper
Auvergne during much of the second half of the fourteenth century was peppered
with fortresses. They were crowded with French men-at-arms engaged by the
regional Estates, with soldiers of nominally English allegiance, with *routiers*, and
with the garrisons of warring local lords. In this area, *Tuchinerie* was often
directed against companies of pillagers from these garrisons. A typical incident
(more of which will be examined below) which nearly broke the local truce
between the town of Saint-Flour and the English garrison of Saillant in November
1382 was an attack by *tuchins* on a *page* of the garrison, and the capture of his
cob.[24] The firebrand Pierre de Bruyère converted this widespread but small-scale
banditry into something a little more like the *Jacquerie* with some of its characteristics of class-war against the privileged classes who were identified as such by
hands uncalloused by manual labour. Thus enlarged, it challenged more than
merely the foraging soldiers of garrisons, and its repression, which was begun
with typical ruthlessness in 1383 by Enguerrand d'Eudin, now a royal seneschal,
and finished off by the nobles of the mountains of the Auvergne, was hardly less
thorough than that of the northern nobles of a previous generation against the
jacques. "Nothing" remarked Marcellin Boudet in 1895, " for the space of
twenty years was more drowned, hanged, burned, tortured than the *tuchin*."[25]

The *jacques* of the Beauvaisis and the *tuchins* of the Auvergne took their first
steps towards insurrection by attacking members of the garrisons of their immediate neighbourhood. "Under cover of the war", wrote Charles V in 1377,
"which at that time existed between ourselves and our enemies, especially in the
Auvergne country, there rose up in that region a company of robbers and pillagers
who used to be called by the good people of the region *touchis*."[26] As they spread
and grew, this movement adopted some of the revolutionary and egalitarian
doctrines of the popular preachers, seeking in some ill-defined way to destroy the
privileged classes. Philippe de Mézières, always a shrewd commentator, had the
poor labourer in his *Dream of the Old Pilgrim* express the sentiments which
inspired peasant revolt.[27] Even under a Lombard tyrant, his peasant grumbled, the
people would have been protected after they had duly paid their taxes. But in
France, no sooner were the royal sergeants satisfied than what little remained was
snatched up by "our own men-at-arms and their pillagers". It was not only the
sword of the English, he claimed, which had transformed them from freemen into
serfs but also the salt taxes, hearth taxes, impositions, watch-duties, plunderings
and enslavements of their own lords. Mézières' spokesman threatened that the
members of this lowest "hierarchy" (which included merchants and craftsmen)
would attack all forms of lordship and would force nobles and priests to work the

---

[24] Boudet, *Tuchins*, pp. 55–56.
[25] Ibid., p. 79.
[26] Ibid., p. 24.
[27] Mézières, *Songe*, i, pp. 455–56.

land. The men-at-arms whose vital interests, if not their very lives, were threatened by such sentiments were able to appeal to a sense of noble solidarity in order to suppress these movements. In social confrontations of such a sort, peasants were invariably and spectacularly the losers.

Forez, between 1422 and 1431, witnessed a *Tuchinerie* in all but name.[28] It is likely that the small bands of brigands which eventually coalesced into formidable armies of peasants were composed of villagers uprooted by the constant activity of men-at-arms in the region. "Where nobles were numerous", Leguai remarks, "these wretched people who had lost everything saw in the men-at-arms the authors of their ruin."[29] By 1431, some of these brigands were reported pointedly to be asking, in a manner reminiscent of the Englishman, John Ball, whether God, on expelling Adam and Eve from the Garden of Eden, had exempted anyone from having to live off the sweat of their brows. The fifteenth-century nobility was in no better mood to discuss such questions than their predecessors of the fourteenth, and the reaction against the rebels united them as before. In this case it was the nobles of the Bourbonnais and of the Auvergne combined with that most notorious captain of freebooters, Rodrigo de Villandrando.

The peasant rebellions which took place in English-occupied Normandy during the period 1434–1436 enjoy a historiography all of their own because some historians have conferred on them, and others have denied them, the status of patriotic wars against foreign oppression.[30] Here, for the first time in the history of France, can be found a brigandage which was directed exclusively against foreigners and their collaborators and which, because of its tenuous links with garrisons loyal to Charles VII, enjoyed, and continues to enjoy, a certain legitimacy as a genuine war of partisans. Whether or not we deny a sense of patriotism to the brigands who were executed by the English authorities at this time, or to the peasant rebels of the Pays de Caux who were slaughtered in the repression of 1436, we cannot help but observe the familiar rhythm of peasant criminality developing into insurrection. The personnel of lordship may have changed as a result of the English conquest but the problem for the inhabitants of the open county was an old and familiar one: of how (or whether) to support a burgeoning military establishment from their own dwindling resources. In the Pays de Caux it was both the attacking French soldiers, as well as the defending English ones, who had to be supported. When the English soldiers had long since departed Normandy, Norman brigands known as *Galants de la Feuillée*, "companions of the woods", were in action once more against soldiers. By this time, however, they were Breton soldiers who had delayed their return to the duchy, in the winter of 1461–1462, in order to plunder the districts of Coutances, Vire and the Cotentin.[31]

---

[28] Leguai, "Revoltes Rurales", pp. 63–65.

[29] Ibid., p. 67.

[30] Allmand, *Lancastrian Normandy*, pp. 229–40, provides a useful summary of the debate together with some conclusions on the subject of Norman brigandage.

[31] Leguai, "Revoltes rurales", p. 73.

As the implications of a revolt against lordship in the earlier rebellion were absorbed, the hard face of noble solidarity when confronted by an armed peasantry had become once more apparent. The failure of men-at-arms in the service of Charles VII to support the popular army as it threatened the English in Rouen, in 1436, was attributed by Thomas Basin to the old sentiments of class-hatred.[32] The loyalist nobles in Normandy, according to this bishop whose own origins were in the Pays de Caux, were suspicious of the peasant rebels and said that "it would be a great danger to themselves and to the kingdom of France if such people were lucky enough by themselves to drive the English from the country . . .".

Clearly, all four of these peasant revolts during the Hundred Years War showed signs of being wars of "non-nobles against nobles" and it is difficult to imagine how the pulpit rhetoric of the time, which delighted in images of a decadent and vicious nobility incapable of fulfilling its ancient duty of protecting the people, could not have inflamed the passions of a desperate peasantry. Pierre Lasnier, an inhabitant of the parish of Ribemont, voiced some of these clerical platitudes, together with a few conclusions of his own, in a confrontation with two squires in 1420 and paid for it with his life.[33] He said that they were worthless and unworthy to mount a horse, and that he himself, and "other people of the country", should kill all such people. There is something here of Siméon Luce's "fatal cleavage" between the nobility and the people; also of the "crisis of feudalism" of the late Middle Ages which several Marxist historians have announced. The perennial tensions of medieval society between an exploitative military aristocracy and an exploited peasantry appear to have erupted into open violence on a large scale. In this analysis, the *jacques* and *tuchins*, throwing their customary caution and parochialism to the wind, embrace the revolutionary rhetoric of the pulpit, and launch an attack directly on the nobles. The nobles, in their turn, cast aside the distinctions of political allegiance which had hitherto divided them and – French, English, freebooters, all – turn the face of class solidarity against the rebellious peasantry in order to bring them back into a proper subjection. There is no lack of support for this interpretation, but, just as there is a danger in confusing the Hundred Years War with the few major campaigns and battles which punctuate it, so there may be a trap in equating the peasant response to the war with the infrequent major peasant rebellions. In order to avoid this latter danger it is necessary to abandon the tracks left by the blazing demagogues who led their peasant armies to destruction and to turn our attention upon the intimately connected phenomenon of brigandage.

---

[32] Basin, *Charles VII*, i, pp. 224–27.
[33] Douët-d'Arcq, *Choix*, ii, pp. 40–42.

Brigandage

Unfortunately, the tracks of the "brigands" of this period have been obscured almost as much by the semantic confusion of commentators as by their own natural reticence.[34] The word "brigand", even in the fourteenth and fifteenth centuries, accommodated at least two distinct, yet connected, meanings. The brigand first appears in France, under the name of *brigan,* in the aspect of a professional common soldier who wore a metal breast-plate, called a *brigandine.* Jean de Venette, writing in the middle years of the fourteenth century, employed the term *brigantes* to describe the foot-soldiers who fought for the French king, John II, at the battle of Poitiers. Froissart, likewise, reported *brigans de piet* in the opposing army of the Black Prince. While it is impossible to determine their exact function in the battle, Venette nevertheless made it clear that they participated with men-at-arms in the plundering of the French countryside during the years immediately after the battle. It is very likely that these common soldiers, when discharged from paid military service, regrouped into armed bands sheltering in the woods in order to prey on travellers.[35] Perhaps the "brigands" who helped the peasants of Longeuil-Sainte-Marie in 1359 and those of Charny in 1361 were already on their way to such a career. As bandits, highway-robbers, outlaws, they were the humble equivalent of the men-at-arms of the Companies whose formation in similar circumstances was described by Froissart.[36] Here is the brief metamorphosis between the "brigand" as common soldier and the "brigand", of whatever (usually humble) origin, who operated in armed gangs and preyed upon the roads and villages.

By the beginning of the fifteenth century, the chronicler-royal of the abbey of Saint Denis, and the Bourgeois de Paris, were using the term "brigand" specifically to describe peasants who had been driven to desperation by the predatory activities of soldiers and who, in the process of arming themselves in their own defence, had been led into a similar existence of their own.[37] Some years later, Thomas Basin, in his *History of Charles VII,* described *brigandi* as "lost and desperate men" who had abandoned their homes and their fields to fight like wild animals from bases in the impenetrable forest.[38] This was a relatively new name,

---

[34] Wright, "Pillagers and Brigands", pp. 19–20. An interesting example of the difficulties which may arise from multiple meanings is Hilton, *Bond Men,* p. 117, where pillaging bands of soldiers are called "brigands" and the *tuchins* merely "counter-brigands". At the same time the *tuchins* are credited with being the "prototype of . . . social banditry".

[35] R. Memain, "Les Misères de la Guerre en Bas-Poitou (XIVe–XVe Siècles)", *Société des Antiquaires de l'Ouest,* 3rd series, xii (1941), pp. 653 and 668, defines "brigands" as discharged soldiers who lived by pillaging, but, inexplicably, he specifically excludes artisans and peasants who, according to the author, had neither the wish nor the ability to "brigander".

[36] Froissart, *Chroniques,* ed. Luce, vi, pp. 59–61.

[37] R. Jouet, *La Résistance à l'Occupation Anglaise en Basse-Normandie, 1418–1450* (Caen, 1969), p. 18.

[38] Basin, *Charles VII,* pp. 106–8.

which could be interchanged with *godin, tuchin* or simply "companion", for an old phenomenon. By this time, however, the chroniclers had recognized that the brigands, far from being soldiers, were very often the enemies of all soldiers.

Even as early as 1377, when one Gieffroy Queton presented his case at the royal castle of the Louvre, all these characteristics of the brigand were in place, and under that name.[39] When the king's enemies, he explained, first occupied La Charité-sur-Loire (presumably he was refering to the Anglo-Gascon occupation from October 1363 until the first months of 1365), he had been a man of good and upright life, peacefully cultivating his fields. He was robbed and harassed by these enemies to such an extent, he declared, that he felt himself ready to join the other "country people who were fleeing to the fields, ditches, caves and woods like desperate men". Because he did not have the means which would allow him to live for a while in a walled town, he joined a company of men "popularly known as *tuchins, brigans*" and *godins*. He said that this company did "much harm" to the enemy, and their services appear to have been acknowledged by the marshals of France. But it appears that he also supplied these enemies with all manner of provisions as well as robbing pilgrims and murdering other travellers on the open road. After the expulsion of the Anglo-Gascons from La Charité, he returned to his honest labour. A similar story was told by the peasant Jean le Jeusne, who had been forced by circumstances into joining a company of twelve *compaignons* who lived by brigandage in the Oise region during the period immediately preceding the treaty of Brétigny. So many fortresses, such as Chaversy and Crépy-en-Valois, were occupied by the king's enemies, he claimed, that "no labouring man, or any other subject of the kingdom, dared venture securely, or to go about their business, in the district where these enemies were, for fear of being killed or taken for ransom". His intention, he insisted, was to bring harm to the king's enemies, but this was achieved, in practice, only by robbing the wretched peasants who were paying *patis* to them and thereby contributing, in no small measure, to the disorder from which he wished to escape.[40] The fact that Jean de Bonval told an almost identical story, in almost identical words, but to officials of Henry VI, king of France and England, exactly half a century later, suggests that we are faced with an important and enduring social phenomenon.[41] The Hundred Years War created the circumstances of social disorder in which peasant brigandage thrived. It even gave it a new name. But the capacity of medieval people, whatever their social position, to drift in and out of armed criminality according to circumstance was certainly not a novelty of this place and period. John Bellamy remarks, in the context of late medieval England, that "unlike today, a man might break the law quite seriously when an opportunity for profit or revenge offered itself but then revert back to obedience to the law, even to upholding it, for the rest of the year,

---

[39] AN, JJ 110, no. 207.
[40] AN, JJ 107, no. 11.
[41] Lewis, *Later Medieval France*, p. 286. It is also, as one must acknowledge, a fine example of the durability of bureaucratic formulae.

the decade, or even a lifetime. There was . . . less of a gulf between honest men and criminals than in modern society."[42]

To all outward appearances, the kind of brigandage with which Queton and Le Jeusne were involved was no great threat to the lives of soldiers, and it seems far removed from the peasant revolts so far described. It must be understood, however, that as thieves, who paid nothing to soldiers in protection-money, these bandits represented competition for scarce resources in the countryside. Their existence undermined the local order which sustained the military structures. What value were "borrowed lordships", or, indeed, any sort of lordship, if the agents of the military captains could not travel the roads to collect their *patis*, and if, when they arrived in the villages, there was no money left to pay them? What value were they if the safeconducts issued by their captains were made worthless by the unpredictable activities of bandits? What value if the rough justice of the brigand lynching-parties usurped the rights of justice which had traditionally belonged to the lord? Furthermore, this brigandage of the woods was a constant and visible alternative course of action for local people when they were faced with the choice of submitting to the demands of the garrison collectors or of resisting them. The flight of peasants from their villages to their secret hideouts in the woods, to caves and tunnels, represented to the arriving soldiers not just the immediate loss of potentially productive labour and of valuable moveable property. It also represented the likely development of alternative centres of power which were completely independent of, and antagonistic to, the more traditional centres in the local towns and fortresses.

Nothing could demonstrate this challenge more clearly than some of the early activities of the *tuchins*, in 1380, which formed no part of any major rebellion. At the beginning of that year, the "English", under Pierre de Galard, had occupied the castle of Chaliers, near Saint-Flour.[43] The consuls of Saint-Flour negotiated a *patis* agreement with this garrison in order to live in peace with the English soldiers, but the truce thus purchased was thrown into jeopardy by the capture of one of the Chaliers garrison by a band of *tuchins*, "*ly companho tochi*". It was Saint-Flour which had to pay for his release. No sooner was this incident cleared away than a band of *tuchins* broke two other local truces by capturing an Englishman of the Montferrant castle garrison and by raiding livestock belonging to the English garrison of Le Saillant. The bandits may, unwittingly, have been fighting the king's war in this remote area, but they were certainly not acting in the interests of the "borrowed lordship" at Chaliers or in the interests of the commune.

The hard core of brigands who did not return to their honest labour when the immediate crisis had passed represented not only a threat to those who did so, but a constant incitement to rebellion against the centres of local authority. We need not, therefore, accept all of the extravagant claims for the Norman brigands of the

---

[42] Bellamy, *Crime and Public Order*, pp. 29–30.
[43] Boudet, *Tuchins*, pp. 30–32.

fifteenth-century English occupation advanced by the nationalist school of historians in order to accept the fact that these bandits posed a huge threat to the whole policy of land settlement initiated by Henry V, just as they had to the so-called "English" occupation around Saint-Flour in 1380. The enormous number of executions of brigands at this time, and the pains which were taken to distinguish between, on the one hand, prisoners of war who were harmless enough to be ransomed, and, on the other, the "people who lie in wait in woods and on highways to take the subjects of our lord the king", who were exterminated as traitors and common criminals, show that the threat was taken very seriously indeed.[44] As seriously, in fact, as the provost of Dijon had done in the entirely different political circumstances of the five months between June and November 1364, in Burgundy, when he had executed no less than 120 "pillards, larrons and meurtriers".[45]

In the great fear generated in the Aube region by the arrival of an army led by the dukes of Lancaster and Brittany, in September 1373, Jehanart and Colin, the sons of Symon le Tisserrant, together with seven other "poor and wretched labouring men" and their wives and children, fled from their village of Dienville.[46] They fled to the woods between Dienville and Brienne-la-Vieille, with such few articles as could be saved, and there, among the trees, met with many other refugees. While in the woods, they captured and killed two men whom they took to be "English enemies and spies". Their victims (notwithstanding the fact that they "spoke like English" or, at least, some "strange and horrible language", were wearing the red colours of English soldiers, were carrying fire-lighting equipment, and admitted to being spies) may have been law-abiding Frenchmen. Such, at least, was the later claim of the local lord and the seigneurial bailiff of Brienne. In this trivial incident are all the essential elements of an embryonic brigandage, although it was never called by such a name. Here, based in the forests which they knew so well, were desperate and fearful peasant refugees prepared to take the law into their own hands and prepared to challenge, in their feeble way, not only the might of an English invading army but also, and perhaps inadvertently, their own traditional lords. The English army passed away to the south, but the local lords did not. The small band of peasants was forced into the lives of outlaws by the threat of prosecution from their own lord, jealously guarding his rights of justice.

The taking of the law into their own hands by the local communities was a common phenomenon of the French countryside during the Hundred Years War, and it represented, along with that building of community fortresses which will be examined in the following chapter, a serious challenge to lordship. In the same year that the lord of Dienville and the seigneurial bailiff of Brienne-la-Vieille were arresting and confiscating the property of the Dienville eight, the joint-lords of Maizy (Aisne) were arresting six peasants of Muscourt. Their offence was to have

---

[44] Rowe, "Bedford", p. 593.
[45] Petit, *Ducs de Bourgogne*, p. 127.
[46] AN, JJ 105, no. 31.

drowned three men whom they took to be English pillagers and who, they claimed, would not otherwise have been punished because "justice was poorly exercised in these times".[47] Two years later, the dean of Vendeuvre (Aube) had forced his tenant, Garnier le Grangier, into the life of a fugitive because he had killed a soldier who was attempting to steal his horses.[48] These actions of peasants may seem to us (as they were certainly intended to be portrayed by the petitioners themselves) to be simple acts of self-defence. Nevertheless, if lynch-mobs of angry peasants assumed rights of high justice in the localities and attacked all armed strangers; if they built for themselves fortresses and refused to support the seigneurial one with finance and labour; was this not a form of *jacquerie*? And if, under threat of prosecution by properly authorized local justice, the peasant miscreants became fugitives and outlaws, as they so often did, where did they seek sanctuary if not in the local band of brigands?

If the English had stayed in the district, as they did in the nearby fortress of Bragelogne (Aube) between 1358 and 1360, the Le Tisserant brothers and their friends might have taken that next step towards genuine brigandage: one towards which Thevenin de Beauvoir claimed to have been impelled.[49] This man explained that, in order to escape the "great war" which these soldiers at Bragelogne brought to his district, and to "resist and to injure the aforesaid enemies", he had joined a band of "companions of the district" who secretly watched the activities of the garrison and attacked its foraging parties. The band of uprooted peasants was strong enough to mount successful ambushes on groups of eight or nine pillagers operating out of the fortress, and their gains included at least thirty-four horses. The peasant "companions" were not, however, above attacking the persons and property of people in the villages of Bagneux-la-Fosse (Aube) and Arthonnay (Yonne) who did business with the constable of the *forteresce englesche* and they made further gains here in horses, cloth, wine and flour. Thevenin's was an effective and self-confident company of brigands who insisted that they were "good, true and loyal subjects" of the French Crown, interpreting for themselves what was, and what was not, "to the prejudice and damage of the said district and of the common good". Their independent lifestyle was, however, a menace, not only to the English garrison, but to all traditional authority and to all law-abiding folk. Christopher Allmand has reminded us, in the context of Normandy in the fifteenth century, not to "be so preoccupied with studying the activities of the partisans" that we "overlook or underestimate the problems of law and order . . . for which the brigands were largely responsible".[50] When Jean de Venette, in the fourteenth century, reported the execution by the English enemies of the "robbers and thieves" who "grew in power along the highways and roads and in the woods", he praised these enemy soldiers for "showing

---

[47] AN, JJ 104, no. 207.
[48] AN, JJ 107, no. 278.
[49] AN, JJ 110, no. 20.
[50] Allmand, *Lancastrian Normandy*, p. 235.

themselves kinder to the peasants in the villages than were their own natural lords".[51]

It is possible that some of those known as brigands at this time may have shown some of the features of the "social bandit" which has been described by Eric Hobsbawm as a peasant outlaw whom the lord and state regard as criminal, but who remains within peasant society and is considered by his own people as a hero.[52] Venette, once described as "the poor man's Homer",[53] did not think of them as heroes, however. Nor, one may safely guess, would the peasant inhabitants of Bagneux-la-Fosse and Arthonnay, between the years of 1358 and 1360. There can be no doubt, however, that some brigands did offer useful services to local people, many of whom must have been old friends and neighbours. In October 1358, when the English occupied La Ferté-sous-Jouarre (Seine-et-Marne), two "brigands of the woods" (clearly distinguished from the common soldier type) captured a woman who had been assisting the English to identify the rich men of the district. Having consulted with some peasant refugees who were sheltering behind the walls of Provins and who urged them to kill all such collaborators, the brigands duly obliged by drowning the wretched woman in the River Morin.[54] The peasants on the battlements of Provins and those who had become brigands in the woods were probably different branches of the same community: the former the more substantial members of the village society, able to pay for town accommodation, and the latter the most destitute. The brigands showed a loyalty to their own people, but they defined "their own" very narrowly indeed.

We can be sure that there were plenty of "social bandits" in late medieval France, just as there must have been plenty of brigands whose protestations of loyalty to the French Crown were meant quite genuinely. If the natural enemy of the brigand, the soldier of the nearby garrison, spoke and behaved in a way which suggested that he was also the enemy of the legitimate king of France, loyalty to the Crown neatly equated with self-interest. This was as true of fourteenth-century Champagne as it was of fifteenth-century Normandy. But it would be foolish to suggest that the brigand of the woods was not an enemy both to lordship and to the peaceful cultivation of the soil, and, if we are determined to place the brigands of this period in a wider context, it must, ironically, be at the much more local level. We must contemplate, with Simplicissimus, the natural hostility between peasants and soldiers in the particular circumstances of the individual villages.

There is more to peasant rebellion than peasant revolts, and these latter were rare and extreme manifestations of a much more general phenomenon: that of village solidarity when faced with threats to its existence from outsiders. Villages, as communities of individual peasants, were not necessarily eliminated when the

---

[51] Venette, *Chronicle*, p. 105.
[52] E. Hobsbawm, "Social Banditry", chapter 4 in *Rural Protest: Peasant Movements and Social Change*, ed. H. Landsberger (London, 1974).
[53] Delachenal, *Charles V*, ii, p. 140.
[54] AN, JJ 109, no. 12.

physical structure of the village was destroyed by flames. Even in the very rare circumstances when the community had been wiped out altogether they could be rebuilt by new settlers much faster than any seigneurial mill or castle. Le Roy Ladurie has described vividly the rebirth of the hamlet of La Cicogne which had been destroyed in the 1440s and re-created by the single individual, Perrin Bordebure, in the 1450s, with the aid of some split logs, reeds and broom.[55] La Cicogne was, however, most unusual in that its human community had disappeared with its physical structure. In other cases of abandonment, the community was preserved by the groups of parishioners such as Jean de Venette saw behind the walls of Paris, with their own parish priests, anxiously awaiting the opportunity to return to their ruined houses and their devastated fields. "On Easter Day [1360]" he wrote, "I myself saw priests of ten country parishes communicating their people and keeping Easter in various chapels or any spot they could find in the monastery of the Carmelite friars at Paris."[56] Continuity was preserved for the less fortunate in the forest-refuges such as that in which Prior Hugh of Montgeron sheltered from the soldiers of the Chantecocq garrison. The community was also preserved, at the more active level and at the expense of other communities, in the robber-bands of brigands.

The "outsiders" who provoked these manifestations of village solidarity were the old enemies of the village: the occupants of the local strong-point seeking to appropriate the village surplus of labour and goods, and the collector of hearth, and other, taxes for the Crown. Often, as has been observed of this period, they were one and the same person, as soldiers, under royal licence or no, appropriated all the local taxes for their own maintenance. The natural solidarity of each community against outsiders such as these could manifest itself in many traditional ways. The group of village oligarchs, often called "the better and wiser part" of the community, could agree to a tax or *patis* and then share out the burden of it amongst the parishioners. They could attempt to co-ordinate the tactics of disobedience and petty sabotage which had been honed to a fine cutting edge by centuries of use against more traditional lords. When these tactics proved themselves inadequate to secure the survival of the community, or when they provoked vicious reprisals against it, the flight of all, or part, of the community to the woods was called for, with a likely evolution into brigandage. Brigands "of the woods", *tuchins*, *godins*, were the enemies of all society except their own immediate community, but they were also the scaffolding around which peasant revolt was constructed when the natural parochialism of the peasantry briefly gave way to a larger hatred. Outlaws would have been the natural leaders, certainly the backbone, of such revolts when caution was so spectacularly thrown to the wind.

---

[55] E. Le Roy Ladurie, *The French Peasantry 1450–1660*, trans. A. Sheridan (Aldershot, 1987), p. 21.

[56] Venette, *Chronicle*, p. 99.

5

PEASANT RESISTANCE: COMMUNAL DEFENCES

PEASANT REVOLT AND brigandage represent manifest failures of rulership, whether we like to consider this lordship at the central or at the local level. They were clear threats to the social order even if, as was so often the case, that "order" was an undisguised tyranny which breached all the norms of traditional, peace-time, lordship. In a well-ordered state, moreover, collective ransoms and individual ransoms should never have been paid by non-combatants to soldiers. Their payment represented an obvious breakdown either of the system of national defence or of proper military discipline and control. The sovereign lord, together with the lesser lords, were supposed, according to the conventional political wisdom of the day, to protect their non-combatant subjects from external attack and from domestic injustice.[1] They were to do so by confronting external enemies, in the field, in order to defeat or to expel them, and by exercising a strict control over the men-at-arms in their own service. When the external enemy could not be defeated, it was their duty as lords to provide havens of temporary security for the country-dwellers behind the properly maintained and defended walls of royal and seigneurial castles, and within the enclosed towns. Each village community was, theoretically, within the protective umbrella, the *réssort*, of one of these safe areas. A soldier who demanded tribute from non-combatants of his own allegiance might always claim some form of official sanction for his actions, but the non-military classes, understandably, viewed this behaviour as criminal. It was seen as an act of war where there was no proper state of war. Effective justice and effective war were the twin responsibilities of kingship and of all medieval lordship. Where either was lacking, there was no political community and no order.

If, as historians, we rely too heavily upon the records of failure in the political and social order – the frequent cases of dispute between peasant communities and their lords in the records of the Paris *parlement* ; the registers of the royal chancery which are redolent of rural criminality; the denunciations of contemporary society by clerics – we are very likely to see nothing but disorder. The writing of the history of the twentieth century from the front pages of the daily newspapers might be almost equally misguided. The chronicle of Jean de Venette, for example, to which reference has so often been made in this present work, creates (as was its author's intention) an almost overwhelming impression of French society in the middle years of the fourteenth century in a state of crisis and collapse. Yet, even

---

[1] Kaeuper, *War, Justice,* Part ii: "Royal Justice and Public Order".

within this chronicle, as a muted sub-text, there is clear evidence of systems working as they were designed to do. The farmhouse at Longeuil, for example, which sheltered Grandferré and his peasant companions in 1359, belonged to the lord of this village, the abbot of Saint-Corneille at Compiègne, and had been fortified with his, and with the regent's, permission.[2] This was an affair of Jacques Bonhomme, as the author himself proudly proclaims, but not of *Jacquerie*, the horrible memories of which were still fresh in everyone's mind. It was a fine example of mutual co-operation between a lord and his subjects. If the dominant theme of Venette's account of the previous year is the destruction of the Ile-de-France by the Anglo-Navarrese soldiers encircling Paris, the sub-text may be found in the description of the stout and well-guarded walls of Paris and of other towns which sheltered the refugees from the countryside. "Men hastened to the cities, with their carts and their goods, their wives and their children . . ."[3] It must frankly be admitted, therefore, that, although we can describe the frequent (and "newsworthy") disasters which befell the French peasants at the time of the Hundred Years War, and can deduce many more of them from the certain evidence of population decline, we have no way of distinguishing between the exception and the rule; the rarity and the commonplace. In the context of this present chapter, we must resist the tendency to assume that all communal defence was self-defence by autonomous peasant communities in defiance of the traditional power-structures. The Crown and traditional lordship were, on the contrary, rarely far from the scene when their rights were seen to be challenged.

Flight to the parish church, to the woods, to the hills, to islands in a nearby river, or underground into caves and disused quarries, was probably the most common immediate reaction of villagers to the sudden approach of unknown soldiers, and the cry "The English are coming!" was often enough to empty an entire village. The arrival of two lightly-armed pillagers in the parish of Saint-Romain-sur-Cher (Loir-et-Cher) was enough to clear the village for ten days, and it was only at the end of this period that a handful of the menfolk ventured back under cover of night.[4] If the danger did not pass quickly, when soldiers set themselves up in a strong-point and prepared for a prolonged occupation, the peasants, as they watched their crops rotting in the fields beyond the woods and their livestock starving for lack of grazing within them, had only three realistic survival options remaining. The first of these options, that of brigandage, challenged, in ways which have been described in the previous chapter, the traditional social order of the countryside. The second, that of *appatisation*, preserved the essential structures which had for centuries tied the village to the castle, even though the ancient customs which had mitigated that relationship were thrown into jeopardy. It also allowed agricultural labour to continue. The third was to take advantage of fixed defences in the vicinity and to eke out a scanty existence, consuming reserves, within the relative security of a passive redoubt.

---

2 Venette, *Chronicle*, p. 90.
3 Ibid., pp. 75–6.
4 AN, JJ 106, no. 77.

If peasant refugees stayed in hiding in the woods and wasteland their able-bodied members would often join gangs of brigands attempting to support their families off the profits of banditry. Alternatively, they could appoint representatives to negotiate a collective ransom with the local garrisons. The first option depended heavily for its success on very careful pre-planning by the village community for just such an emergency: one which allowed the social structure of the village to be preserved within carefully-prepared "shadow" villages located in inaccessible places. It relied upon the peasants' superior local knowledge and upon that strict solidarity of the village community which dealt quickly and savagely with anything which smacked of collaboration with the enemy. The second option, which permitted the village to function more normally, relied on the capacity of the garrison soldiers who received the *patis* – or tribute – payments to protect from further attacks and ransoming the peasants who paid them. As with the other, more desperate, option, it too required a solid communal organization which could distribute the burden of *patis* within the local community with a fair measure of acceptance, if not of equity.

If a sudden flight to the woods, followed either by a more prolonged period of brigandage or of *appatisation,* may have represented the norm, there were other options open to peasants which exploited the fixed defences of stone walls and other places of refuge. As always, some of these options threatened, or were seen to threaten, the social order, and some did not. Of those which did not, the most important was the retreat of country communities, together with their moveable property and livestock, behind the walls of the local royal or seigneurial castle, whose bailey had been prepared for just such an eventuality, or into the local walled town.[5] This was the method most favoured by the Crown because it deprived the enemy of profits from the countryside while it contributed to the general defence of the kingdom. Usually it appealed strongly, too, to the lords of castles, and the captains of town garrisons, whether these were self-appointed officers or no, because it offered them the possibility of securing easy access to labour-services and foodstuffs without the inconvenience of foraging for them. It is clear that the right of offering refuge in the *basse-cours* of castles was one which lords valued highly, because of the labour- and watchkeeping-services which went with it. In 1443, Charles, duke of Bourbon and the Auvergne, allowed the prior of Azerat to retain the fortress made in his priory only on the condition that he did *not* offer refuge there to the duke's subjects.[6] It was also, despite its obvious drawbacks, a favoured option of many country-dwellers. A priest of the late fourteenth-century Cahorsin reckoned that there were more peasants at that time in the cities of Montauban and Toulouse than in the surrounding countryside.[7] In the fifteenth century, and much further to the north, Thomas Basin reported that no cultivation was done except in the immediate vicinity of cities, towns and castles, to which the peasants and their livestock could run as soon as the alarm

---

5   *Guerre de Cent Ans*, ed. Timbal, chapter 3.
6   Fournier, "La Défense", p. 163, note 1.
7   Mollat, *Guerre de Cent Ans*, p. 139.

was sounded. "It was a common and frequent thing", he continues, obviously warming to the theme, "and to be seen almost everywhere, that oxen and horses which had heard the watchkeepers' signal and were detached from their ploughs, would, without further prompting and out of sheer habit, rush to the nearest place of safety. Sheep and pigs, too . . .".[8] It would be foolish, in the light of such evidence, to underestimate the importance of towns and castles, whether in royal or seigneurial hands, to the defence of the French country-people.

Although such a retreat from the "flat" lands into the "enclosed" lands in theory was available to all who lived in the open country, it involved several difficulties of a very practical nature for the country-dwellers. Peasants, who are well-known for their doubting natures, might have considered this move from the "outside" to the "inside" as one from the frying-pan into the fire: an escape from one set of rapacious soldiers only to fall into the jaws of another. And, even if they were prepared to take this chance, the castles and towns which were the official centres of a *réssort* were often too far removed from the villages which they were supposed to shelter for any rapid, but orderly, evacuation. In October 1367, for example, the inhabitants of Saint-Mard-sur-le-Mont complained before the judges of the Paris *parlement* that they were being forced by the royal castellain of the castle of Passavant to perform sentry-duty there, even though, for protection, they would not retreat to Passavant but to either of two castles which were much nearer.[9]

The expense of life in a town or fortress without a trade to support that existence was also a constant disincentive to refugees. Although "no good Frenchman" in the period after the battle of Poitiers dared live or conduct his business in the open country (declared one petitioner for a royal pardon), only those with money retreated into fortresses where they "suffered many costs and expenses and lost all to wickedness. The others fled to the marshes and the woods."[10] Gieffroy Queton claimed that he and his neighbours, in the early 1360s, were forced into brigandage because they "dared not work and cultivate their lands and inheritances in the open country" and because they did not have the means to live in a "closed town".[11] Poor peasants were not welcome in such places.

For their part, the captains of castles and walled towns, whatever their legal obligations may have been to the people of their *réssort*, had to be careful not to put at risk their own capacity to resist a siege by accepting too many refugees, or by allowing too many makeshift dwellings in the vicinity of the curtain walls. The competition for scarce space within the walls or barriers must often have been intense and none but the most privileged of tenants would have enjoyed the guaranteed accommodation of a "lodge" within the bailey walls like those which flanked the inside of the curtain wall at Aulnat.[12] Guillaume Jeurbers, the "poor

---

8 Basin, *Charles VII*, i, p. 87.
9 Timbal, *Guerre de Cent Ans*, pp. 153–56.
10 AN, JJ 92, no. 272.
11 AN, JJ 110, no. 207.
12 G. Fournier, "La Défense des Populations Rurales Pendant la Guerre de Cent Ans en

labourer" of Perreux (Yonne), became a useful member of the garrisons of Saint-Fargeau and Ratilly in the three years after 1357, but the widow Wyette, without such a useful skill, had to hide in the bushes. In February 1374, three inhabitants of Besse-en-Chandesse (Puy-de-Dôme), who were attempting to drive about eleven of their cows and bullocks into the local fortress, were met by another labouring man who attempted to chase them away with a stick, saying that there was no room for them there.[13] It was only after a brawl at the barriers of the fortress, in which knives and sticks were employed to lethal effect, that the refugees gained entry. Even then, the cattle could hardly have been considered secure from the hungry garrison inside.

Town captains faced exactly the same problem as castellains in their duty to place their obligations to refugees in the balance with their capacity to resist a siege. As the English army under Henry V approached Rouen in the summer of 1418 the town's captain commanded that only those with provisions for a full ten months could stay in the city: a tall order, by the standards of any age. By December, the "useless mouths" which had not made suitable provision for themselves were expelled from the town and trapped, in a pitiable state, in the ditches beyond the walls to perish between the two armies.[14]

The alternative to the stone defences which were under the control of royal or seigneurial captains and *châtelains*, who represented local power, were the refuges which belonged, fully or in part, to the communities themselves or which they had appropriated for their own defence. The makeshift dwellings in the woods to which many communities retired at times of military threat, and which often must have formed the bases for banditry, were noted by Victor Hugo in the context of the eighteenth-century revolutionary wars in Brittany. "In several of these forests and woods", he wrote, "there were not only villages beneath the soil, grouped around a central shaft, but there were also veritable hamlets of low huts hidden under the trees, so numerous that sometimes the forest was full of them."[15] The woods and wasteland afforded some sort of refuge to people like La Wyette and her infants who were not parties to any co-ordinated strategy and who merely sought temporary hiding places.[16] The woods also, as in eighteenth-century Brittany, concealed those shadow-villages of makeshift huts in which Prior Hugh of Montgeron lived with his peasant neighbours in October 1358 "eating their bread with fear, sorrow and great anguish".[17] If the soldiers did not depart quickly, the inhabitants of these shadow-villages might face a very stark choice: either to let their refuge become a lair of brigands, such as those described in the previous chapter, or to be starved into submission. Garnier le Grangier, the poor labourer

Basse-Auvergne", *Actes du 90ème Congrès National des Sociétés Savantes, Section Archéologique* (Paris, 1966), p. 167.
[13] AN, JJ 106, no. 383.
[14] M. Labarge, *Henry V: the Cautious Conqueror* (London, 1975), pp. 139–40.
[15] Hugo, *Quatrevingt-treize*, p. 257.
[16] AN, JJ 105, no. 362.
[17] Venette, *Chronicle*, note 137, p. 253.

of Amance (Aube), spent three weeks in the woods near to his village, with his wife, his young family and several neighbours, before they was obliged to take their famished horses out to graze by the village pond. There, they were immediately assailed by a "pillager of foreign tongue" who demanded their horses.[18] The Amance parishioners could not live for long in such circumstances and the aftermath of this confrontation between peasant and pillager is worth noting. Garnier killed the pillager; was prosecuted by his lord, the dean of Vendeuvre (possibly for a homicide on one of the dean's own men); and then became an outlaw, leaving his wife and children to fend for themselves. The progression from "poor labourer", to refugee, then to brigand was enacted in less than a month, and Garnier may have been able to complete the full circle back to "poor labourer" when, thanks to his wife's efforts on his behalf, the king offered him a pardon in October 1375. Taking to the woods or wilderness was an option in an emergency for most peasants but it could never remain a viable alternative to their ordinary life unless they ceased to be "poor labourers" and became "brigands of the woods".

The type of subterranean refuges which were available to the Vendéens of 1793, in Hugo's account, were also available to, and may indeed have been excavated by, the great numbers of displaced villagers of the fourteenth and fifteenth centuries. It is very likely that many of these refuges may have been cut from the rock or developed from old quarries at this time. The ones in the Rouergue, at least, which were called "the English caves", may confidently be located in the fourteenth century. It was in 1923 that Adrien Blanchet attempted to catalogue over a thousand *souterrains-refuges* in France, many of which he believed to have been created in the chaotic period after the battle of Poitiers, and to describe the more typical ones.[19] He showed that every province had some of them and no province more of them than Picardy which included the area of intense military activity to the south-west of Calais. The characteristic refuge consisted of a long central corridor, approximately two-and-a-half metres high and wide, with chambers running off it. The principal entrance was often in, or near to, the parish church, and they usually contained a well for water and ventilation shafts whose surface outlets were suitably concealed. An accidental land-slip in 1840 revealed a stairway of fifty-seven steps leading from the church tower of Hermies (Pas-de-Calais) into a vast network of about three hundred underground cells.[20] These subterranean complexes could be connected directly to the houses on the surface, as at Bulles (Oise). More often they were virtually independent of the surface village, like Naours (Somme), which consists of two thousand metres of corridor and three hundred chambers, whose six ventilation chimneys broke the surface in the miller's house. This latter refuge certainly

[18] AN, JJ 107, no. 278.
[19] A. Blanchet, *Les Souterrains-refuges de la France: Contribution à l'Histoire de l'Habitation Humaine* (Paris, 1923). The information for most of this paragraph derives from this work.
[20] Ibid., p. 186.

existed, although probably not on this scale, in 1331. It would have been a brave soldier who attempted to penetrate these dark labyrinths, and although there are records from the fourteenth century of the use of smoke to force peasant troglo- dytes to the surface, such a technique would have been ineffective against underground cities such as these, with several exits and ventilation shafts. Enguer- rand d'Eudin, the independently-minded captain of Loches, was accused of having smoked eight poor women from a cave and of having then killed them all,[21] and the *Black Book* of Périgueux contains the report of twenty or so peasants returning from the market of Périgueux who were chased by a band of English soldiers into a cave, and then smoked out.[22] But these shallow caves must have been poor examples of the type.

Of the fixed defences, above ground, which did not form part the of a network of royal and seigneurial fortresses, there was an enormous variety. These commu- nity enterprises ranged from the joint-enterprises between the local lord and his people, sanctioned by the Crown, to the creation of dangerously *de facto* com- munes set up in defiance both of the king's right to control the building of fortified places and the lord's right to control local affairs and to ensure the proper maintenance of his own castle at the community's expense. They ranged from the fortification of parts, or all, of the village – often incorporating the parish church, sometimes a seigneurial tower, in the encircling wall – to the use of some local strong-point which was large enough, like the Longeuil farmhouse, to accommo- date people, livestock and property. Traces still remain at Charbonnier (Puy-de- Dôme) of the castle which was owned by the Hospitaller Order and which was reconstructed in the late fourteenth century by a joint effort of the lord and his subjects. Both parties contributed to the expense, and the local people, who were offered places to rent within, or close to, the castle, guaranteed the watch-keeping.[23]

Although the most durable of these enterprises in communal self-defence were the fortified parish churches, their survival may be due as much to the continuity of religious service within them, throughout the modern period, as to any particu- lar merits they may have had as fortresses. Their roof chambers and towers once accommodated scores of families and their precious possessions; their walled cemetery enclosures offered some security to livestock, and their "slanting, squinting" windows watch our passing today in much the same way as those of Michelet's Taillebourg and Tancarville. The sturdy bell-towers of these, and other, village churches remind us that soldiers rarely took peasants completely by surprise, whereas the reverse was by no means the case. Victor Hugo noticed that, in the royalist peasant rebellion of 1793, the communications between peasants over large distances were like lightning. "One would believe that they had the telegraph."[24] The news of the approach of soldiers in the fourteenth and fifteenth centuries could be transmitted by the telegraph of church bells even though, as

21 Martin, "D'Eudin", p. 138.
22 Blanchet, *Souterrains-refuges*, p. 119.
23 Fournier, "La Défense", pp. 174–5.
24 Hugo, *Quatrevingt-treize*, pp. 260–61.

already observed, this form of communication was not always viewed favourably in official circles. In such circumstances, flags were almost as effective.[25] Jean de Venette, always a useful guide in such matters, reported that the peasants of the Ile-de-France, in 1358, "kept lookouts on top of the church towers, and little boys stood there and kept watch. When they saw the enemy coming in the distance, they blew a horn or rang bells."[26] Thomas Basin, more than three generations later, described how "from the vantage point of a high tower or turret, the eye of the watchkeeper could detect the approach of pillagers".[27] They could then give the alarm signal, by bell or horn, to those who were working below in the fields and among the vines. So much had the idea of watch-towers and warning bells entered the collective consciousness that Jean Gerson, in 1405, called his University of Paris the watch-keeper of the kingdom, ready at all times to ring the bell when danger threatened.[28]

Jean de Venette identified the fortified parish church as the typical village fortress of the period, and so it must have been. Nevertheless, there were other sorts of communal refuges whose construction and defence obligations fell almost exclusively upon the communities. Gaston Fébus of Foix, who had played host to Froissart at Orthez and had assisted in the slaughter of the peasants at the Market of Meaux, encouraged within his Pyrenean lands the development of the walled villages with their own hinterlands in the countryside around them, called *recul-hides*.[29] The maintenance and surveillance was largely in the hands of the communities, as was the appointment of captains, the disposition of the gate-keys, and the organization of the watch. This process of encircling the villages with defensive walls had started in other parts of France during the twelfth and thirteenth centuries, as villages acquired charters of liberties modelled on those of the towns, but the fifteenth century has been identified as a golden age for the building of such walls, especially in areas of France such as the Allier plain where lordship was "less coherent" than elsewhere and where the village communities were strong.[30] There were, of course, infinite variations on the basic theme, ranging from the 1443 plans for a fully-developed walled village at Sainte-Eulalie-du-Larzac, complete with moats, curtain walls and flanking towers, to the ones which made the best of what was already there by joining houses together in a rough circle with connecting palisades.[31] La Couvertoirade (Aveyron) is a fine example of a fifteenth-century fortified village whose curtain wall and flanking towers were constructed in a fruitful partnership between the Hospitaller lords of the place and the villagers themselves.[32]

[25] Fournier, *Château*, p. 247.
[26] Venette, *Chronicle*, p. 85.
[27] Basin, *Charles VII*, p. 87.
[28] Gerson, *Oeuvres*, vii, p. 1145.
[29] Fournier, *Château*, p. 245.
[30] Ibid., pp. 194–98 and 215–16.
[31] Ibid., pp. 243–44.
[32] C.-L. Salch, *Dictionnaire des Châteaux et des Fortifications du Moyen Age en France* (Strasbourg, 1979), p. 382

Where it was not possible to defend the village as a whole, there were normally places, within or nearby, from which a defence could be co-ordinated. The famous resistance of Grandferré and his peasant companions at Longeuil, in 1359, was based in a farmhouse which belonged to the monastery of Saint-Corneille.[33] According to Jean de Venette, the farmhouse was stocked with provisions and sheltered about two hundred men, "all labourers who supported their humble existence by the work of their hands", and all under the orders of a captain whom they had elected. The captain was Guillaume l'Aloue, and his servant was Grandferré, "as humble and modest as he was strong". The English in Creil Castle determined to make this fortress their own and attacked it in strength, penetrating the courtyard and killing the captain. They were repelled by the other peasants, including Grandferré, who laid about them "as if they were engaged in their wonted task of flailing wheat in a barn". A revenge attack on the farmhouse by the English of the surrounding garrisons was also beaten back with heavy losses, and no prisoners taken. Grandferré, mortally ill though he was after this second engagement, was still able to fight off a party of English who tried to murder him in his own house. After this third great effort with his mighty axe, he expired, like Roland at the pass of Roncevaux. This has been a famous story ever since, especially after its resuscitation by Michelet in the middle of the nineteenth century, and Grandferré's triumph over the English men-at-arms is today commemorated by a fine nineteenth-century bronze statue in the market-place of Longeuil. Roland Delachenal, in his magisterial history of the reign of Charles V, wondered whether Guillaume l'Aloue and Grandferré had their emulators in other parts of the kingdom and concludes that this was "infinitely probable . . . But these obscure heroes did not have, as did those of the Beauvaisis, a Jean de Venette, who, despite his wretched Latin – so living and so French – knew how to be the Homer of these poor people."[34] Without effective stone defences, and elaborate pre-planning, however, heroism would have availed nothing.

The fortified parish churches are still the most tangible reminders in the French countryside of the enduring quality of peasant communities in wartime. Not all of the surviving examples were constructed during the Hundred Years War although it is likely that the majority of them were.[35] Certainly, there were plenty of them. In a mere fifty, or so, square kilometres in the region south of the Fontainebleau forest, the inspectors of fortresses counted no less than twenty-eight fortified churches in 1357.[36] They outnumbered all the castles, towers, fortresses and fortified houses of the area put together. Of these, many would certainly have been

---

[33] Venette, *Chronicle*, p. 90.
[34] Delachenal, *Charles V*, ii, pp. 139–40. The peasants of Cergy also held out against many enemies from their island fortress in the river, under their captain Thevenin Manessier, and even launched small offensives from it. Fournier, *Château*, p. 356.
[35] Fournier, *Château*, p. 205. R. Crozet, "Les Eglises Fortifiées du Poitou, de l'Angoumois, de l'Aunis et de la Saintonge: Conclusion d'une Enquête", *Bulletin de la Société des Antiquaires de l'Ouest*, 4th series, i (1951), p. 815.
[36] Contamine, *Guerre, Etat*, p. 9. See map, p. xi.

the joint enterprises of the local lord and his subjects. Some would have been created by self-appointed captains in the teeth of local opposition. Nevertheless, it is clear that the metamorphosis of many a small parish church into a fortified refuge with a ground-level chapel and with chambers in the tower and above the vault was the product of a combination of circumstances of which the general insecurity of life in the countryside during the Hundred Years War and an active village organization were the vital elements. "The peasants in open villages", wrote Jean de Venette, "with no fortifications of their own made fortresses of their churches by surrounding them with good ditches, protecting the towers and belfries with planks as one does castles, and stocking them with stones and crossbows."[37] They slept in these strongholds at night and worked in the fields around them by day, always within earshot of the warning bells.

From the point of view of the parishioners, their own church was a logical, if occasionally disastrous, choice as a place of refuge. Even in its unfortified state the church and its adjacent cemetery was a privileged enclave in custom and in law. Canon law afforded asylum to any person who sought it within the church, and Pope Nicholas II as early as 1059 had fixed an inviolable territory of thirty paces in radius around every church.[38] It is true that neither the fear of divine, nor that of ecclesiastical, retribution appears to have acted as much of a restraint on a medieval army hungry for profits and victuals. The melancholy fates of Orly and Châtres in the Easter week of 1360 demonstrated this all too clearly. The disciplinary ordinances of kings which imposed secular penalties on those guilty of tarnishing a just war with sacrilege rarely extended an immunity beyond the clergy and the church's possessions,[39] and the efforts of military commanders who cared about such matters, such as Henry V, were usually directed only against soldiers who robbed churches. It is possible that such prohibitions extended to the possessions of peasants within the churches and to their cattle in the churchyard, as seems to have been intended by the "Constitutions to be Made in the Army of our Lord the King" of King John of England, in 1214.[40] But who would have placed their faith in such a security? French history, at least from the middle of the eleventh century when 110 persons sheltering in the church of Saint Bris (Yonne) were massacred, to the middle of the seventeenth when two hundred persons in the church of Dampierre-sur-Vingeanne were killed and burnt "along with their coffers, furniture and grains", is full of stories of military assaults on churches.[41] Perhaps the stories of divine retribution which were retailed by clerical chroniclers had some restraining effect. Froissart's chronicle, which circulated widely amongst knights, recounts how an English squire, fresh from stealing the chalice at the

[37] Venette, *Chronicle*, p. 85.

[38] Fournier, *Château*, p. 202.

[39] Articles 2 and 3 of Richard II's Durham ordinances (1385) and of Henry V's Mantes ordinances (1419), *Black Book*, ed. Twiss, pp. 453 and 459–60 respectively. The latter did, however, include a protection for working peasants within the king's obedience (p. 469).

[40] Meron, *Henry's Wars*, p. 143.

[41] A. Colombet, "Les Eglises Fortifiées de la Bourgogne: à Propos d'une Etude Récente", *Annales de Bourgogne*, xxxi (Oct–Dec 1959), pp. 253–54.

moment of consecration, had witnessed his horses madly strangling themselves in their own reins and vowed never again to rob or violate a church. "I do not know" added the chronicler cautiously, "whether he kept this promise."[42]

The peasants had to look to more concrete defences than canonical prohibitions.[43] The knight in the fourteenth-century *Le Songe du Vergier* spoke for many of his kind when he rejected as irrelevant to his secular lifestyle the decretals of the pope.[44] The parish church was often the only stone building in the village, and its high bell tower was an excellent look-out point and potentially a formidable passive redoubt. The church's central location within the working area of the community often made it more convenient as a refuge than the more distant castle or walled town. Furthermore, the local church was a possession of the community, and a symbol of the community's existence, in a way which the seigneurial castle never was, and parishioners were undoubtedly more willing to contribute towards the maintenance and the guarding of their own church-fortress than they were to the *corvées* and sentry-duties (or their monetary substitutes) on the lord's residence. This was just as well, because the conversion of a country church into a small fortress represented a massive financial investment for the community. Even the crudest of such fortifications which involved little more than the construction of a defensible entrance to the tower and the raising of the church walls in order to accommodate chambers in the area between the nave vault and the roof entailed unusually heavy expenditure. But few parishes were satisfied, or, for that matter, were permitted by royal inspectors of fortresses to be satisfied, with such elementary modifications.

In the rich, vine-growing lands to the east of Auxerre in northern Burgundy lies the substantial village of Chitry.[45] Its parish church, the church of Saint Valerian, was built in the thirteenth century, but massively fortified during the second half of the fourteenth. Many of these fourteenth-century works remain intact, including the handsomely restored eastern tower topped by a timber-framed corbelled upper chamber, although the moat and curtain wall which once encircled the cemetery have now disappeared.[46] The village, when this fortification was under construction, was large and quite prosperous, containing at least sixty-four adult males, and assessed for taxation purposes at thirty-nine hearths. Although permission to fortify the church was not granted by the royal captain-general in the diocese of Auxerre until August 1364, the idea may have painfully been implanted by an English freebooter whose company had already occupied the village, perhaps even from a base in the church itself. The justification which was

---

42 Froissart, *Chroniques,* ed. Luce, v, p. 176.

43 N. Wright, "French Peasants in the Hundred Years War", *History Today,* xxxiii (June 1983), pp. 38–42.

44 *Songe du Vergier,* p. 22.

45 N. Wright, "The Fortified Church at Chitry", *Fort,* xix (1991), pp. 5–10. This article is based largely on the file E 548 in the AD de l'Yonne, Auxerre, as is much of the information on Chitry which follows.

46 P. Barbier, *Auxerre et les Auxerrois: Pays d'Art et d'Histoire* (Paris, 1936), pp. 218–19.

advanced at this time for the building of a village fortress was the general one of having been reduced to "wretched poverty" by the "wars of the king of England and of the enemies who daily come and go through the aforesaid village, pillaging, robbing, injuring and laying waste". We are able to be more precise. The parish had, in the eight years previous to the petition, been paying protection money to the English captain of the "fortress" of Chitry, as well as "money, wine, victuals and other things" to William Starkey, the English captain of Ligny-le-Châtel. It had also been the victim of plundering raids by nearby French garrisons, including that of Auxerre itself. The force of the argument in favour of a community fortress impressed itself so effectively upon the count of Auxerre, who was the royal lieutenant of the area, that he ordered Guillaime d'Orgelot, captain of Auxerre, to take charge of the construction works and to make the necessary arrangements for watch-keeping. Although the conversion work was carried out under the watchful eyes of the military experts from Auxerre and from Sens, and under the suspicious eyes of the local lords (who had every reason to fear for their rights), the parishioners themselves bore the entire expense. Local assemblies periodically apportioned the building levies of up to several hundred *livres tournois* and disbursed them in stages to the builders and the military captains. Indeed, it was these assemblies, directed by Chitry's "greater and wiser part" and summoned by the bells of Saint Valerian, which eventually aroused the opposition of the local lady of the manor and of the royal bailiff of Sens who had to be hurriedly bought off with concessions and fines.

Within five years of the original order to proceed, the inhabitants of Chitry had a church-fortress which was capable of offering a successful resistance to "men of the Companies". Within nine years they had dared (though not with impunity) to challenge a royal sergeant whose attempts to deliver a summons were thwarted by a large stone, hurled from the new parapet: a stone which "would have hit the sergeant had he not been on his guard". Within seventeen years they had overcome challenges by the Crown and by the joint lords of Chitry to appoint the squire-captains of the new fortress and had secured the right of nomination for themselves. The church of Saint Valerian at Chitry stands today not as a monument to the weakness of peasant communities in wartime, but to the strength of some of them. If there was a "mad hurricane of massacre" sweeping from one end of the century to another, the peasants who worked the vines around Chitry were not going to be blown away by it. The confident footseps of this little community can be followed into the next decade as they paid their captains, demanded and received confirmation of their charters from a new joint-lord of Chitry, and put up finance towards the building of a windmill at Le Cry by the other one. Their story is an admirable illustration of the point which Gabriel Fournier made that "the undertaking of their own defence by the inhabitants helped to reinforce the village communities not only at the military level, but equally on the judicial level"[47] as they defended their new fortress not only

---

[47] Fournier, *Château*, p. 250.

against the English, but also at the court of the royal bailiff of Sens and even at the king's court in Paris. As a collectivity, they ceased to be clod-hopping peasants and became something like lords, closing their gates to royal sergeants, giving orders and wages to squires, and dealing with their own lords almost on terms of equality. Before long they may have been constraining reluctant neighbouring villages to contribute to the costs of the fort at Chitry, as were the villagers of Gonesse (Seine-et-Oise) through the *parlement* of Paris, in 1365,[48] or stocking their moat with fish which had hitherto been a seigneurial monopoly.[49]

If the fortification of parish churches was a popular form of self-help among the country communities, it was certainly less popular amongst those who claimed some authority over the villages and their churches. Church authorities, whilst vigorously championing the right to asylum on an occasional basis, were reluctant to countenance the more permanent unbalancing of the sacred and secular functions of parish churches effected by the construction of cemetery enclosures for the accommodation of livestock and of semi-permanent residences within the church itself. Not only would the resident families and livestock have disrupted the church services, but the presence of armed men inside the churches encouraged attacks by soldiers. The bishops of Rodez in the thirteenth century had turned this concern to some advantage by levying a special tax on all peasants in the diocese who used a church as a refuge, but this action did little to inhibit the development. Indeed, the fourteenth- and fifteenth-century bishops of Rodez made an important contribution, as lords of Sainte-Radegonde and Inières, to the construction of two of the finest surviving examples of the medieval fortified parish church: ones upon which the encrustation of towers and turrets, machicolation and parapets, has almost obliterated the church embedded beneath them.

Sainte-Radegonde is one of the most conspicuous of French medieval fortified parish churches, thanks largely to a twentieth-century restoration programme.[50] The enormous burden of expense fell upon a community rather larger than that of Chitry, of fifty-four hearths.[51] The new fortress had a total of about forty chambers which were built into the space between the vault and the roof, and into the impressive north and south towers.[52] There were five floors built above the nave vault, each with four chambers; four floors were above the choir, and six and four, respectively, in the two towers which had been built over the chapels of the north and south transepts. The topmost chamber in the north tower, and probably the most luxurious in the fortress, with its large fireplace, was reserved for the captain of the place. It was strategically sited, close to the watch-tower and to the bells. The prior, who served the church, had similar accommodation but closer, as was

---

[48] *Guerre de Cent Ans*, ed. Timbal, pp. 166–67.
[49] Fournier, *Château*, p. 203.
[50] J.-M. Cosson, *Sainte-Radegonde et Inières en Rouergue* (Rodez, 1991), p. 68. (I am grateful to Dr Simon Cotton for this source.)
[51] Ibid., p. 67. This was the assessment for the 1349 tax census.
[52] B. de Gauléjac, "Sainte-Radegonde", *Congrès Archéologique de France* (Paris, 1938), pp. 401–7.

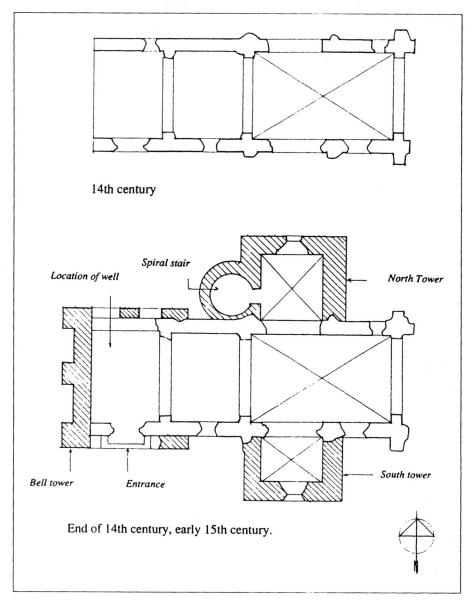

5. Plan of Sainte-Radegonde, a fortified parish church
(after J.-M. Cosson, *Sainte-Radegonde et Inières en Rouergue* (Rodez, 1991), p. 64)

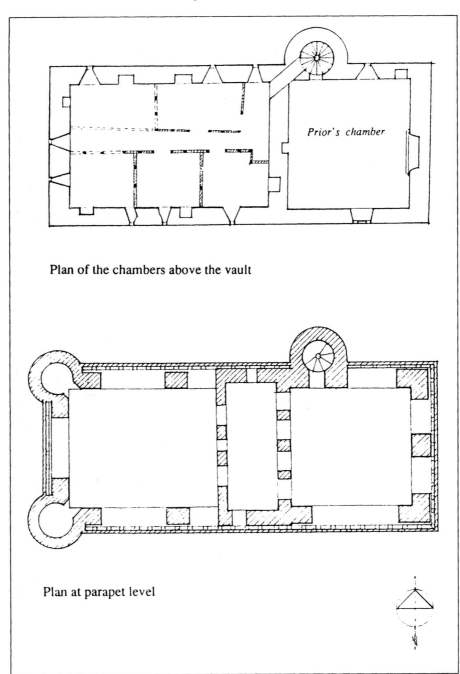

Plan of the chambers above the vault

Plan at parapet level

6. Plan of Inières, a fortified parish church
(after J.-M. Cosson, *Sainte-Radegonde et Inières en Rouergue* (Rodez, 1991), p. 82)

appropriate, to the level of the nave. The other chambers belonged to families of the parish and could be sold and bequeathed within the parish community. The market in rented chambers was as lively as ever in the mid-seventeenth century when Georges Rey, rector of Sainte-Radegonde, negotiated a perpetual lease on a chamber "situated in the fortress of the said place, above the tribune of the church and adjacent, on one side, to the chamber of Georges Burgière, peasant of the parish, and, on the other, to the choir-vault of the church".[53] There is a well in the nave which never dries. Access to the upper-level chambers was by way of a narrow spiral staircase whose entrance can still be seen, two metres above the nave floor. It would then have been accessible by means of a removable ladder. The top of the church, crowned with parapets and with towers, up to thirty metres from the ground, is, to all intents and purposes, that of a small castle. Inières, nearby, is only slightly less impressive. The transformation of this latter church was begun rather later than that of Sainte-Radegonde, in 1442, but a committee of parishioners, under the bishop's authority, was already selling rooms in the fortress by September 1455. Raymond Trogan at that time bought a chamber at the upper level for five gold *moutons* and an undertaking to contribute to watch-duties and defence-works.[54]

In other cases, where churchmen were not lords of the village, it would appear that the church authorities were engaged in a losing, and possibly half-hearted, battle between canonical theory, on the one hand, which insisted on their exclusive rights over church buildings, and, on the other, local necessity, which largely ignored these rights. The local *curé* was sometimes involved in the enterprise, as happened at Fayet (Puy-de-Dôme) in 1370.[55] Sometimes his rôle was entirely passive, as seems to have been the case at Chitry in the 1360s. Bishops occasionally took action to prevent the desecration of graves by men engaged in the digging of moats, as did the bishop of Clermont at Saint-Dier (Puy-de-Dôme) in 1379.[56] More often they turned a blind eye to a development which they could not control and for which they may have harboured a certain natural sympathy. Some of them, as we have seen with the bishops of Rodez, even encouraged it, at least in their own temporalities. The bishop of Clermont, for example, who had rushed to the defence of the bones in the Saint-Dier graveyard, was content to see some of his own property taken over by a partnership between the canons of the church of Saint-Pierre and the local inhabitants, "so that the people of our aforesaid village can retire there".[57]

The opposition of secular authorities towards community initiatives which might usurp their own rights of lordship was probably more robust, although they too were swept along in the torrent. The French Crown, often represented by its *procureur* in the local bailiwick, vigorously resisted anything which might be

---

[53]　R. Durand, *La Commune de Sainte-Radegonde* (Rodez, 1961), p. 102.
[54]　Ibid., p. 85.
[55]　Fournier, *Château*, p. 242.
[56]　Fournier, "Défense", p. 177.
[57]　Ibid., pp. 181–82.

construed as a challenge to its right to control the building of new fortresses in the kingdom. It is most unlikely, however, that any properly-constructed church-fortress was demolished for want of such authorization. Such oversights could be redeemed by the payment of fines. The suggestion has been made that the royal strategy of defence of the kingdom "in depth" actually encouraged the construction of community fortresses, and this has been identified as a policy in the north-eastern part of medieval France.[58] It is difficult, however, to imagine how the rather primitive fortified churches of the Barrois could have presented much of an obstacle to an invading army, and there is some evidence that armies, far from treating them as hazards, used them as convenient larders which had been obligingly stocked by the local people. The inhabitants of Fismes (Marne) may have put up a stout resistance for three consecutive weeks in their fortified church against an army of the Companies which they estimated to have been six thousand strong, and equipped with siege engines.[59] The infamous siege by the Marshal of Saint-Pol of the fortified church of Quincy-en-Brie (to look ahead to the year 1590) was brought to an end only after Saint-Pol had lost eighty men and the great fire in the nave had started to melt the bells in the tower.[60] These stories, however, are altogether exceptional. The French military experts who were advising the king of Castile, in 1386, held no illusions about the strategic value of these church-forts. They stated that, "when the English ride out, these little fortresses in churches and bell-towers will not hold out against them. Rather will they be nourished by what they find within them."[61] The ease with which the knights and squires and captains of companies overwhelmed these fortified churches and minsters inside which the Castilian peasants had withdrawn their "goods, furnishings, wines, grain, flour, meats and other things" in the plundering spree which followed showed scant respect for these "castles of the poor". The horrible slaughter of peasants in the fortified churches of the Ile-de-France, as Edward III approached Paris in 1360, also gives no suggestion of a defence in depth.

The Crown shared, although in a somewhat attenuated form, the profound anxiety of the local aristocracy in the face of the development of *de facto* communes throughout their lands: communal organizations within the villages which usurped rights of lordship and which might be directed towards open rebellion. Certainly, the local aristocracy was alarmed when the building of village fortresses threatened to divert manpower away from the maintenance and defence of its own castles in the area: castles whose walls had been repaired and whose battlements had once been patrolled by local men pressed into service. Many a rearguard action was fought through the courts by a lord determined to safeguard his *corvée* and *guet*. The inhabitants of Is-sur-Tille (Côtes-d'Or) had a long-standing dispute with the castellain of Saulx-le-Duc on this matter, which was

---

[58] C. Gaier, "La Fonction Stratégico-defensive du Plat Pays au Moyen Age dans la Région de la Meuse Moyenne", *Le Moyen Age*, lxix (1963), pp. 753–71.

[59] AN, JJ 104, no. 226.

[60] R. Rey, *Les Vieilles Eglises Fortifiées du Midi de la France* (Paris, 1925), pp. 52–53.

[61] Froissart, *Chroniques*, ed. Luce, xii, pp. 323–24.

only settled in 1421 when the villagers successfully demonstrated that they had an effective fortress of their own, with good walls, four or five towers, moats, two drawbridges and a curtain wall.[62] The lords often insisted upon the right of entry and visitation, a key, perhaps even on the right to nominate to the occupancy of one or two of the chambers and to be consulted over the appointments of captains, but this often appeared very much as a rearguard action.[63] The French aristocracy seems to have reserved its deepest suspicion for the frequent, and often unlicensed, assemblies of parishioners for the purpose of organizing their own defence and (no doubt) all sorts of rebellion. The "son de cloche", the sound of church bells for the purpose not of announcing the mass, but of assembling the people of the district to deal with an emergency, was the subject of strict control. Royal ordinances repeatedly banned the use of church bells even to summon aid from nearby villages against attack.[64] The church bell was undoubtedly feared as an instrument of rural insurrection, and when it rang from the keep of a community fortress it must have been doubly suspect.

If fortified churches represented nothing more to an enemy than valuable concentrations of moveable wealth and victuals, and to the public authority little more than nurseries of *jacquerie* which compromised an otherwise sound defensive strategy, it would be a matter of no small wonder that the people of the French countryside doggedly persisted with this form of self-defence from at least the eleventh century until well into the eighteenth. They persisted with it because they had few alternatives, but also in the knowledge that for every one disastrous encounter between a large company of soldiers and a pathetically vulnerable parish garrison, there would have been a hundred encounters between parishioners and very small companies of pillagers whose outcome might well be determined by the existence or absence of a community fortress.[65] That they were allowed to persist by the secular and ecclesiastical powers in the land when public and sectional interests seemed to be pointing in the opposite direction may be explained not least by the demoralization of traditional community leaders. Preachers and writers had not been slow to denounce the powerful for their failure to protect the weak, and they had presented the plight of the people of the open country so effectively in high places that narrowly selfish, or even sound strategic, considerations were sometimes swept aside before the dogged persistence of the peasant communities.

In the continuous and highly localized Hundred Years War which has been the

---

[62] Colombet, "Eglises Fortifiées", p. 258.

[63] Durand, *Sainte-Radegonde*, p. 85. Conditions laid down by the bishop of Rodez in 1442 for the permission to fortify the church at Inières.

[64] E.g. in the French royal ordinance of 28 December 1355: "lesquelles se porront assembler par cry ou autrement selon ce que bon leur semblera, sanz son de cloche, pour resister aus prenneurs". *Ordonnances*, iii, p. 29.

[65] Rogers, "By Fire and Sword", p. 10, shows that even the raiding parties, consisting of about thirty men, which operated out of much larger armies on campaign, had no time to organize the assault of fortified buildings while attempting to keep up with the main army which was moving along at about ten miles per day.

subject of this book, the main participants were not, primarily, the professional soldiers of the large armies which came and went. It was rather the war of small companies of pillagers operating out of local strongholds on behalf of their masters whose difficult and dangerous task it was to extract money and provisions from a peasantry which did not part with such things easily and which was not without its own defences. The centres of this war were the fortresses whose garrisons supported themselves from the nearby villages. They were ranged not only against other garrisons of a different allegiance, but also against the peasant strongholds. These strongholds consisted of the thousand virtually impregnable subterranean refuges, thirty or more metres beneath the ground. They were the secret, alternative, villages in the forest shadows which hid the peasant refugees and which were bases for ambushing parties. They were the walled villages and the fortified farmhouses whose walls were built and patrolled by peasant volunteers and whose captains were the servants of the community. More important than any of these community enterprises in self-help were the fortified parish churches whose smouldering ruins dotted the tracks of English and *routier* armies, but whose many survivals in the French countryside of today testify, at least in some part, to their successful rôle in the much more generalized and small-scale warfare of the open country.

Joan of Arc, the village girl of Domrémy, had plenty of experience of the baneful effects of war long before she was captured at Compiègne in May 1430 and became the prisoner of the English. Burgundian soldiers had raided and burnt her village in Champagne. When soldiers such as these approached her village, it had been her responsibility to herd livestock to a refuge on an island in the Meuse. She herself had been forced to flee into the town of Neufchâteau in order to escape from soldiers. It should not, however, be forgotten that she was captured as a soldier: a situation as far removed as was possible from that of the non-combatant peasant which Bouvet so often described "who has never borne arms and would not know how to put on a coat of mail, or fasten a greave or a helmet",[66] and her answers to her judges at the trial in Rouen were not, for the most part, those of a cowed or browbeaten victim. Joan's love of bells and the fact that her visions were often associated with the ringing of church bells have often been remarked. Marina Warner has observed that bells had much more than a religious function in this period and that they rallied the village communities in times of local emergency in a way which frightened both their enemies and their natural lords. "When a peasants' revolt in the Angoumois was crushed by the king, the bells were broken up and the bell-ringers castrated."[67] Joan's father was responsible for the local defences of Domrémy and for the organization of its watch. Thus, Joan had direct experience of that local solidarity in the face of the threat of armed outsiders which many historians have since described and in which the church bells played such an important part. Jehan le Jaqueminart of Thièblemont, also of the Champagne region, was one of these village leaders of an earlier generation who had been

---

[66] Bonet, *Tree*, p. 153.

elected to defend the interests of his parish and to use the bells as a tocsin.[68] He, together with several other elected leaders, had confronted a large group of men-at-arms under the lord of Saint-Dizier at the time of the *Jacquerie* and demanded to know their intentions. The nobles had replied with fair words (about wishing to live and die with the people of the district), but in their hearts they suspected Jaqueminart and his companions of rebellion. One can understand their suspicion. Joan's self-confidence when amongst soldiers is recognisably within this tradition of peasant assertiveness.

The idea that a peasant without a lord was like a sheep without a shepherd, easy prey to any passing predator, was popular with preachers but not much supported by the evidence. The arrival of soldiers in the localities did not, usually, result in a scattering of the community but a drawing together of that community around the political organization of the village which had served it so well in previous crises. These structures, the structures of self-governing communes in all but name, are elusive because they were so often disguised within the more widely acceptable religious associations of the village. The very large number of religious confraternities at this time, the confraternities "of the Holy Spirit", which maintained the day-to-day life of the parishes by repairing the church, mending the roads, administering low justice, clearing the wells, distributing charity and organizing the celebration of feasts, were often the fundamental, "grass-roots", building-blocks of late medieval French society.[69] It was through these associations that the "better and wiser" part of each village community exercised its authority. They operated independently of the local lords, and as a constant rival to their fitful authority: less open, perhaps, than that of the bands of brigands in the woods, but hardly less dangerous for their subtlety. It was a natural part of their functions to preserve against outsiders not only the physical body of the village, but also the soul of the community and its rights. In time of peace the outsider was represented, at this grass-roots level, by the seigneurial bailiff: the *prévot, maire, bayle*, or *juge*, who often had been raised by his association with the functions of lordship from a fairly low status in the local community to a position of uneasy power in the village.[70] In time of almost continuous military activity, or rumours of such, the outsider was represented by royal sergeants responsible for the collection of taxes and by the varlets and pillagers of men-at-arms. Like the seigneurial bailiffs, these latter were also, very often, men of low status in the communities, suddenly elevated by association with powerful outsiders, and whose arrogance was a constant affront to the dominant peasant families of the village. The Hundred Years War at this grass-roots level is altogether different from the one with which Jean Froissart has made us familiar, but a deal more

---

[67] M. Warner, *Joan of Arc: the Image of Female Heroism* (Harmondsworth, 1983), pp. 43–44.

[68] Luce, *Jacquerie*, pce. justif., 8.

[69] P. Duparc, "Confréries du Saint-Esprit et Communautés d'Habitants au Moyen Age", *Revue Historique de Droit Français et Etranger*, 4th series, xxxvi (1958), pp. 349–67 and 555–85.

[70] Bloch, *French Rural History*, pp. 191–93.

savage than his one. In the final analysis, Michelet was not entirely wrong when he declared that Froissart's war was dominated by rival military aristocracies which, by and large, understood each other well, liked each other, and fought according to mutually accepted rules. The war between combatants and non-combatants, on the other hand, was fought by people who, by and large, hated each other, with no rules, and over issues which mattered even more than honour. The issue here was survival: an art which peasants understood better than anyone else.

CONCLUSION

IT IS VERY TEMPTING to describe the Hundred Years War in the French country-side in terms of a tyranny which professional soldiers, especially English ones, exercised over a generally defenceless peasantry. The most powerful spokesman for this point of view, since the second half of the nineteenth century, has been Jules Michelet whose third volume of *The History of France* appeared in 1837 and has often been referred to in this present work. It should be clear by now that, although the tyrannies and attempted tyrannies of garrison soldiers were a major feature of this war, the tyrants were multi-national, and the peasants not without their own defences. To return, then, as we have constantly done, to the work of this substantially discredited historian may appear perverse unless we are prepared to admit his pioneering rôle in Hundred Years War studies and the truths which are so often concealed beneath the rhetoric, or contradicted by rival passions.

The high point of Michelet's personal fortunes was under the Orleanist monar-chy, for it was during this period that he was appointed director of the historical section of the French national archives and to the chair of ethics and history at the Collège de France. His lectures at this time were popular events as he drew upon his understanding of the history of his country to propagate a fiery mixture of democracy, republicanism, anti-clericalism and nationalism. His books and his oratory are all of a piece and it is difficult, in a purely literary medium such as this present work, to appreciate them fully without any sense of the physical presence of Michelet himself; also, perhaps, with less sympathy than his Parisian audiences for his emotional attachment to the fatherland. The nearest twentieth-century approach to his manner of presenting the events of the Hundred Years War may be found not in the recent scholarly studies of that war, but in the emotionally-charged pages of Frantz Fanon's *The Damned of the Earth*, which appeared in 1961 and which championed not the downtrodden peasants of late medieval France, but the downtrodden peasants of colonial Africa. By merely substituting Michelet's Hundred Years War peasants for Fanon's "natives" and "colonised peoples", and Michelet's English knights for Fanon's European colonists and settlers, the phrases by which they are described may be found to be surprisingly interchangeable.

It is not an uncommon thing in France to hear Michelet described as the country's greatest historian, and this not only by the writers of history text-books for schools, for whom he must have been something of a godsend, but also, with more or less reserve, by the luminaries of the so-called *Annales* school.[1] These historians often admire Michelet's largeness of vision – precisely the quality

[1]   Le Goff, *Autre Moyen Age*, p. 22.

which is least apparent to foreigners – and hail him as the father of the "new" history which seeks to capture the past at all levels, from material culture to "mentalities". His popular appeal in France may be attributed to his eye for picturesque detail which is combined with an over-arching vision of the development of French national identity through the centuries. All sorts of contradictions and inaccuracies are forgiven a man who so magnificently fills the ancient rôle of the national historian: one who identifies connections with the past which give meaning to the present and confidence in the nation's future. The non-French world has been less enthusiastic about Michelet, tending to ignore the messiah in favour of his disciples, Lucien Fèbvre, Fernand Braudel and Jacques Le Goff. The stern Dutchman, Pieter Geyl, was willing to acknowledge a certain grandeur – even greatness – in Michelet the man, but as historian, none at all.[2] English historians, who might have been prepared to lay aside their suspicion of political rhetoric, have not been encouraged to do so by Michelet's violent anglophobia: by his opinion, often expressed, that the English were proud, bloodthirsty, satanic and detestable and that the French were not only a great deal better, but – to make no bones about it – the best people in the world.

Not surprisingly, that great Anglo-French conflict of the late Middle Ages, the Hundred Years War, abundantly sustained Michelet's anglophobia. His most obvious impact on the historiography of this period has been his treatment of this troubled period as the birth-pangs of the French nation, and his focus upon the French peasantry as the embodiment and symbol of the young nation. There are two climaxes to his Hundred Years War. The first is the period between 1357 and 1359 when the Parisian burgesses took control of the government of France in the aftermath of the battle of Poitiers, and when the peasants rebelled in the *Jacquerie*. The second is the period between 1429 and 1431 when Joan of Arc revitalized the French war-effort by raising the siege of Orléans and by prompting the dauphin to his coronation at Reims. As Michelet expressed it, these were the crises in France's seventy-year labour. With the cruel English midwife in attendance, we can watch the birth in blood, sweat and tears. This distillation of more than one hundred years of war into a mere five, loaded with symbolic meaning, is very typical of Michelet's historical method. Because of it, it is possible to identify the fortunes of the infant France in the rough physiognomy of Michelet's suffering peasants. These are not just peasants in the mass but Jacques Bonhomme, the peasant rebel of 1358; Grandferré, the peasant turned warrior in 1359; and Joan of Arc, the peasant girl who reminded France of her destiny in 1429.

Two of these figures, which are at once catalysts and personifications of the young nation, were drawn largely from the documents in the French national archives where Michelet was director. Grandferré, the exception, was discovered in the pages of the chronicle of Jean de Venette. Jacques Bonhomme, the archetypal peasant rebel, came largely from that great series of chancery registers

---

2 P. Geyl, *Debates with Historians* (London, 1955), chapter 4.

classified "JJ" which contain the testimonies of many peasant petitioners reduced to bureaucratic formulae, but which, for Michelet, were authentic "voices" from the past: "murmurs which came to my ear".[3] The voice of Joan of Arc was available to him, *verbatim*, in the records of her trial which (along with those of her later rehabilitation) were being published by Jules Quicherat almost simultaneously with the relevant volumes of his own *History*.[4] There was here, for Michelet, evidence of a clear progression from the peasant rebel of 1358 whose attacks on his natural lord in the *Jacquerie* could not be accommodated in any anti-English scenario; to Grandferré in 1359, the peasant, "half-man, half-bull", who attacked the English of the Creil garrison but without ever, apparently, expressing a patriotic sentiment; and finally to Joan of Arc the peasant-child who clearly identified the English as the arch-enemy. It is true that a great deal of patience is required for those who wish to follow the development of the French nation as it is embodied in Michelet's peasants-in-arms for the intervening years of the Hundred Years War. The nation which was supposed to have been born in the republican constitution of Etienne Marcel, in the brief frenzy of the *Jacquerie* and in the crunch of Grandferré's axe, appears to have fallen asleep in the pages of Michelet's *History*, and his reader is left with some very mixed metaphors. The baby has returned to the womb, the baby is a huge bull-man, the baby is a lady, the lady is asleep, the lady has died of gangrene.[5]

We are left in no doubt, however, when Michelet picks up the thread again with Joan of Arc, in 1429. "Let us always remember, O Frenchmen, that the *patrie* was born with us in the heart of a woman, out of tenderness and tears, of the blood which she shed for us."[6] Michelet's attachment to Joan is very understandable. Her peasant status could be highlighted in contrast to the pseudo-chivalry of her mercenary and bloodthirsty captors, who, like the sinister earl of Warwick, professed chivalry but coolly sent this girl-child to the stake. If the English barons who bullied and harrassed the Inquisition (in Michelet's account) were not, themselves, the scholastic reasoners whom Michelet loved to denigrate by contrast to the primitive simplicity of the peasant,[7] they came from a country which was, or so he claimed, ruled by priests: by the cardinal of Winchester and by the bishops of Canterbury, York, London, Ely and Bath. Joan's peasant simplicity could, at any rate, be highlighted by opposition to the "rationalists", the "scholastics", the "implacable enemies of inspiration" who actually presided over her trial at Rouen and to whom she offered answers of pure and innocent simplicity. Joan, moreover, was a nationalist, ready to identify without hesitation the English as the evil empire. "You, king of England", she declared, "and you, duke of Bedford . . . will not hold the kingdom of France from God, the king of heaven. It

---

3 Le Goff, *Autre Moyen Age*, p. 20.
4 *Procès de Condamnation et Réhabilitation de Jeanne d'Arc*, ed. J. Quicherat, 5 vols. (Paris, 1841–49).
5 Michelet, *Histoire*, iii, pp. 334 and 5; 306.
6 Michelet, *Jeanne d'Arc*, p. 5.
7 J. Michelet, *The People*, trans. J. McKay (Chicago, 1973), p. 119.

is King Charles, the rightful heir, who will hold it."[8] The truth that Pierre Cauchon and all of the other judges were in fact French made little difference to Michelet who declared, as if to settle the matter, that the bishop of Beauvais spoke English "to show himself a good Englishman".[9]

Whether Michelet knew it or not, the Hundred Years War was for him a battleground between his liberal republican principles and his anglophobic nationalism. When he was true to his republicanism he allowed the fortunes of the French Crown and of its knightly armies to provide the colourful, occasionally poignant, back-drop to the principal action which was the emergence of a uniquely republican French national identity. The military disasters at Crécy, Poitiers and Agincourt were, as he described them, "sad events". Consolation was to be found by identifying their "true sense".[10] The French aristocracy which was decimated in these battles could never be considered truly French because, like the clergy, it was an international order, the order of chivalry, which forged closer ties with the enemy aristocracy than with the French people. The corpse-strewn battlefields of the Hundred Years War and the grim series of French defeats should have been viewed with a cool detachment, even exaltation. The decadence of chivalry was there all too clearly demonstrated, as was the dawn of the common man, of the "blind and savage people who knew neither French, nor English, nor chivalry". But Michelet, the anglophobe, was anything but cool about them.

Michelet's contradictions of interpretation and errors of fact are irritatingly legion. Nevertheless, the medieval third, fourth and fifth volumes of the *History of France* have had an enormous influence. His images of peasant France shaking off its shackles are now eternalized in stone and bronze. In the public square of the small town of Longueil-Sainte-Marie stands the statue dedicated by a *conseiller-général* of the 1870s to the peasant hero Grandferré. He towers, with double-headed axe poised to split the head of a prostrate English man-at-arms, on the scene of his triumphs of more than six hundred years ago. Siméon Luce, professor at the Ecole des Chartes and a true disciple of Michelet, asserted that Grandferré should occupy a place of honour in every history of France, "even the most elementary".[11] It is true that Joan of Arc, especially in the Bonapartist and Restoration period, had started to establish herself in the national pantheon well before Michelet took up the cudgels on her behalf,[12] but he certainly gave the process an enormous boost. His influence is manifested in the iconography of innumerable parish churches, especially in northern France, and in the street names of the thirteenth *arrondissement* in Paris. The origins of this cult may be traced back to the third quarter of the nineteenth century when Michelet was at the

---

8   Cited by M.-M. Martin, *The Making of France: the Origins and Development of the Idea of National Unity*, trans. B. and R. North (London, 1951), p. 119.
9   Michelet, *Jeanne d'Arc*, p. 74.
10 Michelet, *Histoire*, iii, p. 262.
11 S. Luce, "Notice sur Guillaume l'Aloue", *Annuaire Bulletin de la Société de l'Histoire de France* (1875), pp. 149–56.
12 C. Lightbody, *The Judgements of Joan: Joan of Arc, a Study in Cultural History* (London, 1961), pp. 154–63.

height of his influence, if not of his career, and when the Voltairean sneers of *The Maid of Orleans* were distinctly out of fashion. From the middle of the nineteenth century, too, the English occupation of Normandy under the Lancastrian kings, and the resistance to it by peasants, were being put to all sorts of contemporary uses by French scholars. As early as August 1849, Léon Puiseux delivered a lecture on the popular insurrections in Normandy during the English occupation in which the "aristocratic pretensions" of the English "usurper of the national soil" were set against a "democratic movement" of national resistance.[13] The distant thunder of Puiseux and Michelet may still be heard in the continuing debate about the brigands of fifteenth-century Normandy. Were they patriotic peasants of a medieval *maquis*, as many French historians infer, or were they simply members of a permanent class of petty criminals and outlaws, as the English described them at the time and are still, sternly, inclined to do?

Not only was Michelet's interpretation of the Hundred Years War influential in France but it also, despite all of the bombast, performed the valuable service of reminding historians of the vast peasant dimension to this war. His idea that this conflict had more of the features of a war between a multi-national aristocracy and a national peasantry than one between national aristocracies professing allegiances to different crowned heads, is a fruitful one. His occasional attempts to treat the English as the exclusively aristocratic party, ranged against a France which was essentially peasant, is really nothing more than a "red herring": a diversion which, as we have noted above, was attractive to Léon Puiseux. His insistence on a decadent late medieval aristocracy, hurrying to its own extinction, moreover, would not find much favour amongst modern historians of this period. "One has to wait a long time", wrote one contributor to a conference on late medieval and early-modern aristocracies, "before the conventional phrase 'very respected and very powerful lord' is no more than an empty formula."[14]

His theory of late medieval warfare as a nation-builder, however, although constantly undermined by overstatement, is by no means entirely discredited. The habit of peasants in many parts of France at that time of identifying any armed stranger who arrived unannounced in their village, and who spoke a "strange and horrible language" as "English" was undoubtedly a stimulus to the development of national consciousness, as was their touching, and often misplaced, faith in the French Crown's capacity to bring eventual justice and healing. The much more sober work of Jacques Krynen has claimed a clear evolutionary process during the Hundred Years War from a "feudal" to a "national" conflict, and one in which Joan of Arc played a key, if symbolic, rôle.[15] Not only did Michelet draw attention to the literary and documentary sources upon which a study of warfare in the

---

[13] Cited by Allmand, *Lancastrian Normandy*, pp. 306–7.

[14] *L'Etat et les Aristocraties*, ed. Contamine, p. 19. This was part of the paper delivered by Philippe Contamine, "L'Etat et les Aristocraties" (pp. 11–26), which argued that neither feudalism nor aristocratic power were spent forces by the late Middle Ages.

[15] J. Krynen, *Idéal du Prince et Pouvoir Royal en France à la Fin du Moyen Age, 1380–1440: Etude de la Littérature Politique du Temps* (Paris, 1981), pp. 258–77.

French countryside, such as this present one, must be heavily dependent, but he also captured some of the anger, fear and bitterness which brought them into being. "Mine is the first time", he boasted in 1869, and with some justification, "that history has had such a serious foundation."[16] The petitioners for royal pardons were desperate men, often forced by circumstance into the shedding of blood and then into the life of outlaws; usually with a powerful sense of injustice and with their necks dangerously close to the hangman's noose. Michelet's imagination penetrated the bland conventions of the chancery bureaucracies and exposed the frightened individual whose experiences they strove feebly to encapsulate. The rage of the author of the *Complaint on the Battle of Poitiers*, who believed that the cowardly and treacherous French aristocracy was plotting with its enemies to keep the war going for their own mutual advantage,[17] and of the mass of clerical commentators who longed for peace at this time and blamed the wickedly self-seeking nobles for frustrating its achievement, was absorbed by Michelet in a manner which has never been matched. We need not doubt that it was a rage which Michelet adopted because it sustained the feverish cocktail which made up his own passionate republicanism and powerful prejudices, while, at the same time, being able to recognize sentiments which were genuinely rooted in the realities, certainly in the perceptions of those realities, of late medieval France.

Nevertheless, as Roland Delachenal cautioned, in his great *History of Charles V*, historians have a duty to "keep their heads" when faced with Michelet's hyperbole.[18] In attempting to trace the origins of the French nation, and to rehabilitate the forgotten peasants in the process, Michelet concentrated too heavily on this one important, but only faintly detectable, factor of change within French society while ignoring those continuities which were at least as important and rather more obvious.

A long war, such as the Hundred Years War, which was played out almost entirely in the countryside within a society which was overwhelmingly a peasant one, will inevitably share many features with other wars conducted in similar circumstances. A long war of this sort, almost inevitably, will be fought by ill-paid or unpaid soldiers. If the soldiers are "friendly", in the sense that they are of the same nominal allegiance as their victims, their very existence interrupts the work of the ramshackle fiscal structures and prevents a fair distribution of the tax-yield. If they are "enemy" soldiers they must live off the country and their very purpose is to wreck, or intercept, its taxable resources. We need not cast doubt upon the high level of official corruption within the military leadership, which seems to have been widespread at this time, to realize that an unpaid and ill-disciplined soldiery is structurally inevitable in wars of this nature, an inherent quality of them. Before we despair of finding anything new under the sun, however, we must appreciate that soldiers do not operate entirely in a moral vacuum, entirely

---

16 Cited by Le Goff, *Autre Moyen Age*, pp. 19–20.
17 *Complainte*, ed. Beaurepaire, p. 260.
18 Delachenal, *Charles V*, i, p. 396.

cocooned from the values of their society by their professional codes. The circumstances of almost limitless local power open up infinite possibilities of murder and mayhem, but only the most unusually independent and unscrupulous of soldiers are not restrained in some way by the conventional morality of the wider society.

The ideal of knightly soldiers fighting for their lord and people can be traced back at least as far as the epic poems of the late eleventh and twelfth centuries.[19] The idea of a personal obligation to the weak and defenceless elements of their society was largely the product of the Church's efforts to Christianize the military profession during that period, when the knight was urged to take an oath that his sword "may be a defence of churches, widows, orphans" and of all those who were not entitled to bear arms.[20] Furthermore, in western Europe since the time when the military manuals of imperial Rome, of Vegetius, Frontinus and the rest became popular as manuals of "chivalry", there was also a strong attachment, at least within the military leadership, to the ideal of a tight military discipline.[21] During the Hundred Years War this tradition is represented by Jean Gerson's dictum "by discipline, I mean obedience to the prince and to the captain so that no-one may be permitted to follow his own pleasure and fleshly delight";[22] by Philippe de Mézières' advice to captains that they expose in a very public place the instruments of justice, the block and the sword, so that all may know that justice will be done to the "great, middling or small who break the law of chivalry and the command of the leader";[23] by the strict military codes recommended in the *Tree of Battles* of Honoré Bouvet and in the *Book of Chivalry* of Christine de Pisan which was modelled upon it. Few soldiers who find themselves in positions of strong, sometimes absolute, local power will not be corrupted by that power. But few will not also be reminded, often with irritating insistence, of their obligations to the common weal to act with justice and restraint. The knightly soldiers of the Hundred Years War were endlessly reminded of their obligations to society, usually, but not always, by priests. If they refused to recognize their professional obligations to society, then the Crown had the right to impose their recognition through a proper chain of command.

The connection between military discipline and the payment of wages was an obvious and important one. No-one was a fiercer champion of military discipline, in the fourteenth century, than the lawyer-monk Honoré Bouvet, and no-one laid greater stress on the importance of regular and sufficient wages.[24] A knight's loyalty to the Crown should, he argued, override all obligations to any other lord.

---

[19] R. Barber, *The Knight and Chivalry* (London, 1970; new edition, Woodbridge, 1996), chapter 3.

[20] R. Bonnaud-Delamare, "Fondement des Insitutions de Paix au XIe Siècle", *Mélanges Louis Halphen* (Paris, 1951), p. 23.

[21] N. Wright, "Honoré Bouvet, the Tree of Battles and the Literature of War in Fourteenth-Century France", unpubl. Ph.D. thesis (University of Edinburgh, 1972), pp. 153–63.

[22] Gerson, *Oeuvres*, vii, p. 1169.

[23] Mézières, *Songe*, i, pp. 511–17.

[24] Wright, "Tree of Battles", p. 18.

He must be loyal to his lord and obedient to him "who is acting in the place of his lord as governor of the host". Instead of engaging in spontaneous acts of individual prowess soldiers "should go nowhere at all" without the licence of the military commander, and amongst the numerous capital offences in the military catalogue were ranged "striking the provost of the army with intent to injure him", disobedience to the governor of the host, absence without leave in order to show great courage, causing riots and dissensions within the army, and desertion.[25] His insistence that soldiers who went to war for the sake of pillage were not entitled to wages and that those who were paid wages had no rights over booty and prisoners captured in the war held implications of the utmost significance to the military class, though little immediate relevance to the Hundred Years War.[26] It implied that any man engaged in the profession of arms, be he knight or commoner, was a paid servant of the state who "does all that he does as a deputy of the king or of the lord in whose pay he is".[27] A modern soldier in the French or British armies might recognise himself here, but not one who was brought up on a diet of Arthurian romance.

Regular pay for soldiers was thought to be the key: not, of course, to an end to the horrors of war, but to an end to the justifications which soldiers habitually used to excuse abuses of power within their own society. "Payment for soldiers has been wisely instituted in order that they do not turn themselves into brigands to recover their expenses."[28] This was written not in the fourteenth century, but eight hundred years earlier, in the sixth, by Saint Augustine of Hippo. His message was not wasted in the fourteenth, however, and Jean Gerson, in 1392, preached a sermon before Charles VI which made the point that taxes which were levied for the defence of the public weal were, in fact, wasted on luxuries and gifts.[29] If these subsidies, he continued, had been directed towards the war-effort then men-at-arms would have been content with their wages, and the "poor people" would not be obliged to flee with their meagre belongings when they heard of the approach of soldiers. A few years later, Christine de Pisan advised the "good captain who wishes to maintain and conduct his war justly before God and truly towards the world" to see that "his soldiers be so well paid that they need live off no pillage in the country of their friends".[30] That this was good and practical advice for soldiers, even though it came from the mouth of an academic theologian and from the pen of a foreign courtier, neither of whom had any direct experience of war, has no less a testimonial than the words of a member of Charles VII's military high command, Jean de Bueil. His Jouvencel received instruction to support himself, if possible, out of his own wages and from booty taken in enemy territory; but out of "contributions" from friendly territory if neither of these were

25 Bonet, *Tree*, 4:8–10 and 4:15–17.
26 Ibid., 4:34; 4:14 and 4:43.
27 Ibid., 4:14.
28 Cited by A. Vanderpol, *La Doctrine Scolastique du Droit de Guerre* (Paris, 1919), p. 296.
29 Gerson, *Oeuvres*, vii*, p. 440.
30 Pisan, *Livre de Paix*, p. 77.

forthcoming.[31] It is quite clear that, for the Jouvencel, as for the majority of professional soldiers of the Hundred Years War, sufficient and regular wages were not forthcoming and "friendly" contributions were very much the order of the day.

But if "chivalry" departed by the back door as soon as necessity rapped at the front, where was the honour in it? Such was the question which was posed with deadly insistence by the clerical commentators of the Hundred Years War, and it is still one of the most interesting questions which arises from a study of that period. It might be answered, correctly, but inadequately, by suggesting that the interpretation of chivalry which insisted upon a tripartite division of society, of clergy, warriors and peasants, all working in mutual harmony, was a clerical construction which had no part in the codes of honour which prevailed among knights and squires, and no part in real life. Theirs was a different kind of chivalry altogether, a law of arms, which regulated the dispersal of glory and profits exclusively within the knightly group. The rest of society was irrelevant to it. But we know that from the very beginning of the Hundred Years War (with Geoffroy Charny), to the very end of it (with Jean de Bueil), experts such as these in the customs and practices of men-at-arms were deeply concerned about the justice of wars and the moral justification for their own way of life. Charny was able to defend it by describing the way in which knights, like himself, hazarded their comfort and their very lives for the defence of the kingdom. He did not survive the battle of Poitiers and therefore, at one and the same time, demonstrated the truth of his assertion while escaping the widespread cynicism which greeted such claims in the years after 1356. Jean de Bueil, who grew up in this new world, was forced to go beyond the plea of risks and hardship to relate his experience as a soldier to that of a lord who exercised a "borrowed" lordship on behalf of the Crown. By doing so, he took the soldier's self-justification onto another level which more closely corresponded with actual experience and which tapped new sources of the noble tradition which even its most strident critics could easily recognize.

Michelet was too concerned with the drama of change, the emergence of a nation, the dying gasps of a decadent aristocracy, to perceive how, even in the direst of circumstances – perhaps especially in these – people tend to cling for security to the traditional structures. The traditions to which we must refer in the context of late medieval France are those of chivalry, in all of its multitude of meanings, and of village solidarity. In the ideal world in which much of the chivalric ideal is rooted, in the world of romance literature and clerical utopias, there need have been few points of conflict between the world of the warrior and the world of the peasant. The two groups worked in mutual harmony, the one protecting and supporting the other. In the real world they came into very serious conflict, and never more so than during this period of nearly continuous warfare when a massively swollen warrior caste could sustain its increasingly expensive

---

[31] See above, p. 40.

lifestyle neither from the ordinary revenues of lordship nor from the extraordinary revenues of national taxation converted into wages. In such circumstances, the traditions of lordship, the enjoyment of it, subjection to it, and resistance to it, became much more relevant to the daily lives of soldiers and peasants. Another familiar tradition was thus adapted to meet the new situation.

We must, in short, not be so dazzled by the novelties of the situation to recognize the more familiar rhythms of medieval society. The knights and squires who found themselves in occupation of castles and other strongholds within the French kingdom could, and did, fit themselves into some over-arching pattern of political conflict between the Crown of France and its enemies to which their own activities supposedly made a tiny contribution. Their Frenchness and Englishness undoubtedly had a meaning, although it was not always related to language or culture or to any of the other trappings of national identity with which the modern reader is familiar. They did, however, fit themselves much more securely into the traditions of territorial lordship which allowed them to control and profit from traffic on the nearby roads and waterways, to extract payments from the local people in goods, money and services in return for a protection from their enemies which may have been more or less illusory, and to live in a style which accentuated their differences from the common people. Their sergeants and bailiffs may have been disreputable local criminals who had been recruited and armed as pillagers and varlets; their pages, kidnapped youths from the villages; their manorial dues, *patis* extracted at knife-point. Their war-horses still may have borne the marks of the plough-traces on their flanks, and their cups the traces of the communion wine; but they were lords of land, and eager to exploit the joys which went with that status. There was, no doubt, more fighting to be done against the public enemy than in more orderly times, and the insecurities of life were more pronounced, but the familiar patterns of lordship were everywhere apparent.

The peasants who lived in the vicinity of these strongholds may have had only a passing familiarity with that form of warfare which Froissart understood so well: one which consisted of the clash of men-at-arms encased in their metal plates, identifiable by their banners and coats of arms. With lordship, however, they were very familiar. Indeed, the village communities had identified and defined themselves over generations not merely by the collective routines of husbandry, but also by the collective response to lordship. The charters of liberties which freed them from the worst excesses of arbitrary lordship and which were, as often as not, stored in a strong-box of the tower of the parish church, were the precious trophies of this long struggle. These privileges were not to be surrendered lightly, even to a garrison of soldiers which knew little about them, and cared less. So difficult was it at the time to distinguish peasant action against enemies of the kingdom from rebellion against all forms of lordship, between homicides committed in loyal service to the Crown and sedition against the entire social order, between the defence of customary rights and opposition to all proper authority, that an official distinction between them was rarely attempted. Peasant petitioners for pardons often insisted upon their attachment to the legitimate Crown. They may even have felt it. But this claim was largely irrelevant to their plea of provocation and self-defence, and it was too convenient to be taken very seriously. If we ourselves take it too seriously, as Michelet sometimes did, then we are in danger of substituting a weak and ill-developed motivation (that of patriotism, expressed as loyalty to the Crown) for a healthy and fully-developed one (that of village solidarity) and of moulding Jacques Bonhomme into a strange anachronism.

It has been pointed out that, in order to understand the effects of the crisis of the later Middle Ages, we must not forget that the population which suffered it had evolved in an environment which was both narrow and strictly codified, and in which disturbances were, in consequence, bitterly resented.[32] From the point of view of the French village communities, the entire Hundred Years War may be seen in terms of "l'éspace perturbé". The disturbers of the village "space" were the outsiders to it: above all the tax collectors and the soldiers, both of whom pleaded necessity of war to justify their disregard for traditional justice. There was often so little to distinguish between the tactics of a bullying royal or seigneurial official, collecting his fines, and those of a soldier collecting his *patis* and contributions, that they were often lumped together as "enemies" and "English" and resisted as aliens and intruders.[33] Although the chancery clerks may have required a motive of loyal service to the French Crown in order to grant a remission for a homicide, a reasonable assumption that the victim was indeed English, the actual spur to violence may often have been very different. This spur was very frequently an act of abusive lordship: the demand for a tax or a service which was not normally due. The association in the popular mind of the English with the exercise of abusive lordship in the latter years of their occupation of northern France spelled the doom of the Lancastrian land-settlement in France during the fifteenth century and perhaps explains some of the distrust which still lingers between these close European neighbours. Nevertheless, the quality of French lordship was equally in the dock as it was accused by the preaching clergy, from the beginning to the end of this war, of turning from sheep-dog into wolf.

The tyrannies of knights over peasants are all too evident in the French countryside of the Hundred Years War. This was an old tradition of warlordship revived to meet the new needs of late medieval war. But the warlords were not, as Michelet sometimes liked to portray them, all English. They belonged to the mass of men-at-arms who made a permanent living out of the war. These were either men who "borrowed" lordships by force of arms as conquerors or freebooters, or who "borrowed" them under commission from the Crown or from the actual landowners, incapable, themselves, of mounting an effective defence of their own property. They were tyrannies exercised or attempted over peasants, certainly, but not over defenceless ones. *Appatisation* was the result of a negotiation in which neither side held all the cards. The fact that most village communities in France survived this great war, battered but intact, suggests that the bonds which united

[32] Gauvard, *Grace Especial*, ii, p. 523.
[33] Ibid., ii, p. 557.

the village community under its "better and wiser part" were at least as strong as those bonds of "chivalry" which united their enemies, the men-at-arms.

Michelet, it would appear, was right to draw the attention of historians to the social conflict which was part and parcel of the Hundred Years War in the French countryside. He was right to insist that this war between soldiers and civilians was fought with at least as great an intensity as any of the great battles of that war, and in a much more continuous and ultimately decisive way. He was right to draw our attention to the voices of the peasant petitioners in the chancery registers and to attempt an understanding of them; also to take seriously the bitter complaints of the generality of non-combatants: those of the clergy, the lawyers, the merchants and the disillusioned old soldiers. His faults, as always, were in his willingness to distort, even fabricate, evidence in order to prove a point; in his inability to remain neutral and dispassionate in his account of the struggles between peasants and lords, between French and English; in his contradictions. Serious faults, indeed, but ones which the late medieval French non-combatant, at least, would have been eager to forgive.

BIBLIOGRAPHY

Manuscript Sources

Archives Nationales (Paris)

The JJ evidence is the product of a survey of *rémissions* issued during the 1370s (Chancery registers JJ 104–112), many of which refer back to events which took place in the first decades of the war. It is hoped that this northern French, and fourteenth century, bias has been balanced by reference to a wide variety of regional and local studies in printed sources. Of the petitions examined, 93% of the *rémissions* were heard within fifty kilometres of the centre of Paris, and 83% in Paris itself. Charles V was personally responsible for over 30% of the letters; his *Requêtes de l'Hôtel* and Council for another 30% each. 43% of the petitioners came from the bailiwicks of the original royal domain: the viscounty of Paris, Orléans, Senlis, Vermandois, Amiens, Sens, Tours, Bourges and Mâcon. The five Norman bailiwicks of Caux, Rouen, Caen, Cotentin and Gisors accounted for a further 17%. The records of the Paris *parlement* have also been used, and I am grateful to Maurice Keen for having directed my attention to them. They are:

X1a 4798
X2a 7
X2a 12
X2a 18

Archives Départementales

Pyrénées Atlantiques (Pau) E 49 La information feyte en la castelannie de Castet Gelos lo ix jorn del mes de Jener l'an mil ccc lxxxiiii (9 fos.)
AD (Yonne) E 548 (Chitry dossier)

Bibliothèque Nationale (Paris)

Fonds Français 1243 (Christine de Pisan, *Le Livre des Fais d'Armes et de Chevalerie*)
Fonds Français 1971 (Ramon Lull, *Le Livre de l'Ordre de Chevalerie*)
Nouvelles Acquisitions Françaises 4736 (Geoffroy Charny, *Demandes pour la jouste, le tournoy et la guerre*)

British Library (London)

Royal 20 c viii (Honoré Bouvet, *L'Arbre des Batailles*)

Bibliothèque Royale (Brussels)

MS 9079 (Honoré Bouvet, *L'Arbre des Batailles*)

Printed Sources

Allmand, C., *The Hundred Years War: England and France at War c.1300–c.1450* (Cambridge, 1988)

Allmand, C., *Lancastrian Normandy, 1415–1450: the History of a Medieval Occupation* (Oxford, 1983)

Allmand, C., ed., *Society at War: the Experience of England and France during the Hundred Years War* (Edinburgh, 1973)

Allmand, C., "The War and the Non-combatant", *The Hundred Years War*, ed. K. Fowler (Edinburgh, 1971), chapter 7

Allmand, C., ed., *War, Literature and Politics in the Late Middle Ages* (Liverpool, 1976)

"Annales Avignonaises de 1382 à 1410 extraites des Archives de Datini", ed. R. Brun, *Mémoires de l'Institut Historique de Provence*, xii (1935), pp. 17–142; xiii (1936), pp. 58–105; xiv (1937), pp. 5–57; xv (1938), pp. 21–52 and 154–92

Arcq, Douët d', L., ed., *Choix de Pièces Inédites Relatives au Règne de Charles VI*, 2 vols. (Paris, 1863–4)

Avesbury, Robertus de, *De Gestis Mirabilibus Regis Edwardi Tertii*, ed. E. Thompson (London, 1889)

Baratier, E., *La Démographie Provençale du XIIIe au XVIe Siècle* (Paris, 1961)

Barber, R., *The Knight and Chivalry* (London, 1970; rev. edn, Woodbridge, 1996)

Barbier, P., *Auxerre et les Auxerrois: Pays d'Art et d'Histoire* (Paris, 1936)

Barnie, J., *War in Medieval Society: Social Values and the Hundred Years War, 1337–99* (London, 1974)

Basin, Thomas, *Histoire de Charles VII*, ed. C. Samaran, 2 vols. (Paris, 1933–44)

Bates, D. and Curry, A., eds., *England and Normandy in the Middle Ages* (London, 1994)

Bellamy, J., *Crime and Public Order in England in the Later Middle Ages* (London, 1973)

Bentley, Gauthier de, "Mémoire Présenté à Edouard III par G. de B. sur les Affaires de Brétagne, 1352", *Oeuvres de Froissart*, ed. K. de Lettenhove, xviii, pp. 339–43

Bessen, D., "The Jacquerie: Class War or Co-opted Rebellion?", *Journal of Medieval History*, xi (1985), pp. 43–59.

Black Book of the Admiralty, ed. T. Twiss, 1 (London, 1871)

Blanchet, A., *Les Souterrains-refuges de la France: Contribution à l'Histoire de l'Habitation Humaine* (Paris, 1923)

Bloch, M., *Feudal Society*, trans. L. Manyon, 2 vols. (London, 1965)

Bloch, M., *French Rural History: an Essay on its Basic Characteristics*, trans. J. Sondheimer (Berkeley, 1966)

Bois, G., *Crise du Féodalisme* (Paris, 1981)

Bois, G., "Noblesse et Crise des Revenus Seigneuriaux en France au XIVe et XVe Siècles: Essai d'Interpretation", *La Noblesse au Moyen Age, XIe au XVe siècle*, ed. P. Contamine (Paris, 1976), pp. 219–33

Bonnaud-Delamare, R., "Fondements des Institutions de Paix au XIe Siècle", *Mélanges d'Histoire du Moyen Age dédiés à la Mémoire de Louis Halphen* (Paris, 1951), pp. 19–26

Bossuat, A., "Les Prisonniers de Guerre au XVe siècle: la Rançon de Guillaume, Seigneur de Chateauvillain", *Annales de Bourgogne*, xxiii (1951)

Boudet, M., *La Jacquerie des Tuchins, 1363–84* (Riom, 1895)

Bourgeois de Paris, *Journal d'un B. de P.*, ed. A. Tuetey (Paris, 1881)

Bourret, E., *Essai Historique et Critique sur les Sermons Français de Gerson* (Paris, 1858)

Boutruche, R., "The Devastation of Rural Areas During the Hundred Years War and the Agricultural Recovery of France", *The Recovery of France in the Fifteenth Century*, ed. P. Lewis, trans. G. Martin (London, 1971), pp. 23–59

Boutruche, R., *La Crise d'une Société: Seigneurs et Paysans du Bordelais Pendant la Guerre de Cent Ans* (Paris, 1947)

Bouvet, H., *L'Arbre des Batailles d'Honoré Bonet*, ed. E. Nys (Brussels, 1883)

Bouvet, H., *The Tree of Battles of Honoré Bonet*, trans. G. Coopland (Liverpool, 1949)

Bouvet, H., *L'Apparicion Maistre Jehan de Meun et le Somnium Super Materia Scismatis d'Honoré Bonet*, ed. I. Arnold (Strasbourg, 1926)

Bueil, Jean de, *Le Jouvencel par J. de B. Suivi du Commentaires de Guillaume Tringant*, ed. C. Favre and L. Lecestre, 2 vols. (Paris, 1887–89)

Calendar of the Patent Rolls, preserved in the Public Record Office, Edward III, 16 vols (1891–1916), vol. 14, pp. 392–454

Cazelles, R., "La Jacquerie: Fut-elle un Mouvement Paysan?", *Academie des Inscription et Belles Lettres, Comptes Rendus* (July–Oct 1978), pp. 654–66

Cazelles, R., "La Réglementation Royale de la Guerre Privée de Saint Louis à Charles V et la Précarité des Ordonnances", *Revue Historique de Droit Français et Etranger*, 4th series, xxxviii (1960), pp. 530–48

Cervantes Saavedra, M. de, *The Adventures of Don Quixote*, trans. J. Cohen (Harmondsworth, 1970)

Chandos Herald, *Life of the Black Prince by the Herald of Sir John Chandos*, ed. M. Pope and E. Lodge (Oxford, 1910)

Charny, Geoffroy, "Le Livre de Chevalerie", *Oeuvres de Froissart*, ed. K. de Lettenhove, 25 vols. (Brussels, 1867–77), i, pp. 462–533

Charny, Geoffroy, "Le Livre Messire G. de C", ed. A. Piaget, *Romania*, xxvi (1897), pp. 394–411.

Chartier, A., *Le Quadrilogue Invectif*, ed. E. Droz (Paris, 1950)

Chavarot, M.-C., "La Pratique des Lettres de Marque d'après les Arrêts du Parlement (XIIIe–début XVe Siècle)", *BEC*, cxlix (1991), pp. 51–89

Colombet, A., "Les Eglises Fortifiées de la Bourgogne: à Propos d'une Etude Récente", *Annales de Bourgogne*, xxxi (Oct–Dec, 1959), pp. 250–58

Combat de Trente Bretons contre Trente Anglais, ed. G. Crapelet (Paris, 1827)

"Complainte sur la Bataille de Poitiers", ed. C. de Beaurepaire, *BEC*, ii (1851), pp. 257–63

Contamine, P., ed., *L'Etat et les Aristocraties (France, Angleterre, Ecosse) XIIe–XVIIe Siècle: Actes de la Table Ronde, Maison Française d'Oxford, Sept. 1986* (Paris, 1989). Contamine's own paper, "L'Etat et les Aristocraties", is on pp. 11–26.

Contamine, P., "The French nobility and the war", *The Hundred Years War*, ed. K. Fowler (London, 1971)

Contamine, P., *Guerre, Etat et Société à la Fin du Moyen Age* (Paris, 1972).

Contamine, P., ed., *La Noblesse au Moyen Age, XIe au XVe Siècle* (Paris, 1976)

Contamine, P., "Rançons et butins dans la Normandie Anglaise, 1424–44", *Actes du 101e Congrès National des Sociétés Savantes, Lille, 1976, Philologie et Histoire* (Paris, 1978), pp. 241–70

Contamine, P., "La Théologie de la Guerre à la Fin du Moyen Age: la Guerre de Cent

Ans fut-elle une Guerre Juste?", *Jeanne d'Arc: une Epoque, un Rayonnement: Colloque d'Histoire Médiévale, Orléans, 1979* (Paris, 1982), pp. 9–21

Contamine, P., *La Vie Quotidienne Pendant la Guerre de Cent Ans: France et Angleterre (XIVe Siècle)* (Paris, 1976)

Contamine, P., *War in the Middle Ages*, trans. M. Jones (Oxford, 1984)

Cosson, J.-M., *Sainte-Radegonde et Inières en Rouergue* (Rodez, 1991)

Crozet, R., "Les Eglises Fortifiées du Poitou, de l'Angoumois, de l'Aunis et de la Saintonge: Conclusion d'une Enquête", *Bulletin de la Société des Antiquaires de l'Ouest*, 4th series, i (1951), pp. 813–20

Curry, A., and Hughes, M., eds., *Arms, Armies and Fortifications in the Hundred Years War* (Woodbridge, 1994)

Curry, A., "The First English Standing Army? Military Organization in Lancastrian Normandy, 1420–50", *Patronage, Pedigree and Power in Later Medieval England*, ed. C. Ross (Gloucester, 1979), pp. 193–214

Delachenal, R., *Histoire de Charles V*, 5 vols. (Paris, 1909–31)

Denifle, H., *La Désolation des Eglises, Monastères et Hopitaux en France Pendant la Guerre de Cent Ans*, 2 vols. (Macon, 1897)

Deschamps, Eustache, *Oeuvres Complètes*, ed. le Marquis de Queux de Saint-Hilaire and G. Raynaud, 9 vols. (Paris, 1878–1903)

Diez de Gámez, Gutierre, *The Unconquered Knight: a Chronicle of the Deeds of Don Pero Niño*, ed. J. Evans (London, 1928)

Duby, G., *Hommes et Structures du Moyen Age* (Paris, 1973)

Duparc, P., "Confréries du Saint-Esprit et Communautés d'Habitants au Moyen Age", *Revue Historique de Droit Français et Etranger*, 4th series, xxxvi (1958), pp. 349–67 and 555–85

Durand, R., *La Commune de Sainte-Radegonde* (Rodez, 1961)

Durrieu, P., *Documents Relatifs à la Chute de la Maison d'Armagnac-Fezensaguet et à la Mort du Comte de Pardiac* (Paris, 1883)

Durvin, P., "Les Origines de la Jacquerie à Saint-Leu-d'Esserent en 1358", *Actes du 101e Congrès National des Sociétés Savantes; Philologie et Histoire jusqu'à 1610* (Paris, 1978)

Flammermont, J., "La Jacquerie en Beauvaisis", *Revue Historique*, ix (1879)

Fournier, G., *Le Château dans la France Médiévale: Essai de Sociologie Monumentale* (Paris, 1978)

Fournier, G., "La Défense des Populations Rurales Pendant la Guerre de Cent Ans en Basse-Auvergne", *Actes du 90ème Congrès National des Sociétés Savantes; Section d'Archéologie* (Paris, 1966), pp. 157–99

Fourquin, G., *Histoire Economique de l'Occident Médiévale* (Paris, 1969)

Fowler, K., "Les Finances et la Discipline dans les Armées Anglaises en France au XIVe Siècle", *Cahiers Vernonnais*, iv (1964), pp. 55–84

Fowler, K., *The Age of Plantagenet and Valois: the Struggle for Supremacy, 1328–1498* (London, 1969)

Fowler, K., ed., *The Hundred Years War* (London, 1971)

Fowler, K., "Truces", *The Hundred Years War*, ed. K. Fowler (London, 1971)

François, M., "Note sur les Lettres de Rémission Transcrites dans les Registres du Trésor des Chartes", *BEC*, ciii (1942), pp. 317–24

Froissart, Jean, *Chroniques de J.F. Publiées pour la Société de l'Histoire de France par Siméon Luce [et al.]* (Paris, 1869–continuing)

Froissart, Jean, *Froissart, Chronicles*, ed. G. Brereton (Harmondsworth, 1968)

Froissart, Jean, *Oeuvres de J.F. Publiés avec les Variantes des Divers Manuscrits*, ed. K. de Lettenhove, 25 vols. (Brussels, 1870–77)

Froissart, Jean, *J.F., Voyage en Béarn*, ed. A. Diverres (Manchester, 1953)

Gaier, C., "La Fonction Stratégico-defensive du Plat-Pays au Moyen Age dans la Région de la Meuse Moyenne", *Le Moyen Age*, lxix (1963), pp. 753–71

Gallia Regia, ou Etat des Officiers Royaux des Bailliages et des Sénéchaussées de 1328 à 1515, ed. G. Dupont-Ferrier, 6 vols. (Paris, 1942–61)

Gaulejac, B. de, "Sainte-Radegonde", *Congrès Archéologique de France* (Paris, 1938), pp. 401–7

Gauvard, C., *De Grace Especial: Crime, Etat et Société en France à la Fin du Moyen Age*, 2 vols. (Paris, 1991)

Gerson, Jean, *J.G.: Oeuvres Complètes*, ed. Mgr. Glorieux, 10 vols. (Paris, 1960–73)

Geyl, P., *Debates with Historians* (London, 1955)

Gillingham, J. and Holt, J., eds., *War and Government in the Middle Ages: Essays in Honour of J.O. Prestwich* (Woodbridge, 1984)

Goff, J. Le, *Pour un Autre Moyen Age* (Paris, 1977)

Gray, Sir Thomas, *Scalacronica: The Reigns of Edward I, Edward II and Edward III as Recorded by Sir T.G.*, ed. H. Maxwell (Glasgow, 1907).

Grimmelshausen, J. Christoph, *Simplicissimus the Vagabond*, trans. A. Goodrick (London, 1912)

Guenée, B., *Tribunaux et Gens de Justice dans le Baillage de Senlis à la Fin du Moyen Age (vers 1380 – vers 1550)* (Paris, 1963)

Guerre de Cent Ans vue à travers les Registres de Parlement, ed. P. Timbal *et al.* (Paris, 1961)

Guigue, G., *Récits de la Guerre de Cent Ans: les Tards-Venus en Lyonnais, Forez et Beaujolais, 1356–69* (Lyon, 1886)

Gutmann, M., *War and Rural Life in the Early-Modern Low Countries* (Assen, 1980)

Hay, D., "The Division of the Spoils of War in Fourteenth-Century England", *Transactions of the Royal Historical Society*, 5th Series, iv (1954), pp. 91–109

Hewitt, H., *The Black Prince's Expedition of 1355–57* (Manchester, 1958)

Hewitt, H., *The Organization of War under Edward III* (Manchester, 1966)

Hilton, R., *The English Peasantry in the Later Middle Ages: the Ford Lectures for 1973 and Related Studies* (Oxford, 1975)

Hilton, R., *Bond Men Made Free: Medieval Peasant Movements and the English Rising of 1381* (London, 1973)

Hilton, R., "Y eut-il une Crise Générale de la Féodalité?", *Annales: Economies, Sociétés, Civilisations*, 6th Year (Jan.–March 1951), pp. 23–30

Hobsbawm, E., "Social Banditry", *Rural Protest: Peasant Movements and Social Change*, ed. H. Landsberger (London, 1974)

Hugo, V., *Quatrevingt-treize* (Paris, 1880)

Jones, M., ed., *Gentry and Lesser Nobility in Late Medieval Europe* (Gloucester, 1986)

Jones, M., "War and Fourteenth-Century France", *Arms, Armies and Fortifications in the Hundred Years War*, ed. A. Curry and M. Hughes (Woodbridge, 1994), pp. 103–20

Jorga, N., *Philippe de Mézières, 1327–1405, et la Croisade au XIVe Siècle* (Paris, 1896)

Jouet, R., *La Résistance à l'Occupation Anglaise en Basse-Normandie, 1418–50* (Caen, 1969)

Kaeuper, R., *War, Justice and Public Order: England and France in the Later Middle Ages* (Oxford, 1988)

Keegan, J., *The Face of Battle* (Harmondsworth, 1978)

Keen, M., *The Laws of War in the Late Middle Ages* (London, 1965)

Keen, M., *Chivalry* (New Haven, 1984)

Krynen, J., *Idéal du Prince et Pouvoir Royal en France à la Fin du Moyen Age, 1380–1440: Etude de la Littérature Politique du Temps* (Paris, 1981)

Labarge, M., *Henry V: the Cautious Conqueror* (London, 1975)

Ladurie, E. Le Roy, *The French Peasantry 1450–1660*, trans. A. Sheridan (Aldershot, 1987)

Ladurie, E. Le Roy, *Montaillou: Cathars and Catholics in a French Village, 1294–1324*, trans. B. Bray (Harmondsworth, 1978)

Lafavrie, J., *Les Monnaies des Rois de France* (Paris, 1951)

Lalande, D., *Jean II le Meingre dit Boucicaut 1366–1421: Etude d'une Biographie Héroïque* (Geneva, 1988)

Landsberger, H., ed., *Rural Protest: Peasant Movements and Social Change* (London, 1974)

Leach, E., Mukherjee, S., Ward, J., eds., *Feudalism: Comparative Studies* (Sydney, 1985)

Lefranc, A., *Olivier de Clisson, Connétable de France* (Paris, 1898)

Leguai, A., "Les Révoltes Rurales dans la Royaume de France du Milieu du XIVe Siècle à la Fin du XVe", *Le Moyen Age*, lxxxviii (1982), pp. 49–76

Lewis, P., "War Propaganda and Historiography in Fifteenth-Century France and England", *Transactions of the Royal Historical Society*, xv (1965), pp. 1–21

Lewis, P., *Later Medieval France: the Polity* (London, 1968)

Lightbody, C., *The Judgements of Joan: Joan of Arc, a Study in Cultural History* (London, 1961)

Livre du Bon Messire Jean le Maingre dit Boucicaut, Mareschal de France et Gouverneur de Genes, ed. C. Petitot (Paris, 1819)

Livre de Vie: les Seigneurs et les Capitaines de Périgord Blanc au XIVe Siècle, ed. E. Labroue (Bordeaux, 1891)

Luce, S., *La France Pendant la Guerre de Cent Ans: Episodes Historiques et Vie Privée au XIVe et XVe Siècles* (Paris, 1890)

Luce, S., *Histoire de la Jacquerie d'après des Documents Inédits* (Paris, 1859)

Luce, S., *Histoire de Bertrand du Guesclin et de son Epoque: la Jeunesse de Bertrand, 1320–64* (Paris, 1876)

Luce, S., "Notice sur Guillaume l'Aloue", *Annuaire Bulletin de la Société de l'Histoire de France* (1875), pp. 149–56

Madeiros, M.-Th. de, *Jacques et Chroniquers: une Etude Comparée de Recits Contemporains Relatant la Jacquerie de 1358* (Paris, 1879)

Mandements et Actes Divers de Charles V, 1364–80, ed. L. Delisle (Paris, 1874)

Martin, H., "Enguerrand d'Eudin, Capitaine Royale de Loches, Sénéchal de Beaucaire, Gouverneur de Dauphiné, 13..–1391", *Bulletin Trimestriel de la Société Archéologique de Touraine*, xxxii (1958), pp. 131–59

Martin, M.-M., *The Making of France: the Origins and Development of the Idea of National Unity*, trans. B. and R. North (London, 1951)

Mas Latrie, A. de., "Du Droit de marque au Droit de Répresailles au Moyen Age", *BEC*, 6th Series, ii (1866)

Massey, R., "Lancastrian Rouen: Military Service and Property-holding, 1419–49",

England and Normandy in the Middle Ages, ed. D. Bates and A. Curry (London, 1994), pp. 269–86

Mémain, R., "Les Misères de la Guerre en Bas-Poitou (XIVe–XVe Siècles)", *Société des Antiquaires de l'Ouest*, 3rd series, xii (1941), pp. 651–76

Meron, T., *Henry's Wars and Shakespeare's Laws: Perspectives on the Law of War in the Later Middle Ages* (Oxford, 1993)

Mézières, Philippe de, *Le Songe du Vieil Pelerin*, ed. G. Coopland, 2 vols. (Cambridge, 1969)

Michelet, J., *L'Histoire de France*, iii (Paris, 1837)

Michelet, J., *Jeanne d'Arc by J.M.*, ed. J. Sacret (Oxford, 1909)

Michelet, J., *The People*, trans. J. McKay (Chicago, 1973)

Mollat, M., *La Guerre de Cent Ans Vue par Ceux qui l'ont Vécue* (Paris, 1992)

Monicat, J., *Les Grandes Compagnies en Vélay, 1358–92* (Paris, 1928)

Ordonnances des Rois de France de la Troisième Race, various eds., 21 vols. (Paris, 1723–1849)

Orville, Jean Cabaret d', *La Chronique du Bon Duc Loys de Bourbon*, ed. A. Chazaud (Paris, 1876)

Ouy, G., "Le College de Navarre, Berceau de l'Humanisme Français", *Actes du 95e Congrès National des Sociétés Savantes: Philologie et Histoire jusqu'à 1610*, i (Reims, 1970), pp. 275–99.

Ouy, G., "Honoré Bouvet (appelé à tort Bonet), Prieur de Selonnet", *Romania*, lxxx (1959), pp. 255–59

Owst, G., *Literature and Pulpit in Medieval England* (Cambridge, 1933)

Perroy, E., *The Hundred Years War* (London, 1965)

Petit, E., *Les Ducs de Bourgogne de la Maison de Valois: Philippe le Hardi, 1363–80* (Dijon, 1909)

Petrarch, F., *Letters from Petrarch*, ed. M. Bishop (London, 1966)

Piaget A. and Droz, E., *Pierre de Nesson et ses Oeuvres* (Paris, 1925)

Pisan, Christine de, *The Epistre of Othea to Hector, or the Boke of Knyghthode, Translated from the French of C. de P. by Stephen Scrope, Esquire*, ed. G. Warner (London, 1904)

Pisan, Christine de, *Le Livre des Fais et Bonnes Meurs du Sage Roy Charles V*, ed. S. Solente, 2 vols. (Paris, 1936–40)

Pisan, Christine de, *The "Livre de la Paix" of C. de P.*, ed. C. Willard (The Hague, 1958).

Pisan, Christine de, *The Book of Fayttes of Armes and of Chyvalrye*, ed. A. Byles, trans. W. Caxton (Oxford, 1932)

Portal, C., "Les Insurrections de Tuchins dans le Pays de Langue d'Oc, vers 1382–84", *Annales du Midi*, xvi (1892), pp. 433–74

Procès de Condamnation et Réhabilitation de Jeanne d'Arc, ed. J. Quicherat, 5 vols. (Paris, 1941–49)

Procès de Gilles de Rais, ed. G. Bataille (Paris, 1965)

Quicherat, J., "Récit des Tribulations d'un Religieux du Diocèse de Sens Pendant l'Invasion Anglaise de 1358", *BEC*, xviii (1857) pp. 357–60

Registre Criminel du Châtelet de Paris du 6 Septembre 1389 au 18 Mai 1392, ed. H. Duplès-Agier, 2 vols. (Paris 1861–64)

"Relation de la Visite des Forteresses du Bailliage de Caen", ed. A. de Caumont, *Société des Antiquaires de Normandie, Mémoires*, 2nd. series, i (1840), pp. 185–204

Rey, R., *Les Vieilles Eglises Fortifiées du Midi de la France* (Paris, 1925)

Rogers, C., "By Fire and Sword: *Bellum Hostile* and 'Civilians' in the Hundred Years War", unpublished paper presented at "Civilians in the Path of War Conference", Ohio State University, 5–6 November 1993

Ross, C., ed., *Patronage, Pedigree and Power in Later Medieval England* (Gloucester, 1979)

Rowe, B., "John Duke of Bedford and the Norman 'brigands' ", *English Historical Review*, xlvii (1932), pp. 583–600

Rowe, B., "Discipline in the Norman Garrisons under Bedford, 1422–35", *English Historical Review*, xlvi (1931), pp. 194–208

Russell, F., *The Just War in the Middle Ages* (Cambridge, 1975)

Salch, C.-L., *Dictionnaire des Châteaux et des Fortifications du Moyen Age en France* (Strasbourg, 1979)

Songe du Vergier, ed. M. Schnerb-Lièvre (Paris, 1982)

Spencer, H. Leith, *English Preaching in the Late Middle Ages* (Oxford, 1993)

Sumption, J., *The Hundred Years War*, 1, *Trial by Battle* (London, 1990)

Tessier, G., *Diplomatique Royale Française* (Paris, 1962)

Thomas, A., "Une Oeuvre Patriotique Inconnue d'Alain Chartier", *Journal des Savants* (Sept.–Nov.1914), pp. 442–49

Tuchman, B., *A Distant Mirror: the Calamitous Fourteenth Century* (Harmondsworth, 1979)

Ullmann, W., *The Medieval Idea of Law as Represented by Lucas da Penna* (London, 1946)

Upton, Nicholas, *The Essential Portions on N. U.'s "De Studio Militari"*, trans. J. Blount, ed. F. Barnard (Oxford, 1931)

Ursins, Jean Juvenal des, *Les Ecrits Politiques de J.J. des U*, ed. P. Lewis, 3 vols. (Paris, 1978–92)

Vale, M., "The Gascon Nobility and the Anglo-French War 1294–98", *War and Government in the Middle Ages: Essays in Honour of J.O. Prestwich*, ed. J. Gillingham and J. Holt (Woodbridge, 1984), pp. 134–46

Vale, M., "Seigneurial Fortification and Private War in Later Medieval Gascony", *Gentry and Lesser Nobility in Late Medieval Europe*, ed. M. Jones (Gloucester, 1986), pp. 133–57

Vale, M., *War and Chivalry: Warfare and Aristocratic Culture in England, France and Burgundy at the End of the Middle Ages* (London, 1981)

Vanderpol, A., *La Doctrine Scolastique du Droit de Guerre* (Paris, 1919)

Venette, Jean de, *The Chronicle of J. de V.*, trans. J. Birdsall, ed. R. Newhall (New York, 1953)

Verrier, M., "Le Duché de Bourgogne et les Compagnies dans la Second Moitié du XIVe Siècle", *Académie des Sciences, Arts et Belles Lettres: Mémoires*, 4th series, viii (1901–2), pp. 219–320

Warner, M., *Joan of Arc: the Image of Female Heroism* (Harmondsworth, 1983)

Whiting, B., "The Vows of the Heron", *Speculum*, xx (1945), pp. 261–78

Wood, M., *The Spirit of Protest in Old French Literature* (New York, 1966)

Wright, N., "Feudalism and the Hundred Years War", *Feudalism: Comparative Studies* (Sydney, 1985), pp. 105–23.

Wright, N., "The Fortified Church at Chitry", *Fort*, xix (1991), pp. 5–10

Wright, N., "French Peasants in the Hundred Years War", *History Today*, xxxiii (June, 1983), pp. 38–42

Wright, N., "Honoré Bouvet and the Abbey of Ile-Barbe", *Recherches de Théologie Ancienne et Médiévale*, xxxix (1972), pp. 113–26

Wright, N., "Honoré Bouvet, the Tree of Battles and the Literature of War in Fourteenth-Century France", unpublished Ph.D. thesis, University of Edinburgh (1972)

Wright, N., " 'Pillagers' and 'Brigands' in the Hundred Years War", *Journal of Medieval History*, ix (1983), pp. 15–24

Wright, N., "The Tree of Battles and the Laws of War", *War, Literature and Politics in the Late Middle Ages*, ed. C. Allmand (Liverpool, 1976), pp. 12–31

Zola, E., *The Earth*, trans. D. Parmée (Harmondsworth, 1980)

INDEX

The numbers shown in bold typeface indicate illustrations.

CPSIA information can be obtained at www.ICGtesting.com
Printed in the USA
LVOW071222191212

312094LV00002B/21/A